the
KETO CURE

A Low-Carb, **High-Fat** Dietary Solution to
Heal Your Body & Optimize Your Health

Adam S. Nally, DO
& International Bestselling Author **Jimmy Moore**
with recipes by **Maria Emmerich**

VICTORY BELT PUBLISHING
Las Vegas

First Published in 2018 by Victory Belt Publishing Inc.

ISBN-13: 978-1-628601-29-9

The information included in this book is for educational purposes only. It is not intended or implied to be a substitute for professional medical advice. The reader should always consult his or her healthcare provider to determine the appropriateness of the information for his or her own situation or if he or she has any questions regarding a medical condition or treatment plan. Reading the information in this book does not constitute a physician-patient relationship.

Cover design by Justin-Aaron Velasco

Interior design by Charisse Reyes

Recipe photos by Maria Emmerich

Printed in Canada

TC 0218

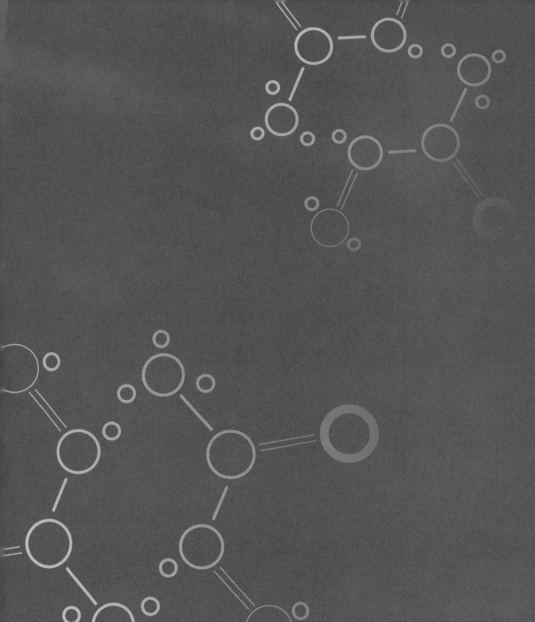

PART 1
THE BASICS

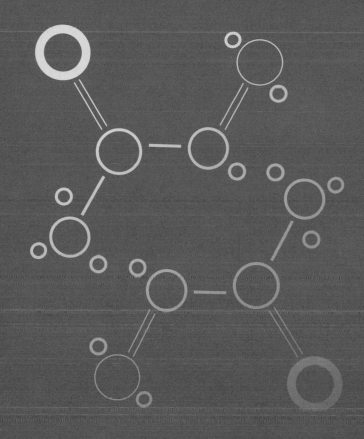

INTRODUCTION

JIMMY SAYS

Committing yourself to a permanent lifestyle change can be incredibly challenging when you've tried and failed so many times before. But the good news about what we share in this book is that everything you will read within these pages is based on practical information that is grounded in the latest nutritional health science and is being used daily by many physicians in clinical practice around the world. Once you get the basic tenets of keto nailed down, optimal health will logically follow.

I don't believe in coincidence. Everything happens for a reason, including why you and I have come together through the medium of this text. I hope you will take a moment and think about how you came to be holding this book in your hand. You've probably been searching, and maybe even praying, for answers. Picking up this copy of *The Keto Cure* is your first and most powerful step to changing your life.

Improving your health, and your life, is not something you can do occasionally. Health is a lifestyle, a mindset, and a cause that moves you to action. This book was written for people just like you. It is designed as a guide to help you understand the basic principles that enhance your metabolism. We've known about these foundational principles for more than 100 years, but they've become clouded and gray. Applying these principles will help you achieve a healthy weight and dramatically improve your overall health. The six principles of the ketogenic approach laid out in this book are metabolically essential to reversing the causes of the "diseases of civilization."

But what are these "diseases of civilization"? They are diseases that either didn't exist or occurred rarely until our cultures became more civilized. They include heart disease, elevated cholesterol, diabetes, pre-diabetes, impaired fasting glucose, hypoglycemia, kidney stones, gout, psoriasis, eczema, inflammatory diseases—including arthritis and polycystic ovary syndrome (PCOS)—and autoimmune disorders such as hypothyroidism. These diseases, the ones that keep me in business, weren't problematic when people lived in smaller villages and tribes. They began to rear their ugly heads when our societies began to incorporate "civilized" eating and the mass production of foods that contained higher quantities of starches, sugars, and carbohydrates. When you follow a ketogenic lifestyle, you return to the kinds of eating habits that humans living in those smaller, less industrialized societies had. Consequently, your body can reverse the progression of the diseases of civilization and return to a healthier state.

Is the ketogenic lifestyle just a Paleolithic approach? No. It's a lifestyle that revolves around the use and cooking of natural, whole foods, with an emphasis on those foods that have positive hormonal effects on disease at a cellular and genetic level. The ketogenic lifestyle is an intentional way of eating wherein you restrict carbohydrates, moderate protein, and use fat as your primary fuel.

WHO I AM

Why do we need another book about ketosis and ketogenic diets? Many other wonderful authors have written books on the topic. I have bookshelves full of them. What makes me special enough to write another? You may even be wondering, "Why do you call yourself *DocMuscles*? Are you bragging about your physique?"

I'm not particularly special, but I do have more than seventeen years of personal and professional experience with the ways that eating habits can affect how you look and feel. Although I am proud of keeping myself healthy today, I haven't always been healthy. In fact, after medical school and residency training, even though I exercised an hour a day, restricted my food intake to 1,200 to 1,800 calories per day, and limited fat in my diet, I was 65 pounds overweight, always tired, very moody, and pre-diabetic. I spent so much time in the gym trying to maintain my health that my trainer said, "If you keep this up, Doc, you'll become the doctor of muscles." (A friend heard this and started calling me DocMuscles. The nickname stuck.) My problem, as you also might have experienced, is that no matter how much I exercised, I couldn't outrun or outlift the wrong diet.

I come from a family with a strong history of insulin resistance, diabetes, heart disease, high blood pressure, and stroke, to name just a few medical issues. I've tried vegetarian diets, calorie-restricted diets, and all the fad diets in between. Nothing worked for me.

I found the same problem in my patients. A few had found success with rigorous exercise and calorie restriction, but the rest of them (myself included) plateaued at around 20 pounds of weight loss; were left with ravenous hunger, moodiness, and fatigue; and saw no improvement in blood pressure, cholesterol, or diabetes numbers. In fact, these numbers often worsened with calorie restriction, and the patient would end up being prescribed yet another pill a few months later.

I saw this pattern repeatedly throughout my residency and the first five years of private practice, and it's disheartening to the physician and discouraging for the patient. In fact, it is so discouraging that most patients begin to lose trust in their doctors' competence and advice. Patients get the impression that we doctors *enjoy* dispensing pills. I don't know a single physician who doesn't truly want to help his or her patients succeed. However, giving out dietary advice that doesn't work leads our patients to believe that we intentionally try to keep them unhealthy just to prescribe them more medication.

My father's health journey ended with his death after his fifty-eighth birthday. He weighed almost 400 pounds, was on one hundred fifty units of insulin, and took thirty-two pills per day. I watched him struggle with symptoms of fatigue, weight gain, and poor sleep while he tried to limit calories and exercise—just as I had been struggling. My father died after multiple heart attacks, kidney failure, liver failure, and essentially all the complications of diabetes. It was a real wake-up call for me when I realized that my lab work (cholesterol, blood sugar, and so on) in my early thirties and his lab work from his early thirties looked almost identical.

So, I began looking for answers, both for myself and for my patients. I went through three separate training programs and obtained a second board certification in obesity medicine. I took a five hundred–hour advance curriculum fellowship in obesity medicine and carbohydrate restriction. I looked for anyone who was successfully treating what I was seeing in my office, and I picked their brains for answers and solutions.

When I started down this path, much of the information we have today didn't really exist anywhere that was easily accessible to the general public, so I began blogging and tweeting about it. I created DocMuscles.com so that I could have a place to send patients who had questions I didn't have time to answer during our office visits. In order to bridge the gap between science and day-to-day application, I still blog and livestream regularly, and you can find that content at DocMuscles.com. Over the years, I've found a number of other wonderful physicians, dietitians, authors, and bloggers who are on the same journey that I've been on. They provide great insight and information for both the physician and the layperson.

In my office, I see and treat patients who've read these books and blogs, yet they still seem to be missing some basic principles of application both for health and for disease. That's my goal with this book—to translate the science DocMuscles-style in a way that you and your family can understand and apply.

So, where do we start?

My goal is not to sell you a program, although for some people, programs can be effective, and I'd be happy to sell you one if you really want to buy it. However, I'd rather give you the foundational principles that, if followed, can change your health and body composition over your lifetime. The intent of this book is to give you the pathway and stepping-stones of daily practice that allow for effective physical, emotional, and spiritual remodeling of your body. Throughout the last seventeen years of working in my "in-the-trenches" medical practice, I have found that true change involves the mind, body, and spirit. Often, just understanding the basic principles of health and then applying them enables an individual to blossom with previously untapped potential.

ABOUT JIMMY AND MARIA

My co-authors have written many books about ketosis and ketogenic diets: Jimmy Moore has written two of them, and Maria Emmerich has written nine. These two have been focused on helping people understand the basics of ketosis and ketogenic diets for as long as I've been practicing medicine. I'm going to take the knowledge that Jimmy and Maria have and build on it.

- **Jimmy Moore** and his coauthor, Dr. Eric Westman, brought you the book *Keto Clarity*. It tells you what ketosis is in layman's language. In this book, we go one step further, taking the basic principles of ketosis and applying them to disease. Jimmy has added comments in the margins to help translate anything you may not understand.

- **Maria Emmerich** brought you *Quick & Easy Ketogenic Cooking* and *The 30-Day Ketogenic Cleanse*, among other great cookbooks. She has provided some great recipes for this book to support your efforts to change your lifestyle and prevent or treat disease.

HOW TO USE THIS BOOK AND FOLLOW THE KETO CURE APPROACH

CHAPTER 1:
INTRODUCTION

JIMMY SAYS

When I first started my ketogenic journey, I found it helpful to track my food intake, test my blood sugar and blood ketone levels, and manage lifestyle factors such as sleep, stress, and exercise. These things aren't optional if you truly want to succeed in your pursuit of health through nutritional ketosis.

Purchasing this book is your first action step and a demonstration of faith. The act of making this purchase solidifies hope and belief that creating change and achieving success in your life are not only possible but also realistic. So many lifestyle books that are written for the layperson don't really help you understand the basics; I want to fill that void. I've also worked to make this more than just another cookbook. I want this to be a guidebook that lives up to the old saying, "If you give a man a fish, he'll eat today, but if you teach him to fish, he'll eat for the rest of his life."

Each principle in this guide is based in a truth—a scientifically sound, reproducible principle. To be successful, the truth must be applied through an associated action. Just as a poison has an antidote that must be taken, a disease has a cause that must be corrected. You must take action to get a result. The Keto Cure is the application of a principle that results in an action.

Benjamin Franklin used a three-step method for planning and pursuing his goals. His planning method was based on values or truths. He identified the value or truth and then prioritized and planned how to apply each value throughout his day. He completed this simple planning and journaling each evening. I recommend that you use the same approach or technique when applying the Keto Cure to your life. Remember: You cannot improve what you don't measure, and actions are most easily completed when you've planned them.

Consequently, I highly suggest that you get a journal, a planner, or some other form of daily diary that you can use to plan the action for the next day so that you can be accountable to yourself the following evening by recording how well you completed the planned action. I have found that most people who don't use a journal or planner fail, whereas most people who follow my advice about journaling have great success. Using a journal makes it easier to follow the principles outlined in the later chapters of this book. It takes four to six weeks of journaling to see the benefits of this tracking. Be patient with its use, and trust me that you *will* see results if you stick with it.

I recommend that you plan and track the following things: daily carbohydrate intake, daily protein intake, daily fat intake, daily water intake, exercise, and sleep patterns. Also, remember that we are more than just physical beings; we are spiritual and mental beings as well. Therefore, I find that adding meditation, scripture reading, positive affirmation, or spiritual reflection as a part of each day plays a solidifying role in helping people stay on track when physical carb cravings kick in, and I encourage you to plan and journal your daily attention to your spiritual and mental needs.

Here's an example of an effective way you might manage your daily journaling:

- Five to ten minutes before bed, write down your next-day plan for exercise, meditation, and meals.

- Throughout the following day, record what you do and what you eat at each meal:

EXERCISE: Upper-body weight-lifting for 40 minutes	BREAKFAST: 3 boiled eggs (Carbs: 0, Protein: 21g, Fat: 21g) and 24 ounces of water
SCRIPTURE READING/ MEDITATION: Read and ponder New Testament Galatians Chapter 5 for 30 minutes	LUNCH: 2 lettuce-wrapped ham-and-cheese sandwiches (Carbs: 4g, Protein: 30g, Fat: 30g) and 12 ounces of water
	DINNER: 12-ounce rib-eye steak with butter and salad (Carbs: 6g, Protein: 30g, Fat: 40g) and 12 ounces of sparkling water

- That night, account to yourself whether you met the goal from the night before. If you did, journal how you feel. If you didn't, journal what you think happened and how you will correct it tomorrow. Then write down the next day's plan for exercise, meditation, and meals.

> **"If you don't design your own life plan, chances are you'll fall into someone else's plan. And guess what they have planned for you? Not much."**
>
> —Motivational speaker
> Jim Rohn

I find that this type of journaling and accounting is a powerful form of cognitive behavioral therapy and helps people quickly identify causes and triggers in a positive way, without shame or guilt.

For some people, applying the Keto Cure principles is simple and intuitive. It might take you a few months (or, for a few people, even years) to wrap your mind around the changes you will be asked to make. No matter which group you fall into, my advice to you is to enjoy the journey!

DISCLAIMER: *The lifestyle changes discussed within this book are very powerful. Changes to weight, blood pressure, cholesterol, blood sugar, insulin levels, and pulse often begin within one or two weeks. If you are currently under the care or supervision of a physician for any medical reason or condition—being treated for blood pressure, blood sugar, cholesterol, heart disease, vascular disease, or other endocrine diseases—it is essential that you are closely monitored and that your medications are carefully and frequently adjusted by someone with a qualified medical license. I strongly advise anyone beginning this or any lifestyle change, nutritional modification, or diet to undergo a physical exam before starting the program and to have yearly checkups. Any program that can cause changes to the metabolism or to weight has the potential to have adverse effects in certain genetic or heritable conditions. It is important that you have clearance from your physician prior to undergoing this or any other weight-management program.*

THE BASICS

JIMMY SAYS

If you understand the basics of keto, then you can add to your knowledge gradually to keep yourself happy and healthy for the rest of your life. Now is your time to take back control of your health and empower yourself with one of the most powerful dietary modalities you will ever experience. Keto is your new superpower!

Let's get started with the basic information you need as you start changing your lifestyle. This section answers a few questions that I am asked every day:

- What are the basic macronutrients?

- Why do I get fat?

- What is the complex science behind weight loss and weight gain, and how can I apply it in a simple way?

My hope is that I can teach you how to adopt a ketogenic lifestyle that you can manage for the rest of your life so you can apply it to disease prevention.

What Are Macronutrients?

Before you begin, you need to understand some fundamental definitions of macronutrients. There are three basic macronutrients:

- **PROTEINS:** Chains of amino acids that are used as building blocks for connective tissue and muscle. Proteins also can be converted into forms of carbohydrate to be used as fuel. Proteins are usually found in varying amounts in meats, cheese, eggs, nuts, and seeds. Some examples of amino acids are glutamine, lysine, phenylalanine, tryptophan, and arginine.

- **CARBOHYDRATES:** Simple sugars, starches, and cellulose (fiber). Some examples of carbohydrates are fructose, glucose, sucrose, and lactose.

- **FATS:** Chains of glycerol and fatty acid esters that are found in organic tissue, especially in the adipose tissue (fat) of animals and in the seeds, nuts, and some fruits of plants. There are three types of fat: saturated, monounsaturated, and polyunsaturated, as well as essential fatty acids.

FIBER AND CARBOHYDRATES

Our bodies usually can't break down and absorb the carbohydrate from long-chain fibers that are found in leafy greens, fruits, and vegetables, but cooking, juicing, or blending those long-chain fibers breaks some of the bonds and makes more of the carbohydrates (simple sugars) available. This means that the carbohydrates from the fiber contribute to your carbohydrate intake, which inhibits weight loss.

Because of the sheer numbers and complexities of these molecules (proteins, carbohydrates, and fats) and the variability of where they can be found, people get confused, even if they've taken high school or college nutrition classes. They walk into my office not understanding what these macronutrients really are, where to find information about the macronutrient content of foods, or how to apply the basic science in selecting foods to eat. My goal is to help you overcome that lack of knowledge.

What Do Macronutrients Do?

Macronutrients provide energy. They are compounds of chemicals that humans consume to provide energy to power the body. Each of these macronutrients can be used as fuel.

The illustration below shows a simplified chemical breakdown of how each of the three macronutrients is processed to provide fuel for energy within a cell. (Some of you—the chemical engineers in the group—will love this illustration and be upset that I didn't include all the chemical reactions. The rest of you will thank me later.) My point is to show you that protein, carbohydrate, and fat all can be used within a cell to create the molecule that gives us energy.

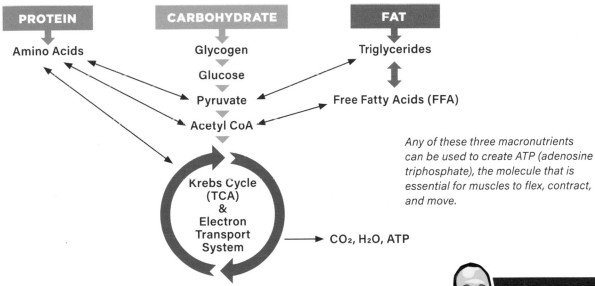

Any of these three macronutrients can be used to create ATP (adenosine triphosphate), the molecule that is essential for muscles to flex, contract, and move.

It's interesting to note that deficiencies in protein or fat cause disease in humans and other mammalian species, but there are no diseases that result from carbohydrate deficiency. In other words, if you don't eat protein or fat, you're at risk for a number of deficiency-based diseases, but if you don't eat carbohydrates, there are no forms of disease that arise.

JIMMY SAYS

There are essential fats and essential proteins that you must consume or you will get very sick and could possibly die. But despite the push by so-called health experts to get you to eat gobs of carbohydrate-based foods like fruits, whole grains, and vegetables, the truth is that there is no such thing as an essential carbohydrate. Look it up!

CAN PEOPLE FUNCTION NORMALLY WITHOUT EATING ANY CARBOHYDRATES?

In the late 1800s, Lieutenant Frederick Schwatka and his men traveled 2,700 miles through the Canadian Arctic. During this trip, Lt. Schwatka, a physician, and his men lived and actually thrived on an Inuit Indian diet that was very high in fat and very low in carbohydrate, which demonstrated that humans can function normally with little to no carbohydrate in their diets.[1]

The Science Behind Weight Gain

The key to understanding why 85 percent of the U.S. population is overweight or obese is that the problem is not caloric; it's hormonal. Your ability to recognize this one factor will change your whole outlook on health, disease, and weight loss. Your choices and actions from here on out must be based on this understanding.

There are actually thirty different hormones that regulate weight and appetite. Among these thirty hormones, insulin is the master hormone.

- Anything that raises insulin halts weight loss and stimulates significant inflammation, which is *the cause of most diseases of civilization.*

- Insulin stimulates lipoprotein lipase, the enzyme that pushes triglycerides (the transportable form of fat in the blood) out of the bloodstream into the fat cells, which is what causes us to gain weight.

- Without insulin, we don't gain weight. (That's why type 1 diabetics are usually very slender).

I will say it again: Insulin is the master hormone regulating weight and the diseases of civilization.

The majority of the people I see in my office—80 to 85 percent—have some degree of insulin resistance. Simply put, insulin resistance is an overproduction of insulin in response to the consumption of sugars or starches. Chapter 4 talks more about insulin resistance; for now, think of insulin resistance as a worn key.

My father was a locksmith. When I was a young man, I often accompanied him as his assistant. One of my jobs was cutting keys to fit the locks. Keys have teeth. The tooth of each key is a specific height from the base of the key. If that height is wrong, or if the tooth is worn, the key won't lift the pin inside the lock to the correct height, which means that the lock won't unlock.

Insulin is a lot like a key. It fits into a number of biological locks within the cells of our bodies. If the key is worn or damaged, it may take a bit of wiggling to get the teeth of the key to turn the lock.

Insulin resistance is like a hotel doorman with a worn key. The key (insulin) opens the door, but not very quickly. The doorman can get the door open, but not until he's done a great deal of wiggling, twisting, and coaxing of the key.

In the case of insulin, instead of getting new keys that work efficiently, the body sends out more keys to open the doors. The body ends up producing two to twenty times the normal amount of insulin.

How do you know if your body is overproducing insulin? Your doctor checks a blood test after you've fasted. The normal lab values for fasting insulin levels were set years ago when insulin was first discovered; those levels range from 10 to 22 mg/dL.

JIMMY SAYS

Many people mistakenly think that weight loss is all about what you eat and the number of calories you consume. But we now understand the tremendous impact of hormones in this battle against the bulge. Knowing what your fasting insulin is and implementing proven strategies (like a ketogenic diet) for lowering this master hormone are the keys to stemming the tide of weight gain. For some of us who have severe insulin resistance, keto alone may not be enough to bring the weight down. Fasting, yoga, meditation, relaxation techniques, and other lifestyle strategies may be needed in conjunction with a ketogenic diet.

The test is called a *glucose tolerance test*. You fast overnight (ten to twelve hours of fasting), and then the doctor tests your insulin and glucose response by giving you 50 to 75 grams of sugar. Over the years of administering these tests, I have found that people routinely test positive for insulin resistance when their fasting insulin level is higher than 5 mg/dL. As you can see, that's *lower* than the standard range (or currently accepted reference range) for what's considered normal, which means that you can be insulin resistant before your insulin level rises to a level that would be considered in the range of being a type 2 diabetic.

The following are additional physical markers that indicate you might have insulin resistance:

JIMMY SAYS

- Skin tags

- Acanthosis nigricans

- Triglyceride/HDL ratio greater than 3.0

- Elevated small-dense LDL particle number (greater than 500)

- Fasting insulin greater than 5 mg/dL

- Fasting blood sugar greater than 100 mg/dL

- Postprandial blood sugar greater than 140 mg/dL (two hours after a meal)

- Waist circumference more than 40 inches in men or 35 inches in women

- Family history of diabetes

- Coronary artery disease

POINT OF FOCUS

Food stimulates hormones, specifically insulin. If you're having trouble managing your weight, look at your hormones and focus on the hormone response to your diet.

Now that you have some essential information about macronutrients and the science behind weight gain, Chapter 2 gets into some of the history of why we've been fueling our bodies the wrong way for the past fifty years.

Several years ago, I had a five-hour glucose tolerance test that revealed the level of insulin resistance I was experiencing. My blood sugar dropped very quickly to hypoglycemic levels, while my insulin jumped to double digits. At that point I sought a nutritional approach to help me manage this condition, and that's where keto came into play for me. I can tell I'm still dealing with insulin resistance because I continue to have skin tags, slightly elevated fasting insulin, a waist circumference over 40 inches, and a family history of heart disease. Getting into ketosis has definitely helped me manage my insulin resistance; I'm sure I would have full-blown type 2 diabetes had I not made this change.

WHY WERE THE LAST 50 YEARS OF NUTRITION WRONG?

Dietary fat reduction and caloric restriction for the treatment of obesity and associated cardiovascular disease, diabetes, cancer, and hypertension have been recommended since the early 1970s. These guidelines are based on questionable or inaccurate evidence and are partly responsible for the dramatic rise in obesity we have seen over the last forty-five years. What is greatly concerning is that the financial cost of obesity has risen dramatically, to almost 28 percent of total healthcare costs in the United States.[1] Unfortunately, the factors upon which dietary guidelines are based are not influenced solely by nutritional science. Knowing some of the history behind the guidelines we've been using might help you understand how we got to where we are today.

SOME HISTORY ABOUT GOVERNMENT POLICY ON CONSUMPTION

President Franklin D. Roosevelt's Agricultural Adjustment Act of 1933 (also known as the Farm Bill) provided subsidies to American farmers in the midst of the Great Depression. Since that time, the federal government has paid subsidies to farmers to encourage them not to grow wheat, feed grain, corn, barley, oats, soybeans, and rice—which are seven crops known as commodities—with the intent of decreasing the supply, increasing the demand, and thereby raising the price.[2] Dr. Susan Blumenthal, former U.S. Assistant Surgeon General and current SNAP to Health project director, writes, "The Farm Bill has since expanded to include many different categories or 'titles.' The last bill to be authorized, in 2008, had 15 titles, including nutrition (food stamps), crop subsidies, conservation, livestock, crop insurance and disaster assistance. The 2008 Farm Bill approved $300 billion in spending: 67% was spent on food stamps; 15% on agricultural subsidies; 9% on conservation; and 8% on crop insurance."[3]

The U.S. Department of Agriculture (USDA) Subsidy Programs tend to favor, either directly or indirectly, foods that increase obesity and other diseases. These subsidies support commodity crops, dairy products, livestock, and federal purchase programs. These subsidies are incentives to grow and produce specific commodities that have a higher monetary return. Subsidies also act as a disincentive for farmers to grow fruits and vegetables that fall under the "specialty crops" category. This restricts both small and large farmers from diversifying their crops and limits fruit and vegetable production.[4] The government's justification for subsidies is that they help stabilize prices by balancing supply and demand.[5]

It's profound that the food guidelines directly influence the way we eat and the food choices we have available to us. For many low-income Americans—especially children—federal programs have a direct and significant influence on food choices. More than 30 million children receive government-subsidized school lunches through National School Lunch Program (NSLP), which is administered by the USDA Food and Nutrition Service.[6]

USDA-purchased meats, dairy products, grains, fruits, and vegetables are supplied to schools for use in meal programs. Current recommendations on calorie intake set by the USDA and The Healthy, Hunger-Free Kids Act of 2010 mandate that school lunches provide 650 to 850 calories per meal to the children enrolled in the program.[7] (Interestingly, that is the same caloric count as a meal comprising a Big Mac, small fries, and Diet Coke from McDonald's.[8]) The rationale for the foods selected and the purchase decisions made by the schools are based on agricultural support goals and adherence to national dietary guidelines.

A CLOSER LOOK AT SUBSIDIES

Let's look at an example of how subsidies favor farmers who grow industrial crops rather than specialty crops that would contribute to healthy diets. I'll use my home state of Arizona.

Between 1995 and 2016, the government paid $353.5 billion in farm subsidies to almost 40 percent of U.S. farmers. From 1995 to 2011, Arizona farms received $25.3 million in dairy subsidies and $29.5 million in livestock subsidies (USDA, 2013).[9] Arizona ranks second nationally in its production of cantaloupe and honeydew melons, head and leaf lettuce, spinach, broccoli, cauliflower, and lemons, all of which are "specialty crops" and do not receive subsidies.[10] The most recent statistics show that the top five states receiving subsidies are Iowa, Texas, Illinois, Nebraska, and Minnesota, with Kansas coming in at a close sixth. From 1995 to 2016, the majority of these subsidies were for corn ($106 billion), wheat ($43.3 billion), cotton ($37.7 billion), soybeans ($35.6 billion), and rice ($15.3 billion).[11] It is important to note that the Renewable Fuel Standard of 2012 (legislation protecting the corn-ethanol lobby) mandates that 37 percent of the corn harvest be used for ethanol production and further affects the availability of food for our tables.[12] The pie chart at left shows the disproportionate distribution of subsidies for various agricultural products.[13]

Where the Money Goes: The Foods That Subsidies Support

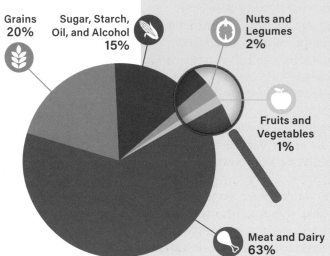

Grains
20%

Sugar, Starch, Oil, and Alcohol
15%

Nuts and Legumes
2%

Fruits and Vegetables
1%

Meat and Dairy
63%

A study published in *Economics and Human Biology* reveals that a person's body mass index (BMI, or height-to-weight ratio) increases faster if that person is on food stamps, and the increase in BMI is greater while a person is on the Supplemental Nutrition Assistance Program (SNAP), formerly known as food stamps. "We can't prove that the Food Stamp Program causes weight gain, but this study suggests a strong linkage," said Jay Zagorsky, coauthor of the study and research scientist at the Ohio State University's Center for Human Resource Research.[14] Many of the foods available through SNAP are refined, subsidized, high-carbohydrate-containing foods. These highly refined, processed, high-carbohydrate foods contribute directly to weight gain and spawn the diseases of civilization.

The price of food influences an individual's consumption choices.[15] Foods that are refined contain greater amounts of sugar or high-fructose corn syrup than nonrefined foods. Refined foods also are more calorie dense and are often cheaper and more readily accessible. These are the foods that are usually found in the center of the grocery store and frequently are on sale at the ends of each aisle. On the other hand, nutrient-dense, higher-fiber foods are frequently associated with higher prices and are consumed less often. These are the foods you usually find around the periphery of the grocery store (fruits, vegetables, and meats).

Food subsidy policy found in the Food, Conservation and Energy Act of 2008 extension mandated by the American Taxpayer Relief Act of 2012 drives up the price of fruits, vegetables, and meats. This policy also turns people toward lower-cost foods that are higher in simple carbohydrates and caloric density. Thus, current government policy is actually making obesity worse and making Americans fatter. Research completed at the University of Illinois at Chicago reveals that small taxes or price changes don't produce a change in a person's BMI. In other words, a ten-cent tax on soda pop wouldn't necessarily change your habit of drinking it. However, the research demonstrates that a more significant price change has a measurable and significant effect on weight in both adults and children. Price increases of 100 to 150 percent have been shown to change purchasing behavior, which thereby affects health.[16] For example, if the price of milk doubled from $3.50 to $7.00 per gallon, you'd probably be less likely to buy it, or at least you would buy less of it.

However, the USDA disagrees with the amount of influence prices have over an individual American's food choices. An article from the USDA's magazine *Amber Waves* states that "Some public health advocates have argued that falling real, or inflation-adjusted, prices for many high-calorie foods encourage people to buy and consume more of these foods, leading to poor diet quality and rising rates of obesity. A closer look at how consumers respond to food price variation—over time, across geographic markets, in different types of stores, and in response to taxes and subsidies—reveals how food prices affect people's food choices, and their waistlines. In short, price matters, but not very much, and it is not the only factor."[17]

JIMMY SAYS

You have a choice as a consumer—you can eat foods that cost less but are less nourishing for your body, forcing you to eat more of them, or you can eat foods that cost more but are nutrient dense, offering complete nutrition that satisfies your micronutrient needs to keep hunger at bay so you naturally eat less. If you think this through to its logical conclusion, then choosing better-quality foods makes more economic and health sense in the long run.

CURRENT POLICY

The most recent Farm Bill was set to expire on September 30, 2013. If it had been allowed to expire, the result would have been a return to the 1949 Farm Bill legislation, which theoretically would have doubled the price of milk. However, this would have had the effect of freeing up more than $5 billion of federal spending per year and also would have led to decreased consumption of major sources of carbohydrates, such as wheat and corn, in the standard American diet. Senator Debbie Stabenow, chairwoman of the Senate Agriculture Committee, had repeatedly said that she was opposed to an extension; however, she agreed to a compromise that extended the bill for another year to help the farmers who were experiencing serious drought conditions in 2012.

Two additional extensions were passed in the House and Senate, but because the two versions differed so significantly, they were referred to a House-Senate Conference Committee to work out a compromise. With only $23 billion in spending reductions, the Agricultural Act of 2014 was passed on in January 2014. The act covers the years 2014 through 2018; what happens when we reach the end of the period covered by this act remains to be seen.

JIMMY SAYS

Americans need to understand that the USDA's Dietary Guidelines for Americans are not at all about improving our health. They are simply about boosting the bottom line of the agriculture industry. This fact alone should make you angry enough to demand that lawmakers in Washington remove national nutrition policy from the Department of Agriculture and assign it to an independent panel of experts to more closely examine the scientific research. The Nutrition Coalition (www. nutritioncoalition.us) led by Nina Teicholz is aiming to do exactly that.

LOSERS AND WINNERS IN THE GAME OF GOVERNMENT POLICY

The graph below shows how the weight of the American population has increased from the 1960s to the early 2000s.[18] If the United States continues along its current course, up to 58 percent of the population will be obese by 2030.[19] Many believe that the USDA Dietary Guidelines are to blame. Richard David Feinman, president of the Nutrition and Metabolism Society and professor of cell biology at SUNY Downstate Medical Center, said, "The previous Guidelines have not worked well. It is unreasonable to ask the Dietary Guidelines Advisory Committee (DGAC) to audit its own work. An external panel of scientists with no direct ties to nutritional policy would be able to do a more impartial evaluation of the data. This would be far better for everyone."[20]

Trends among adults aged 20–74 years: United States, 1960–2008

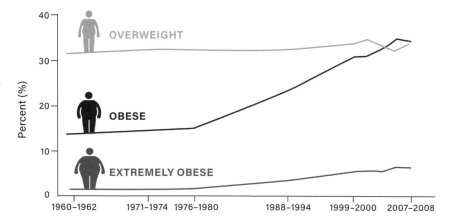

Evidence from the Women's Health Initiative Dietary Modification Trial, which studied 49,000 women, supports Dr. Feinman's conclusion. The study did not show any statistically significant evidence that following a low-fat or calorie-restricted diet had any long-term effect on obesity.[21] The Weston A. Price Foundation, which, according to its website, is "dedicated to restoring nutrient-dense foods to the human diet through education, research and activism," supports the view that the USDA Dietary Guidelines have been a significant cause of obesity. The foundation has been an active voice in promoting legislative change.[22] (Read more about the USDA Dietary Guidelines later in this chapter.)

Attempts at legislation, such as the 2012 DeMint Amendment (SA 2276), have been made to modify the Farm Bill. However, because of a large lobbying agricultural coalition, the amendment was voted down. Changing farm subsidies will be a great challenge, as 40 percent of the farmers in the United States now have some degree of dependence on these subsidies. A number of agricultural groups—including the American Soybean Association, the National Corn Growers Association, and the National Cotton Council—have historically had significant monetary interest in the farm subsidies that these amendments would affect, and they are likely to continue to use their considerable lobbying power to encourage legislators to continue the subsidies. Groups with monetary interests stand to lose large profits if the farm subsidies are changed, reduced, or removed. Many of these groups provide significant employment opportunities in rural areas, and changing these subsidies has the potential to disrupt the economy in those areas. Do the jobs that are preserved because of governmental subsidies offset the ill effects to individuals' waistlines and health? This is a controversial question and not one that will be easy to answer. Perhaps changes can be made slowly to allow for transition.

If certain crops, such as corn or wheat, were no longer subsidized, drastic changes would be likely to occur in the food manufacturing industry, which could be the largest proponent against change. Unintended consequences of modifying the Farm Bill and not extending its subsidies could have the short-term effect of escalating the price of a number of commodities to two to three times their current price. For example, without federal subsidies, the price of milk would increase to $6 to $8 dollars a gallon.[23] This price increase would likely deter the use of carbohydrates that contain dairy products, but it might also increase the price of meats and cheeses.

JIMMY SAYS

The low-fat lie that has been perpetrated on the American people has been exposed as the fraud it always was. The Women's Health Initiative was supposed to be the study to end all studies on nutrition heralding low-fat diets as the undisputed champion—but it did exactly the opposite. Despite never being founded on any solid research, low-fat and low-calorie diets have long been heavily promoted as the "healthy" way to eat for weight loss. Now we know that these diets are neither an effective nor a healthy way to lose weight.

THE COST OF OBESITY IN THE UNITED STATES

Obesity isn't a problem only for the individuals who suffer from it. It affects society as a whole in a number of ways, including the cost of healthcare.

As of 2012, an obese person incurred $2,741 more in medical expenses per year than his or her non-obese counterpart.[24] (This was the increased cost that the insurance company or plan pays out each year. The individual may not be responsible for all of this cost.) As of 2014, that cost had increased to more than $4,000 more per year.[25] That adds up to a minimum of $190.2 billion spent annually on obesity-related medical problems.[26] The Center for Health Policy and Economics has predicted the increase of $600 per year per beneficiary as a trend to continue through 2030.[27] That adds up to an estimated $564 billion cost for obesity-related healthcare per year on Medicare alone. This is a drastic change from previous years. By comparison, healthcare costs related to obesity were $85.7 billion (9.1 percent of overall healthcare costs) in 2006 and $61.2 billion (6.5 percent of overall healthcare costs) in 1998.[28]

As of 2017, the Centers for Disease Control statistics reveal that 36.5 percent of the U.S. adult population is obese, and another 34 percent is overweight. More than 127.9 million adults and 13.2 million children in the United States are obese.[29]

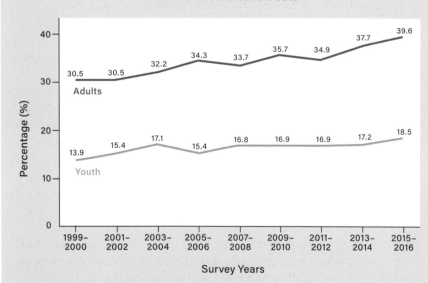

Obesity as a Percentage of Total U.S. Healthcare Costs

WHY WE'VE BEEN DOING IT WRONG

So, now that you know more about how government policy plays a part in which foods we have access to and how much we pay for them, and how different groups influence those decisions, you need to know more about how the dietary recommendations that we've lived with for the past fifty years came to be. Knowing that will help you understand why we've been doing things all wrong.

The man who invented the K-ration (individually packaged military service meals) in World War II was an epidemiologist by the name of Ancel Keys. He became one of the most influential scientists, writers, and researchers in the nutrition community between 1940 and 1970.

Keys introduced what we know today as the Diet-Heart Hypothesis, which basically says that if you eat fat, it makes you fat. This hypothesis also implies that fat causes heart disease and decreases the duration of your life because of the potential for heart attack. The Diet-Heart Hypothesis became popular first because of Keys's political influence. (Remember how we were just talking about how politics play a large role in our eating habits in this country?) The second reason the hypothesis became popular was Keys's staunch position and the media attention he received as a result of his hypothesis. A third factor in the popularity of the Diet-Heart Hypothesis was that, starting in 1952, gas liquid chromatography became an effective way to measure cholesterol.

Lipid science study was just taking off at that time, and so, because of political influence, excitement in the media, and a fascinating new cholesterol measurement tool, Keys's hypothesis that cholesterol in the diet can cause heart attack took off and became a firmly held belief. For the first time in history, science had provided a way for doctors to measure something and then give people medical advice and direction about their heart health. The Diet-Heart Hypothesis became the big thing. It was—and still is—a belief that some people cling to more strongly than religious belief.

Around the same time that Keys was presenting his hypothesis, President Dwight Eisenhower had a heart attack. The President's doctor, Paul White, actually quoted Keys's Diet-Heart Hypothesis as the "true science" that was available at the time, and White's support helped drive the process of legislating nutritional guidelines through the Food Guide Pyramid, which was originally formulated in 1977. In other words, the public put a lot of faith into what the physician to the President of the United States was delineating as "true science" and "false science." (The definition of science as the systematic study of the structure and behavior of the physical and natural world through observation and experiment doesn't seem to matter when it comes to the Diet-Heart Hypothesis, does it?)

JIMMY SAYS

I often refer to Ancel Keys as the Darth Vader of nutrition. He has made a more significant impact on the way Americans eat today than any other single person in our nation's history. And his claim-to-fame Seven Countries Study was flawed from the start; it actually included more than twenty countries that showed varying levels of heart disease and saturated fat consumption rates. He selected the seven that supported his hypothesis that eating more saturated fat leads to more cardiovascular disease. Now that we know Keys fudged the numbers, why do we still believe the Diet-Heart Hypothesis he promoted nearly seven decades ago? If it were presented in a court of law, Keys would be found in contempt for perjury. This is why taking the oath requires you to share the truth, the whole truth, and nothing but the truth. Keys didn't tell the whole truth, and the collective health of the United States has suffered as a result.

JIMMY SAYS

How the Dietary Guidelines for Americans were created to push an unproven low-fat nutritional approach on an unsuspecting public is one of the biggest travesties in U.S. history. Future generations will look back on this period as the dark days of nutrition that threatened our very existence, taking us to the brink of disease and death. I sense we will be closing the books on low-fat dieting soon, as it has proven to be a cataclysmic failure. Just how different would America be today if low-fat diets had never been given the health halo by our government, health organizations, and the medical community?

FURTHER READING ABOUT THE CHOLESTEROL MISCONCEPTION

Nina Teicholz's book The Big Fat Surprise *(Simon & Schuster, 2014) and Gary Taubes's book* Good Calories, Bad Calories *(Anchor Books, 2007) have done a wonderful job of going through the history of this long-held misconception.*

In addition, the American Heart Association endorsed the low-fat diet and the Diet-Heart Hypothesis; the association was likely influenced in this direction because of Keys's political and monetary ties.

Senator George McGovern, the chairman of the Senate Select Committee on Nutrition, staffed his committee with a number of laypeople who didn't understand nutrition. McGovern had a close friendship with Ancel Keys. Because of this relationship and the fact that the American Heart Association endorsed the low-fat lifestyle, significant influence was held in the eyes of the nutritionally naïve committee members. Senator McGovern also had just come from a Pritikin Longevity Clinic, where he was indoctrinated in fat reduction and became a stalwart low-fat follower. Lastly, McGovern directed that the committee's report be written by Nick Mottern, a journalist who had no background in nutrition. As a result, Mottern used Mark Hegsted from the Harvard School of Public Health as his source for the report, which basically said, "Hey, we should stop eating fat!"

The recommendation of the committee was carried on through the American Heart Association and the National Institutes of Health. Because of the political power of these two organizations, anyone who wanted to oppose either of those societies literally couldn't get tenured or funded and couldn't get papers published. Speaking out against the committee's recommendation could seriously affect a person's professional stature.

Another factor that contributed to the widespread acceptance of the Diet-Heart Hypothesis was that the American Heart Association and the National Institutes of Health basically set the financial playing field in the field of nutritional research. They controlled all the research dollars, which meant that money was directed toward looking at and measuring cholesterol and its particles. When some people realized that total cholesterol didn't really correlate with heart disease risk, those two organizations said, "Oh, it's not the total cholesterol that's the problem; it's the HDL and the LDL." So, researchers changed their focus to HDL-C and LDL-C.[30] Then, in 2001, we realized that HDL-C and LDL-C still didn't work as great indicators for heart disease risk.[31]

In a nutshell, that's how we got to where we are today. Because of all the support that the Diet-Heart Hypothesis received from high-profile organizations and individuals, the public believed the "true science" of the Food Guide Pyramid and accepted the idea that fat is bad. We were taught to cut the fat out of our diets and increase our intake of the overall "good" complex carbohydrates.

WHY CURRENT DIETARY GUIDELINES HAVE NOT BEEN EFFECTIVE

Why do we get fat? Why have we not been successful in losing weight via diet and exercise? To answer these questions, we can look to the obesity paradox that was described by Jules Hirsch of Rockefeller University. He proposed two opposing hypotheses:

1 "Obesity is the result of a willful descent into self-gratification," which implies that we gain weight because we overeat (caloric excess), which leads to caloric imbalance.

2 "Alternative hypothesis is that there is something 'biologic' about obesity, some alteration of hormones, enzymes or other biochemical control systems which leads to obesity."[32]

The 1977 Dietary Goals for the United States—the first comprehensive statement by any branch of the federal government about the American diet—supported the first theory. The USDA Dietary Guidelines were heavily influenced by the American Heart Association's position that fat intake alone would cause heart disease. The USDA 2010 Dietary Guidelines state that the "people who are the most successful at achieving and maintaining a healthy weight do so through continued attention to consuming only enough calories from foods and beverages to meet their needs and by being physically active."[33]

Current research contradicts the caloric restriction or "calories in, calories out" theory. Scientific evidence clearly demonstrates the domino effect of carbohydrate or starch intake increasing insulin levels, which stimulates obesity by raising cholesterol and triglyceride levels. *TIME* magazine published evidence that the longstanding recommendations to "eat less high-fat red meat, eggs and dairy and replace them with more calories from fruits, vegetables and especially carbohydrates" are now seen as incorrect.[34] Even our medical textbooks from 1965, like the introductory chapter of the *Handbook of Physiology*, make it clear that carbohydrate intake causes weight gain and raises triglyceride and cholesterol levels.[35, 36]

The USDA Dietary Guidelines need to be revised to reflect current evidence-based obesity prevention and weight-reduction research. The guidelines should include information about limiting intake of foods that are high in carbohydrates.

JIMMY SAYS

The concept of counting calories as a means to manage weight has never made sense to me. So 1,800 calories of hot fudge cake is exactly the same as 1,800 calories of sirloin steak and non-starchy vegetables with butter? I don't think so. The only thing people who push low-fat diets have left is the calorie hypothesis. But medical professionals like Dr. Nally, who work with thousands of patients each year, see the tremendous hormonal impact that food has on them. Choosing foods that minimize this impact regardless of their calorie counts is the key to weight management. This is where a ketogenic diet shines above the rest.

New Science Refutes the Old, "True" Science

Over the years, study after study of the "science" behind the Diet-Heart Hypothesis has failed to show that this hypothesis is true.[37] Studies have shown that avoiding dietary fat neither increases the length of your life nor decreases the number of heart attacks you have, and eating less cholesterol doesn't make your cholesterol go down.[38]

But, hey, when you cling to the "hypothesized science" with the same fervor that you hold on to your religious beliefs, a scary thing happens: People might believe you. The government accepted the hypothesis, and we did, too! We followed right along with the bad science and accepted it like good little lemmings. The question I have for you is this: If the government accepts something as truth, does it make it true, even when it actually isn't? Eventually, though, new facts came to light. As a family physician and an internal medicine doctor who was trying to assess risk in my patients, I saw that even when patients lowered their cholesterol, they didn't live longer or have fewer heart attacks; in fact, they had more. When patients lowered their cholesterol intake, they saw a rise in their total cholesterol, which sold more cholesterol pills. People in my office with lower cholesterol still had heart attacks, whereas people with higher cholesterol didn't.

I started seeing patterns. Giving more people cholesterol-lowering drugs didn't seem to stop the frequency of heart attacks. It didn't seem to lengthen their life spans or lower the frequency with which they died from heart disease. It didn't seem to stop the blockages in areas that can lead to strokes and vascular disease in the legs and other parts of the body.

Cutting out fat just made people fatter—that's what I've seen for the last seventeen years. In my observations, cutting out fat seemed to have the following results:

- It made blood sugar worse.
- It made diabetes worse.
- It made cholesterol worse.
- It made blood pressure go up.
- It increased uric acid levels.
- It increased gout and kidney stones.

Have we been doing it wrong? Absolutely. I was inspired to ask, "Why is it that this approach isn't working? It didn't work for my father, and it didn't work for me. So, what are we going to do about it? How are we going to approach it? How are we going to fix it?" I started to look for alternatives. My search led me to the rarely commented upon science about carbohydrate restriction and to a friendship with a podcaster named Jimmy Moore. That's where I began to find the answers that really work.

CHAPTER 2:
WHY WERE THE LAST 50 YEARS OF NUTRITION WRONG?

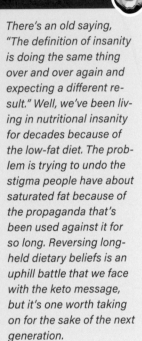

JIMMY SAYS

There's an old saying, "The definition of insanity is doing the same thing over and over again and expecting a different result." Well, we've been living in nutritional insanity for decades because of the low-fat diet. The problem is trying to undo the stigma people have about saturated fat because of the propaganda that's been used against it for so long. Reversing long-held dietary beliefs is an uphill battle that we face with the keto message, but it's one worth taking on for the sake of the next generation.

CHAPTER 3

WHAT IS KETOSIS?

You might have heard quite a bit about ketosis recently, but what exactly is it? What does it do? Why is it important? This chapter answers these questions and gives you the information you need to understand why altering your lifestyle by applying the Keto Cure is not just a good thing; it is *life-changing*.

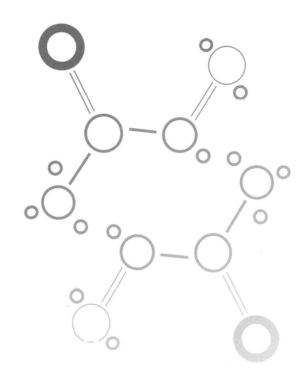

METABOLISM 101

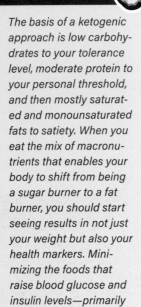

JIMMY SAYS

The basis of a ketogenic approach is low carbohydrates to your tolerance level, moderate protein to your personal threshold, and then mostly saturated and monounsaturated fats to satiety. When you eat the mix of macronutrients that enables your body to shift from being a sugar burner to a fat burner, you should start seeing results in not just your weight but also your health markers. Minimizing the foods that raise blood glucose and insulin levels—primarily carbs but also excessive protein—is the key to success.

As I said in Chapter 1, the body can use three different forms of fuel: protein, carbohydrate, or fat. Any one of these macronutrient fuels is essential for making a molecule called adenosine triphosphate (ATP). ATP is essential for the muscle fibrils to contract. If you don't have ATP, your muscles, including your heart and the diaphragm that moves your lungs, won't move. A lack of ATP leads quickly to a state called rigor mortis. Rigor mortis can really slow you down socially, so you want to avoid that.

A diet high in carbohydrates, just like I described in Chapter 2 as the standard American diet (SAD), drives both weight gain and the diseases of civilization. This is caused by the presence of and, in most cases, overproduction of insulin in response to carbohydrates (absorbable fibers, starches, and sugars).

What about a diet that is predominantly protein? This is essentially what the first low-carb diets—Paleolithic and Atkins-like diets—consist of: lean fat, limited carbohydrates, and high quantities of protein. In these cases, the body uses protein for building blocks, but in the absence of other fuels (carbohydrates and fat), it is forced to convert protein into a form of glucose through a process called gluconeogenesis. The result is increased glucose, which raises insulin and puts you right back where you were with a low-fat, high-carb diet.

Yes, I can hear the bodybuilders and trainers of the world cursing my name and having conniptions as I say this. Many of them, because of their intense exercise regimens, require a much larger amount of protein than the average person, and they can get by with a low-fat, low-carb, high-protein diet. If you are very physically active, meaning that you spend two to three hours or more per day engaged in very physical, high-intensity exercise, your body will use the added protein as building blocks. This type of athlete doesn't experience insulin surges because of the intense exercise. However, for the average Joe or Jane, this method doesn't work. About 85 percent of the people who walk through my office doors end up in tears because low-fat dietary approaches fail, caloric-restriction dietary approaches fail, Paleolithic dietary approaches fail, and even the recently praised Mediterranean dietary approaches fail. Most people lose 10 to 20 pounds, but then weight loss halts, cholesterol rises, kidney stones begin to occur more often, and blood pressure keeps rising. When these things happen, people get discouraged and angry, and they give up.

Let me suggest an alternative: What if your diet was primarily fat based? Yes, you read that correctly. Consider what might be different if your diet was made up predominantly of *fat*.

You're probably saying, "What!? Eat *fat* as my primary fuel source?"

Yes. Fat.

When the body is using neither carbohydrate nor excess protein as a fuel source, it is left with fat. When the body uses fat as its primary fuel source, there is an absence of glucose in the bloodstream, so the body converts fat into ketones to make those fancy ATP molecules. Ketones don't require insulin to form ATP and energy. If you gain nothing else from these first few chapters, make sure you hang onto this one statement: "*Ketones don't require insulin to create energy.*" As you will see in the following chapters, insulin is the master hormone. In excess, insulin Is the hormone that drives weight gain and all the diseases of civilization.

Fat or fatty acids are the long tails of the triglyceride molecule that are broken off and converted into ketones in the liver. There are three forms of ketones: *acetoacetate*, *β-hydroxybutyrate*, and *acetone.* The body can use all three of these forms of ketones for fuel. After the ketones are created in the liver, they are dumped into the bloodstream, and almost every cell in the body can use them for fuel instead of using glucose.

> "Switching from glucose to ketones is like taking you off of unleaded and putting you on diesel."
>
> —Doc Nally

Some people say, "Well, Dr. Nally, you have to have carbohydrates, or you'll die."

You actually won't die. That's an old wives' tale—or, to be more accurate, an old nutritionists' tale. You're seriously not going to die if you don't eat carbohydrates.

Repeat after me: "I won't die if I don't eat carbohydrates."

How do I know that? Because your liver makes about 200 to 280 grams of glycogen, which is a form of glucose that any part of the body can use. A small area of your brain is dependent on glucose or glycogen, but it needs only 100 grams per day. In other words, the liver makes more than twice the amount of glucose you need by processing fat. You can live your whole life and not eat a single carbohydrate, and there is no disease that will arise. Really!

Again, repeat after me: "There are no carbohydrate-deficiency diseases. They don't exist!"

Any dietitian or nutritionist who says, "If you don't eat carbs, you're going to die," needs to go back and reread his or her physiology textbooks, because it's absolutely not true. The world is not flat, and you won't die if you don't eat carbohydrates.

Let's imagine that you live in a carbohydrate-deficient world. Let's also say that your meals are at least 50 to 60 percent fat. The result is that your body will use fat as its predominant fuel by converting it to ketones. You're getting enough protein with the fat you eat to maintain muscle and tissues. (It's kind of interesting that protein and fat usually come together in the same package, but I don't recall seeing the "fishy cracker cut" on the Angus cow I drove by the other day.) The ketones are taken up within the cells and processed through the mitochondria of each cell. The mitochondria process the ketones a little differently than glucose, but

JIMMY SAYS

If not eating carbohydrates is supposed to make you die, then I would have been a goner years ago. It's simply amazing to me how nutritional health experts can be so vitriolic in their rhetoric.

they're still producing ATP, and the by-products are carbon dioxide (CO_2) and water. The CO_2 that you produce drives your respiratory rate and causes you to breathe out (exhale) as its level in your bloodstream rises, and the excess water you produce is filtered out through your kidneys. So, the fat you eat and the fat you store basically produce energy; they drive your breathing and water usage.

JIMMY SAYS

When I first started talking about ketogenic diets, well-meaning but misinformed people would arrogantly tell me to simply cut the carbs and I would be in ketosis. If only it were that easy for the majority of the population dealing with insulin resistance. This is why testing blood ketones (see page 35) is essential. Otherwise, you wouldn't know whether you were producing ketones to get the desired health effects. Knowledge is power.

THE INS AND OUTS OF KETOSIS

Over the years, we've learned that improving health, losing fat, decreasing inflammation, and improving blood sugar are done most effectively when you're in a state of *nutritional ketosis.* However, just cutting out carbohydrates from your diet doesn't always achieve that goal. There are some basic metabolic rules that you need to understand; the following sections help clarify those rules.

Nutritional Ketosis

Let's define nutritional ketosis. It's a state in which blood ketone levels are between 0.5 and 6 millimoles per liter (mmol/L). We've found that the body seems to change its predominant fuel from glucose to ketones as the level of ketones rises higher than 0.5 mmol/L.

All right! But how do you know whether you're in nutritional ketosis? In other words, how do you know whether your body is using ketones as its primary fuel? You can check by testing your blood ketone levels through a simple finger stick and a blood ketone monitor. If your ketone level is 0.5 mmol/L or greater, then you're in nutritional ketosis, and you're burning fat more than you're burning glucose.

Some people freak out because their ketone levels are not up to 2 or 3 mmol/L. Unless you're treating a disease such as epilepsy, you don't have to register ketone levels that high to gain the therapeutic effects of ketosis. Remember, your body's going to try to conserve and/or partition fuels as it needs to, and it can use ketones and glucose at the same time. This is where the magic of treating the diseases of civilization lies, including cholesterol and blood pressure. The benefits of ketosis in treating disease start in the 0.5 mmol/L range. As ketone levels rise, you can start to see a lot of the benefits of ketosis, including increased energy, more efficient fat loss, improvement in blood pressure, improvement in cholesterol, and better control of seizures. This is why a lot of the medical literature talks about ketone levels in the 1 to 3 mmol/L range.

If your insulin levels are high, insulin stimulates an enzyme called *lipoprotein lipase* and drives fat into the fat cells rather than letting it remain in the bloodstream to be processed by the liver. To get into and maintain a state of ketosis, your insulin levels must be low enough to keep fat from being driven into the adipose tissue (fat cells) instead of being processed in the liver.

When insulin is high, it also keeps fat from exiting the fat cell. In other words, having high insulin levels prevents weight loss in two ways: by pushing fat into the fat cells and by keeping the fat in the fat cells. You can think of insulin as your pushy financial adviser or banker who is always trying to get you to save money but is very stingy about letting you take money out of the bank. (Some of us could use a little less fat banking and a little more more precious metal banking.)

Insulin is essentially the master hormone that drives fat storage. It also drives the diseases of civilization. The effect you're looking for from the Keto Cure is to lower the overall signal from insulin. You're not completely turning it off; that would be bad. That's what happens to type 1 diabetics who don't make any insulin. A small amount of insulin is necessary to maintain health, but excessive amounts cause disease. You want to lower insulin enough to turn down the fat storage drive and turn down the other twenty-six hormones that contribute to the diseases of civilization. To do that, you simply cut your carbohydrate intake enough to drop your insulin low enough that your ketone levels begin to rise higher than 0.5 mmol/L. It's actually that easy. *That's* nutritional ketosis.

JIMMY SAYS

The pursuit of nutritional ketosis really comes down to how effective your efforts are at reducing insulin levels to a range that optimizes the way your body functions. High levels make it impossible to be in ketosis, lower inflammation, and lose weight, whereas too-low levels (where you no longer produce insulin) are equally unhealthy. Making appropriate diet and lifestyle changes that put your insulin in the Goldilocks range is what we are trying to help you accomplish in this book.

Ketoacidosis

I told you that nutritional ketosis involves a ketone range between 0.5 and 6 mmol/L. A small amount of insulin present acts as a ketone brake. In a state of ketoacidosis, the body generally has no insulin whatsoever. If for some reason the body is not making *any* insulin (as in a person with type 1 diabetes), blood sugar would shoot higher than 500 mg/dL and often go higher than 700 mg/dL. In this state (the absence of insulin and rapidly rising blood sugar), the body cannot derive any fuel from glucose, and ketone levels rise higher than 20 mmol/L and often up to 25 to 26 mmol/L. Together, high blood glucose and high blood ketones cause a shift in the way the body handles hydrogen, and that leads to an acidic pH shift in the blood. Normal blood pH is between 7.35 and 7.45. When the blood pH drops below 7.35, many of the body's enzymes stop functioning, and that can slow you down. In fact, it can kill you.

⚠️ **CAUTION:**
If you are a type 1 diabetic or you have a predisposition to ketoacidosis due to other rare metabolic issues, you should be closely monitored by your doctor, and your blood sugar should be closely watched to prevent this from happening.

Ketoacidosis is a dangerous condition; however, if you're not a type 1 diabetic, then you shouldn't have to worry about this issue. I say that because when you are producing insulin on your own and your blood sugars are under fairly good control (not higher than about 300 mg/dL), your likelihood of progressing to ketoacidosis is very, very rare.

DISCLAIMER: *Even though it's extremely rare in people who are not type 1 diabetics, ketoacidosis can occur when a person gets horribly dehydrated while also overworking his or her muscles and going beyond the point of heat exhaustion. I've seen this twice in my career. (I live in Arizona.) Both patients were very physically deconditioned borderline diabetics. The severe dehydration affected their pancreatic function as well as caused rapid muscle breakdown, which led to a state of ketoacidosis. If you have any questions about your blood sugar and insulin function, please talk with your doctor.*

For "average bears" like you and me, who produce an adequate amount of insulin (most people who are pre-diabetic or have weight gain issues produce too much insulin) and have our blood sugar under good control, removing carbohydrates from our diet will move us into a state of nutritional ketosis without taking us higher than 6.0 mmol/L. Ketoacidosis will never be an issue.

Keto Adaptation

Over the past ten years, I've had hundreds of patients complain, "I tried that keto thingy, and it didn't work." They claim to have tried a ketogenic diet; they may have lost a little weight, but they felt horrible. Let me discuss a couple of things that help explain why you might feel terrible as you start your ketogenic journey:

- When you transition to a ketogenic diet, you go through a phase called the *keto-adaptation phase*. It lasts for two to eight weeks, depending on your body's adaptation speed.

- A ketogenic lifestyle will cause you to lose sodium, potassium, magnesium, and zinc. These salts are excreted to help your body remove the excess water that comes from burning fat and ketones.

When you follow the generally accepted guidelines for nutrition, your body gets used to using glucose or carbohydrates as its primary fuel. Over time, because your fat intake is low, the body enhances the gut microvilli to be more effective at absorbing glucose. The gut and cells downregulate their ability to absorb and use fat to accommodate a more efficient use of glucose. The lower segment of the small intestine and the large intestine use MCT receptors (there are more than fifteen types) to absorb fat into

JIMMY SAYS

If you are scared of keto-acidosis, then let me assuage your concern: This is a problem experienced primarily by a type 1 diabetic who consumes a high-carb meal and doesn't take insulin, resulting in extremely high blood sugar levels and extremely high blood ketone levels. A type 1 diabetic eating a ketogenic diet can maintain blood sugar levels in the healthy range with a much lower need for insulin and only moderate therapeutic levels of blood ketones—a tiny fraction of what would be considered dangerous.

the bloodstream or the lymphatic tissues. There also are MCT receptors in the cell walls themselves, which allow ketones to be moved into the cells throughout the body at an increased or decreased speed. As you shift away from carbs and increase your fat intake, you're going to see a delay in your ability to adequately use and absorb fat. It takes about two to eight weeks to upregulate those fat receptors in both the gut and the cells of the body. This is the keto-adaptation phase.

People in this keto-adaptation phase experience common symptoms of fatigue, low energy, and even headaches and bloating. Some experience depression and anxiety. I've had patients who have had a sugar withdrawal that's identical to some of the symptoms common to recovering from drug addiction, such as with opiate withdrawal. Carbohydrate withdrawal can cause jitters, shakiness, irritability, nausea, and even tingling sensations in the body. Be patient. These symptoms will pass.

Keto-Adaptation Hacks for the True Ketonian

You can avoid some symptoms and even augment the speed with which keto-adaptation occurs through a couple of metabolic hacks.

Get Adequate Fat in Your Diet
A lot of people who cut out carbs are afraid to add fat, and they increase calories from fat to only 40 or 50 percent, which doesn't quite drive the upregulation of fat receptors to help the cells of the body enhance fat absorption. If you're truly doing a ketogenic diet, you need to increase your fat intake to roughly 60 percent, 70 percent, or even 80 percent. Now, that's a lot of fat on your plate, but it works. Look for food that is high in fat (red meat is 55 percent fat; pork is 45 percent to 50 percent fat), and then add fat to it by cooking it in butter, lard, or coconut oil or by adding some other form of fat.

Replace the Salt
Remember, when you're burning fat, your body is producing carbon dioxide and water. You blow off the carbon dioxide when you breathe, and you eliminate the water through urination. The problem is that water doesn't naturally leave your renal system (kidneys and bladder) unless it follows salt out of the kidneys. Water follows salt just about anywhere, including right out of your kidneys into your bladder and then off to the deep, dark recesses of the sewer system. Your body takes salt (potassium, sodium, magnesium, and zinc) and

UPGRADE YOUR SALT

I find that it's not sufficient just to increase the amount of table salt you use. The challenge is that regular table salt is just sodium, but you also need potassium, magnesium, and zinc. I recommend pink Himalayan salt, which has the extra minerals. You can find it in a grinder at just about any grocery store. I encourage you to consider using pink Himalayan salt so you can replace those electrolytes that you lose by burning fat as your primary fuel.

puts it in the kidneys, and then the water follows the salt into your kidneys and out of your body into the toilet. I cannot emphasize this enough: When you urinate, you're dumping not only water but also salt. So, you *must* replace the salt.

Unfortunately, in the past fifty years in the United States and other medically capable countries, we have become afraid of salt. Everyone thinks that salt will give them high blood pressure. If you're following a high-carb, low-fat diet, yes, you're going to retain salt. The higher insulin levels stimulated by following the SAD tell your body to retain salt, which means you retain water. (I see more leg swelling and varicose veins after the holidays when people cheat on Christmas cookies than at any other time of the year.)

If you are doing a high-fat, low-carb diet, you're going to experience a loss of salt. Making sure you have adequate salt intake seems to alleviate a number of the symptoms that occur during the keto-adaptation period. Again, I can't emphasize that enough. Replace the salt!

Supplement with Methylated Folic Acid

I find that roughly 50 to 60 percent of people who have insulin resistance (read more about it in Chapter 4) have some degree of a methylfolate reductase deficiency. You might hear this referred to as an *MTHFR deficiency.*

People with an MTHFR deficiency don't convert folic acid to the necessary intracellular methylated form. If your folic acid is not methylated within the cell itself, even though you might receive oral or injectable B12 and B6, you can't use that B6 and B12 appropriately inside the cell. This deficiency increases the likelihood of B12 deficiency, B6 deficiency, depression, anxiety, fatigue, and weight gain. The MTHFR deficiency can be screened for by a simple genetic test that uses a blood draw or salivary swab sample.

METHYLATED FOLIC ACID

You can't find methylated folic acid in most health food stores. I found that people were coming into my office with five to ten different bottles of the vitamins I often recommend for general health and weight management. I added methylated folic acid to the multivitamin combination that I found to be most effective, and we ended up with a single cost-effective multivitamin that covers all the bases and aids in keto-adaptation. One of the big reasons we developed the KetoEssentials vitamin, which you can find at www.KetoLiving.com, was to provide the pre-methylated form of folic acid, which helps you use the folic acid correctly within your cells when you eat fat that contains the essential fat-soluble vitamins.

THE ABCs OF VITAMINS AND FAT

One of the challenges with today's nutritional fat dogmas is that the symptoms of depression are often amplified because people restrict fat. Fat contains vitamins. If you're not eating enough fat, you're not getting the vitamins you need. Where I live in Arizona, a lack of fat in the diet is the biggest cause of deficiencies in vitamins B12 and D. We average only two cloudy days per year, so how could someone not get enough vitamin D? Yet one-third of the people I see in my office who follow a low-fat diet are vitamin D deficient. Eat more fat and you'll absorb more vitamins.

How Do You Test for Ketosis?

A lot of people contact me and say, "Dr. Nally, this keto diet doesn't work. I tried it."

I reply, "Well, did you actually test to see if you were in ketosis?"

One hundred percent of the time, the answer is, "No. I didn't know you could test for ketosis. How do I do that?"

Are *you* testing for ketosis? If not, then I have three words for you: "Check your ketones!"

I started following a low-carbohydrate diet around 2005. I followed the plan pretty well, and about five years later, when we realized that a low-carbohydrate diet puts a person into a state of nutritional ketosis, I thought I was in ketosis just because I was eating low-carb. I followed a very-low-carb program and kept my carbohydrate intake to less than 20 grams per day (because I'm horribly insulin resistant), so I just assumed I was in ketosis. However, when we started being able to accurately test for ketosis through either a blood test or a breath test, I realized I wasn't in ketosis all the times I thought I was.

> **"**It's not a *short-term diet.*
> It's a *long-term lifestyle*
> *change.***"**
>
> —Doc Nally

In my case, too many carbs, too much protein, a great deal of stress, a lack of sleep, too much travel, or even a number of artificial sweeteners would kick me out of ketosis. It wasn't until after I started testing that I dramatically improved the way I was able to augment my diet and move those last 15 pounds of fat off. That's when I started truly feeling the benefits of ketosis.

Now I live a ketogenic lifestyle, and I'm predominantly in a ketogenic state.

So, how do you test for ketosis? There are three ways—urine ketone strips, breath ketone monitoring, and blood ketone testing.

Urine Testing for Ketosis

One way to test for ketones is to check your urine with urine-testing strips. The problem with urine ketone testing is that it's effective for only one to two months. After the second month, most of us begin to conserve the ketones in our blood instead of spilling them over into the urine.

Your body thinks, "Hey! Rib-eye steaks and butter are expensive. You're using ketones as fuel now. Stop dumping that extra fuel!" So, it hangs on to the ketones as an adaptive fuel conservation function, which causes your urine test strips to start showing as negative even when you're actually in nutritional ketosis.

This lack of ketones in the urine often causes people to get discouraged by the ketogenic approach because they think that the diet isn't working. "I'm not in ketosis," is what I often hear when people see me after a few months of following a ketogenic diet that was recommended by a Facebook page moderator. Well, you might actually be in ketosis; you just

JIMMY SAYS

If you don't learn anything else from this book, remember this: Testing for the presence of ketones when you are attempting a ketogenic diet is a must, not an option. It would be like using a debit card to pay for purchases without ever keeping records and balancing your account. You know there are deductions being made from your account, but you have no idea where your current balance stands. Don't let your body suffer from an overdraft charge because you didn't prioritize ketone testing!

JIMMY SAYS

When I released my book Keto Clarity in 2014, Ketonix was the only ketone meter available. Now there are several newcomers to the market that are making waves with innovation and ingenuity, including the LEVL meter (www. levlnow.com). There's really no excuse for doing keto without testing.

can't see it in your urine after the second month. Some people still can, but most can't.

If you're interested in trying urine-testing strips, True Test and Ketostix are two brands that I have used in the past. You can find these strips at your local pharmacy or drugstore.

Breath Testing for Ketosis

The second method of testing is with a breath ketone meter. These meters don't directly test β-hydroxybutyrate; they test acetone, which is the ketone expelled through the breath. Acetone is blown off through the lungs in small amounts. The challenge with breath testing is that the amount of acetone breathed off is not the same for everyone at uniform levels of blood β-hydroxybutyrate. That means breath meters can't give you a number that correlates with the level of β-hydroxybutyrate in your blood; they just give you an acetone level that lets you know you're in a certain range of ketosis. If you're trying to find out how a certain food affects your level of ketosis, it's more difficult with a breath meter than with the other testing methods.

As of the writing of this book, breath meters are still fairly expensive. The Ketonix Meter is a reusable breath ketone meter that I have used fairly regularly. There are a couple others available, including The Voyager by Invoy. They are available from online retailers and medical-supply stores.

Blood Ketone Testing

The third method of testing is through the use of blood ketone test strips. To check your ketones, you basically prick your finger like you would to check your blood sugar, drawing up a drop of blood onto the test strip. The monitor gives you a blood ketone reading within about ten seconds. With blood ketone monitoring, the goal is to see blood ketone levels at 0.5 mmol/L or higher.

Blood ketone monitors, which you can usually find at local pharmacies, aren't particularly expensive, but the cost of the test strips will bite you in the wallet. In addition, not all pharmacies carry the strips. You can find them on Amazon, eBay, and other online suppliers.

The available models at the time of this writing are the Precision Xtra, the Keto-Mojo, and the Nova Max. I've used all three, and I recommend the Precision Xtra and the Keto-Mojo. The Keto-Mojo is notably less expensive.

CHAPTER 4

INSULIN RESISTANCE 101

As a family practice physician and obesity medicine specialist, my job is to examine and treat disease. In my career, I have discovered that the majority of the diseases I treat are the *diseases of civilization*, which are those diseases that have come about because of the changes induced by modernizing and industrializing a society or a people. These include diabetes, dyslipidemia (abnormal cholesterol), heart disease, hypertension, gout, vascular disease, and stroke. It is fascinating that these diseases didn't really appear in large numbers until the early 1900s. Yes, some of these diseases have been identified in early Egyptians, but as a society modernizes or industrializes, certain types of disease begin to become more prevalent.[1]

The Canadian cardiologist William Osler, one of the founding professors of Johns Hopkins Hospital, documented the first "syndrome" associated with narrowing of the arteries and heart disease at the turn of the nineteenth century. In 1912, the American cardiologist James Herrick was credited with the discovery that narrowed arteries cause "angina," a form of chest pain associated with exertion.

Today we know that underlying each of these diseases is the phenomenon of "insulin overproduction" or insulin resistance, which seems to occur ten to twenty years prior to the onset of the diseases of civilization. *Metabolic syndrome, dysmetabolic syndrome*, or *syndrome X* is the name we give to cases in which a person has three or more of the diseases of civilization and has insulin resistance. There is still an argument over whether insulin overproduction is the chicken or the egg in this scenario, but what I have seen over time has convinced me that insulin is culprit.

JIMMY SAYS

I was doomed to deal with insulin resistance from the very beginning. My mom weighed well over 300 pounds when she delivered me, I was born via cesarean section, and as a kid I consumed mostly crappy foods that put my body in a position of not responding to insulin signaling like it's supposed to. Now I have severe insulin resistance, so I have to work hard at dialing in my diet and lifestyle to ward off future health complications. It's a battle worth fighting, though!

Insulin is a very powerful hormone and is often called the "master hormone." The main job of insulin (it has a few) is to open the cells so that they can receive glucose when it is present in the bloodstream.

For reasons that appear to be genetic, this key becomes "worn" in a portion of the population and does not unlock the door fast enough or efficiently enough to lower the blood sugar as it rises after a meal or after sugar, starch, or complex carbohydrates have been ingested. As insulin is released, the glucose in the bloodstream goes down as it enters the cells, where it will be used as fuel.

In the case of insulin resistance, blood glucose doesn't enter the cells very effectively, and overall blood sugar remains high after meals. The body panics and stimulates the production of additional insulin. This added insulin in the bloodstream eventually lowers the blood sugar (but overcompensation causes hypoglycemia in a number of people).

Over time, people with insulin resistance begin producing two to ten times the normal amount of insulin. In some people, even higher levels of insulin can occur. Insulin resistance, then, is an excessive production of insulin because the signaling mechanism to let glucose through the door of the cell wall isn't being correctly received by the cells in the body as rapidly as it should. It's not that the insulin is broken; it's just that the speed with which the insulin causes the glucose to be absorbed into the cells is notably slower (or resistant). The insulin that initially was produced eventually kicks in, but it might take one to five hours longer than normal. This extra insulin, acting at a slower rate, is the underlying culprit of the diseases of civilization.

Insulin actually lingers in the bloodstream for up to twelve hours. This is why some pre-diabetic patients who eat only a sugary meal experience a hypoglycemic (low blood sugar) episode two to five hours after eating.

How, you ask? Let me explain. We know that there are two, or maybe more, broken receptor mechanisms in the cell wall of a person with insulin resistance. The first one is impaired transport of the GLUT-2 receptor, which is in the β-cell of the pancreas. Because of changes in the cell surface, fewer receptors are present to identify the presence of glucose, which reduces the rate of insulin release.

The second known mechanism is also in the β-cell of the pancreas. Elevated cholesterol levels and triglyceride levels, as well as the presence of high levels of fructose, impair transcription at the genetic level of an essential transport molecule called Abca1. When this molecule is lacking, it has been shown to worsen insulin signaling when glucose is present.

Which mechanism is really at the center of this issue remains to be determined. Either way, 80 to 85 percent of the people who walk through my clinic doors exhibit some degree of insulin overproduction to glucose or have signs of insulin resistance.

Insulin is supposed to keep the glucose levels in the bloodstream within a normal range (between 70 and 99 mg/dL when fasting). Why is it a problem if it does so just a little slower?

Insulin does more than just open the door to the cell wall in the presence of increased glucose. I talk more about the functions in the following chapters, but for the sake of understanding, the following seven points are important:

- **INSULIN CAUSES WEIGHT GAIN.** We know that at least twenty-seven hormones play a role in gaining or losing weight. Because insulin is the master hormone, from the perspective of treating obesity, you can't fix the other hormones until insulin is corrected. Insulin turns on the storage of fat by activating lipoprotein lipase, an enzyme discussed earlier, which pulls triglycerides out of the cholesterol molecules and deposits them in adipose tissue (fat cells). Insulin also closes the back door to the cell, which makes it more difficult to release triglyceride or fat from the fat cell proportional to its presence in the blood.

- **INSULIN DRIVES INCREASED TRIGLYCERIDE PRODUCTION** in the liver, especially in the presence of fructose. This increases your total cholesterol and your risk for vascular disease.

- **INSULIN TRIGGERS ATHEROSCLEROSIS.** Triglycerides are essentially the passenger in the small-dense LDL (bad cholesterol) molecule. Higher triglycerides cause increased LDL production, which leads to increased atherosclerosis (narrowing of the arteries).

- **HIGHER INSULIN LEVELS STIMULATE INCREASED FREQUENCY OF GOUT AND KIDNEY STONES.** Insulin increases uric acid production. In a complex secondary mechanism, insulin also increases calcium oxylate. Both uric acid and calcium oxylate increase the risk of kidney stones and gout.

- **INSULIN RAISES BLOOD PRESSURE.** Insulin stimulates the retention of sodium, causing an increase in blood pressure by increased water retention as a result of retaining salt.

- **INSULIN MAKES INFLAMMATION WORSE.** Insulin drives the inflammatory cascade. It stimulates the inflammatory hormones that cause arthritis, allergic rhinitis, psoriasis, dermatitis, and inflammatory bowel problems to become amplified.

- **INSULIN INCREASES FREE RADICAL FORMATION.** During the process of normal enzyme reactions within the body (more than thirty-seven thousand billion billion—that's twenty-one zeros after the thirty-seven—reactions in the body per second), unpaired electrons can form when oxygen reacts with various molecules. This can cause a chain reaction of damage to cell membranes, DNA, proteins, and fats. Overproduction of free radicals (without a balance of antioxidants) can lead to the more rapid formation of disease, including cancer.

JIMMY SAYS

Once you realize that the overproduction of insulin is at the heart of everything bad that happens in your health, you should feel motivated to do everything within your power to reduce the insulin load to a healthy range. That's why Dr. Nally and I are so incredibly passionate about the ketogenic diet—it lowers insulin and reduces all the negative effects that come from high insulin levels. I guess you could say we are all about any diet that is a low-insulin diet, and keto fits the bill perfectly.

CHAPTER 4:
INSULIN
RESISTANCE 101

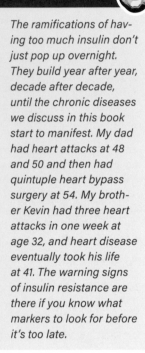

JIMMY SAYS

The ramifications of having too much insulin don't just pop up overnight. They build year after year, decade after decade, until the chronic diseases we discuss in this book start to manifest. My dad had heart attacks at 48 and 50 and then had quintuple heart bypass surgery at 54. My brother Kevin had three heart attacks in one week at age 32, and heart disease eventually took his life at 41. The warning signs of insulin resistance are there if you know what markers to look for before it's too late.

My intent here is not to demonize insulin; it's not 100 percent bad. Fire is a good metaphor for insulin. Fire is used to cook food, warm a home, and run a steam engine. However, too much fire scorches the food, turns a home to ash, and can cause a steam engine to become a bomb with wheels. Similarly, insulin in moderation is essential and life-saving, but too much is dangerous. When your body is producing five to ten times the normal amount of insulin, you're going to scorch, singe, or destroy the organs with which it comes in contact. Five to ten times the normal amount of insulin amplifies the diseases of civilization by five to ten times.

When I first started practicing medicine in the late 1990s, I noticed a correlation and a very scary trend. Patients would present with symptoms including elevated triglycerides, elevated fasting blood sugar, neuropathy, microalbuminuria (a sign of kidney disease), gout, kidney stones, polycystic ovary disease, coronary artery disease, and hypertension. These conditions would appear five to fifteen years before the diagnosis of type 2 diabetes was made, but these patients consistently became diabetic at some point down the road.

Because I saw this pattern, I began doing two-hour glucose tolerance tests (GTTs) with insulin levels. I was shocked to find that 80 to 85 percent of those people were actually diabetic or pre-diabetic, or they had significant abnormality of their fasting or after-meal insulin levels.

The problem with a two-hour GTT is that it's an older test that today is used mostly for pregnant women. It fell out of favor because a much easier hemoglobin A1c (HbA1c) blood test became available. The reason the GTT fell out of favor is that many people feel miserable after the test due to the profound insulin spike and concomitant hypoglycemia that can occur, especially in those who are diabetic or pre-diabetic. Many of my patients got pretty upset with me for ordering the test, both because of how they felt afterward and because I was the only physician in town still ordering it. So, in my attempt to find a better solution, I realized that I could triangulate three tests: fasting insulin, triglycerides, and small-dense LDL particle number. Because these three tests respond to higher insulin levels over a period of twenty-four to forty-eight hours, abnormality in these three tests correlated quite closely with those in my clinic who had positive glucose tolerance tests at the same time. There is absolutely no data in the literature about the use of this triangulation, but I have found it to be a pattern that is clinically consistent.

Dr. Joseph Kraft is a pathologist who began measuring both glucose and insulin levels through a three-hour GTT at the University of Illinois St. Joseph Hospital in Chicago. This test consists of checking the blood sugar and insulin of a patient who's in a fasted state; then the patient drinks a 100-gram glucose load and has his or her blood sugar and insulin tested at the 30-, 60-, 120-, and 180-minute marks. Dr. Kraft completed this test and recorded the results for 14,384 patients between 1972 and 1998. His landmark findings both confirm and clarify the results that I have seen and suspected for years.[2]

I was ecstatic to see that I wasn't alone in my suspicions. Dr. Kraft and his team administered an unpleasant GTT to more than 14,000 patients and provided the data that many of us have had to clinically triangulate. What Dr. Kraft points out so clearly in his research is that huge spikes in insulin occur one to two hours after the ingestion of carbohydrates fifteen to twenty years prior to a person's blood sugar level ever rising into the "diabetic range." He also consistently demonstrates the pattern that occurs in a normal non-insulin-resistant patient and in each stage of insulin resistance progression.

FIVE STAGES OF INSULIN RESISTANCE

Using information extrapolated from Dr. Kraft's research and what I see clinically, I've come up with five stages of insulin resistance, shown in the chart below.

	Fasting Insulin	1-Hour Insulin	2-Hour Insulin	3-Hour Insulin	Notes
Non–Insulin Resistant/ Non-Diabetic	1–5	< 30	< 40	5–15	2 hr + 3 hr < 60
Type/Stage II	6–30	30–120	40–90	16–55	2 hr + 3 hr = > 60
Type/Stage III	11–30	30–120	90–150	50–90	2 hr + 3 hr > 213
Type/Stage IV (DM Type 2)	> 31	120–180	> 150	80–200	2 hr + 3 hr > 320
Type/Stage V (DM Type 1)	0–5	5–20	5–20	5–10	2 hr + 3 hr = 25 or less

Insulin values in mU/mL

From this chart, you can see that the current definition of diabetes is actually the fourth and most prolifically damaging stage of diabetes. From the data gathered in Dr. Kraft's population, it is apparent that hyperinsulinemia (insulin resistance) is really the underlying disease and that a diagnosis of diabetes mellitus type 2 should be based on fasting and an after-meal insulin test instead of an arbitrary blood sugar number. This would allow us to catch and treat diabetes ten to fifteen years prior to its becoming a problem. In looking at the percentages of the 14,384 patients in Dr. Kraft's study, the data also implies that 50 to 85 percent of people in the United States are hyperinsulinemic or have diabetes mellitus "in-situ."[3] This means that up to 85 percent of the U.S. population is in the early stages of diabetes, which is the reason projections state that one in three Americans will be diabetic by 2050.[4]

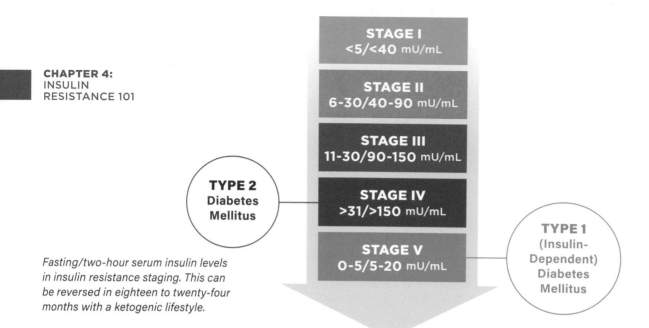

STAGE I
<5/<40 mU/mL

STAGE II
6-30/40-90 mU/mL

STAGE III
11-30/90-150 mU/mL

STAGE IV
>31/>150 mU/mL

STAGE V
0-5/5-20 mU/mL

TYPE 2 Diabetes Mellitus

TYPE 1 (Insulin-Dependent) Diabetes Mellitus

Fasting/two-hour serum insulin levels in insulin resistance staging. This can be reversed in eighteen to twenty-four months with a ketogenic lifestyle.

JIMMY SAYS

People tend to look at fat on their bodies as a disgusting result of a gluttonous overconsumption of calories and not enough exercise. But ancestrally speaking, there is a practical reason why the fat is there: It's a survival mechanism for when food is scarce so the body can maintain energy and vitality. Although many people in the modern world no longer deal with issues of food scarcity, our genetic makeup is exactly the same now as it was then.

Insulin resistance isn't really a disease; it's a genetically inherited syndrome. As demonstrated by the data in the figure above, diabetes has a pattern to its progression. It is my opinion that this "syndrome" was, and is, the genetic mechanism that protected groups of people and kept them alive during famines or harsh winters when no method of food preservation was available. Prior to the advent of refrigerators, food preservatives, and large storage cellars, people ate seasonally and were dramatically more physically active. If looked at from that perspective, insulin resistance is what provided for essential mammalian fuel storage and protection from seasonal swings and food scarcity. It is most likely what kept the Pima Indians of Arizona and other similar groups alive for hundreds of years in arid deserts or other harsh climates that provided only limited access to carbohydrates. This syndrome didn't become an issue among these populations until they were introduced to boxed baking mixes and beer.

SIGNS OF INSULIN RESISTANCE

How do you know if you have insulin resistance? It's actually pretty simple. There are two cutaneous signs of insulin resistance. The first is skin tags. Yes, those little pedunculated, flesh-colored tags of skin in areas where skin folds or experiences friction are "pathognomonic" for insulin resistance. That means if you have skin tags, you have insulin resistance, period.

The second sign is a pronounced thickening and darkening of the skin at the folds of the neck, axilla, and waist. It is called *acanthosis nigricans.* This condition usually is seen in association with diabetes, but I often see it before diabetes has been diagnosed.

The following abnormal lab values also point to insulin resistance:

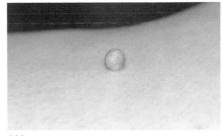

Skin tags.

- Triglycerides greater than 150

- Triglyceride/HDL ratio greater than 3.0

- Elevated small-dense LDL particle number greater than 500

- Fasting insulin level greater than 5 mg/dL

- Fasting blood sugar higher than 100 mg/dL

- Postprandial blood sugar greater than 140 mg/dL (two hours after a meal)

- Waist circumference greater than 40 inches in men and greater than 35 inches in women

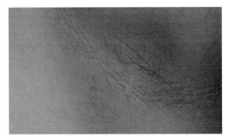

Acanthosis nigricans. Photo by Madhero88 (CC BY).

Lastly, a pattern I commonly see is the onset of polyneuropathy five to ten years prior to the onset of diabetes. Polyneuropathy is a generalized numbness, burning, or tingling in the lower legs and feet that progressively moves up to the knees. When evaluated by a neurologist, the neuropathy is often blamed on other causes because blood sugars after fasting are not always abnormal and the form of demyelination of the nerves is variable based on the degree of inflammation and vascular changes.

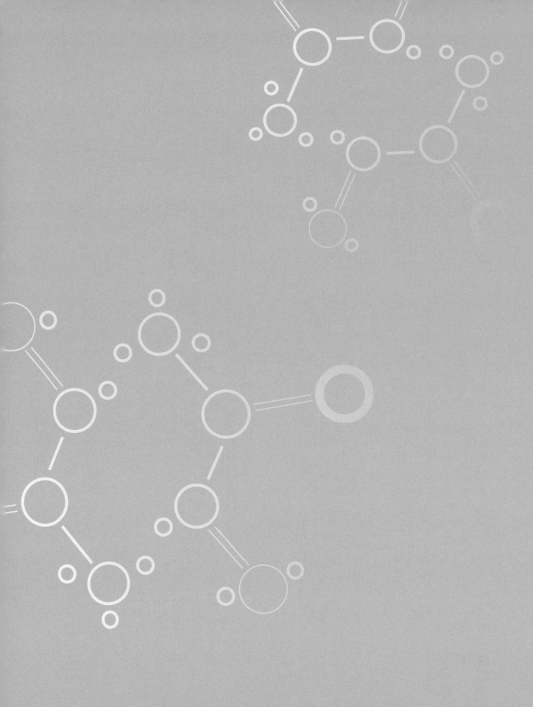

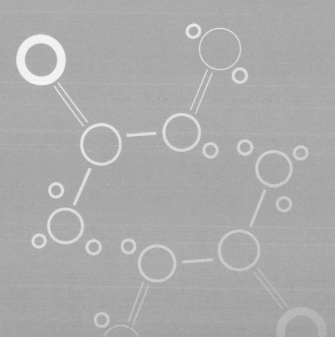

PART 2

THE KETO CURE APPROACH TO DISEASE TREATMENT

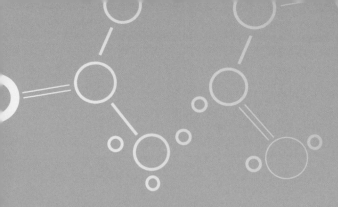

Throughout this book, you are going to see nutritional approaches to the treatment of the diseases of civilization. Each approach is made with the principles on the following pages in mind.

In the almost two decades that I've been practicing medicine and treating the diseases of civilization, six basic principles seem to stand out. I hesitate to write the principles here because I fear that people might treat them like a cookbook or flow chart. However, medicine is an art, and you just can't blindly follow the principles without giving them some thought, because no two people are the same.

One of the things I've learned in the practice of this art is that the human body functions in response to physical laws. Science is based on a hypothesis regarding physical laws and testing. The principles outlined here are those that I have found to be generally effective in changing the function of the body in response to the physical laws we currently understand.

In the chapters that follow, each of which focuses on one disease or class of diseases, I give you information about these principles that is specific to the disease or class of diseases I am discussing in that chapter. If you suffer from any of these diseases of civilization, make sure to read the related chapter(s) to see how the principles apply specifically to the changes you're making as you apply the Keto Cure approach to your life.

PRINCIPLE 1
LOWER INSULIN LEVELS WITH DIET

Insulin is the master hormone. The first step in addressing many diseases is to get insulin back to its baseline. This is done by restricting dietary carbohydrate intake. The goal is to reduce carbohydrate intake to less than 20 grams per day. When this is done correctly, blood sugar drops into the normal range (60 to 100 mg/dl) and fasting insulin returns (over 12-24 months) to less than 5 mU/mL.

PRINCIPLE 2
AVOID ADDITIVES THAT RAISE INSULIN LEVELS

Realize that a number of sweeteners stimulate insulin production without raising blood sugar. These sweeteners need to be eliminated as well. (See Chapter 16 for information about sweeteners to avoid.)

   If your triglycerides are lower than 100 mg/dL but your small-dense LDL particles are greater than 600 mg/dL, you need to examine what you're eating to see what might contain artificial sweeteners. You might think there's nothing in your diet that will raise insulin levels, but if you read labels, you might identify, say, a coffee creamer that includes sweeteners like dextrose, maltodextrin, or acesulfame potassium. Another possible culprit is that you're drinking a leaf-based tea—such as black, green, or oolong—that spikes insulin without raising glucose.[1, 2]

> **WHAT'S CONSIDERED AN ADDITIVE?**
>
> *The term* additives *might make you think only of preservatives and other ingredients in foods that can cause insulin levels to rise. However, in the discussions of certain diseases, you'll see that I also include things such as alcohol and smoking in the section about additives.*

PRINCIPLE 3
MODERATE PROTEIN WHERE APPROPRIATE

Low-fat protein spikes insulin, so low-fat protein sources such as chicken, turkey, and crustaceans will cause a variable rise in insulin due to their higher arginine content. We know that higher-protein and lower-fat diets don't change the inflammation cascade. (See Chapter 2 for more information about that.)

   Remember that your goal is to increase fat to at least 70 percent of total caloric intake, which is easy to do if you make sure that the ratio of your protein to fat intake is 1:1. For example, a boiled egg has 7 grams of protein and 7 grams of fat. Because fat contains more than twice as many calories as protein, the caloric ratio of fat to protein in the egg is 70 percent. You shouldn't have to worry about counting calories; just try to ensure that for every gram of protein you eat, you eat a gram of fat.

A number of amino acids in high concentrations also stimulate a variable insulin response. These include (from the most insulinogenic to the least) arginine, lysine, phenylalanine, leucine, tryptophan, valine, threonine, methionine, isoleucine, and histidine.[3] Amino acids make up the formation of protein. So, use your proteins with prudence. Remember, excess low-fat proteins in your diet could have a stimulatory effect on insulin and a suppressive effect on thyroid function.

The following are great protein sources for a ketogenic lifestyle:

- Beef
- Lamb
- Pork (including bacon)
- Fatty fish (salmon, sea bass)
- Eggs
- Hard cheeses (Velveeta is not real cheese!)
- Almonds/walnuts/macadamia nuts

> **STARTING POINTS**
>
> *The following calculations are starting points that can be adjusted up or down based on your level of hunger, blood sugar, and need for weight control.*

You can calculate your ideal protein needs based on your height in inches with the formulas below:

MEN:

| 50 grams of protein (for the first 5 feet of height) | + | 2.3 grams of protein x each inch over 5 feet | x1.2 = | MALE DAILY PROTEIN NEED |

If you exercise more than sixty minutes five days per week, then multiply daily protein need by 1.6 instead of 1.2.

x1.6

Here's an example for a 6-foot male:

[50 grams + 27.6 grams] x 1.2 = 93.1 grams of protein needed per day

For someone who exercises:
[50 grams + 27.6 grams] x 1.6 = 125.2 grams of protein needed per day

WOMEN:

| 45 grams of protein (for the first 5 feet of height) | + | 2.3 grams of protein x each inch over 5 feet | = | FEMALE DAILY PROTEIN NEED |

If you exercise more than sixty minutes five days per week, then multiply daily protein need by 1.4.

x1.4

Here's an example for a 5-foot, 4-inch female:

[45 grams + 9.2 grams] = 54.2 grams of protein needed per day

For someone who exercises:
[45 grams + 9.2 grams] x 1.4 = 75.9 grams of protein needed per day

PRINCIPLE 4
ELIMINATE PROBLEM MEDICATIONS

Many medications actually stimulate insulin, slow the metabolism, or cause cravings. These medications may be standards of treatment for the diseases in question. Working with your doctor to find alternatives or to eliminate those medications is a key step in improving the diseases of civilization. If your doctor doesn't know how to do that, most obesity specialists have been trained to identify medications that inhibit weight loss or cause weight gain because of their effect on the metabolism or on hormones that stimulate weight gain.

I won't go into the mechanisms of how these medications cause problems, but I'm providing a list so that you can discuss these with your doctor and identify alternatives where necessary.

- **BETA-BLOCKERS**
  - Lopressor, Toprol-X (metoprolol)
  - Tenormin (atenolol)
  - Trandate (labetelol)
- **GLITAZONES**
  - Avandia (rosiglitazone)
  - Actos (pioglitazone)
- **MONOAMINE OXIDASE INHIBITORS**
  - Nardil (phenelzine)
  - Eldepryl; Emsam; Zelapar (selegiline)
  - Parnate (tranylcypromine)
- **ANTI-ANXIETY/ANTI-DEPRESSANTS OR SSRIs**
  - Paxil (paroxetine)
  - Lexapro (escitalopram)
  - Zoloft (sertraline)
  - Celexa (citalopram)
  - Prozac (fluoxitine)
- **MOOD/PSYCHOSIS STABILIZING MEDICATIONS**
  - Seroquel; Seroquel XR (quetiapine)
  - Zyprexa; Zyprexa, Zydis (olanzapine)

 **CAUTION:**
Do not stop or modify your use of any of these medications without direct consultation with your doctor.

PRINCIPLE 5
ADD MEDICATIONS THAT HELP

There are medications that actually help various diseases and work synergistically with a ketogenic lifestyle. I talk about individual medications that are effective for each disease or class of diseases that I discuss. It's essential to work closely with your doctor to identify whether using the specific medications identified in these sections will be beneficial in your ketogenic journey.

PRINCIPLE 6
CONSIDER APPROPRIATE SUPPLEMENTATION

A number of vitamins and herbal supplements can be beneficial for the treatment of disease. Balancing these supplements so that they help without interacting with prescription medications is also something to consider, and you need to work closely with your doctor to manage your use of them.

> **NOTE**
>
> *As a physician, I view any supplement, vitamin, or herbal remedy the same way I see prescription medications. Many people think that because a supplement is "natural," it is safe. That isn't always the case. I've had plenty of people cause themselves significant harm by using "natural" or herbal supplements that interact with other supplements or prescription medications. This principle focuses on using supplements in a way that is synergistic and less likely to interfere with other treatment approaches that are being used at the same time or cause an overmedicated state.*

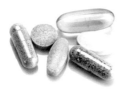

CHAPTER 5

TYPE 1 AND TYPE 2 DIABETES

I distinctly remember being in medical school and sitting in an auditorium-style, tiered section of seating. A gargantuan computer screen sat at the front of the class. I was staring at the back of the head of the student sitting in front of me when my pathology professor stated, "Diabetes isn't reversible; it just keeps getting worse. You can't cure it." It was a painful thing to hear, and I will never forget it.

That statement struck me for two reasons. First, my father was diabetic, and, with my family history, it meant that I would probably be diabetic as well. Second, the idea that there was no cure was downright depressing.

So, when a patient came to me a year after applying the principles of a ketogenic diet to his type 2 diabetes and said, "Doc, I'm no longer diabetic. Your diet worked. It cured me," I was shocked.

I ran him through all the testing: two-hour glucose tolerance tests, HbA1c blood tests, fasting blood sugar tests, and insulin tests. Again, I was shocked. He was right! He was no longer diabetic:

- He had normal blood sugar.
- He had normal HbA1c.
- He had normal cholesterol.
- He had a normal two-hour glucose tolerance test.

Could it be real? Just to be sure, we waited a few months, and then I ran the tests again. And again, they all came back normal. After that second set of tests, the patient said to me, "Now will you contact my insurance company and tell them I'm not diabetic?"

The best day of my career was in 2008, when I got to write a letter to this patient's insurance company, attach copies of both sets of tests, and request that the diagnosis of type 2 diabetes be removed from his records.

JIMMY SAYS

Why the medical profession and organizations like the American Diabetes Association fail to lend credence to the keto approach to treating diabetes is beyond me. Reversing type 2 diabetes and minimizing the need for insulin injections for type 1 diabetes is typical of those who embrace a low-carb, high-fat, ketogenic lifestyle. What's it going to take for the powers that be to get on board with a natural remedy for diabetes?

I've now done that eight times since 2008.

When I was asked how this patient went from being a diabetic to not being a diabetic, I said, "It's the Keto Cure!" When we understand that type 2 diabetes is really the fourth stage of insulin resistance, we gain the insight needed to improve, reverse, and—dare I say it?—cure the diabetes.

JIMMY SAYS

My heart breaks for people with type 1 diabetes when they hear exclamations about a cure being found for diabetes, but referring to type 2 diabetes. There is no known cure to completely heal someone who has type 1 diabetes and whose body makes no insulin at all. However, a ketogenic lifestyle helps type 1 diabetics manage their need for insulin better than any other dietary modality.

WHAT IS DIABETES?

First, it is essential that you understand that there are two types of diabetes. They are type 1 and type 2 diabetes, and most people don't know the difference. Sadly, I've even met a few medical practitioners that struggle to explain the difference. So, let me give you a simple definition of them.

Defining Type 1 Diabetes Mellitus

Type 1 diabetes (sometimes called juvenile diabetes) is a state where there is an absolute absence of insulin, meaning your pancreas has stopped producing the hormone. This often happens during one's youth. Most true type 1 diabetics have had damage to their pancreas, which caused it to stop producing insulin altogether. These people require exogenous insulin (insulin through a shot) or they will die.

Now, remember, insulin is the key that opens the sugar door in every cell in the body to enable the glucose to enter the cell to be used as fuel. Type 1 diabetics don't make the key at all. Period. Zip. Nada. There are several reasons that the pancreas stops producing insulin. (In fact, whole books are written about it, so I won't cover that here.) The most important thing for you to understand is that type 1 diabetes is a state where insulin is not being made, and the person requires insulin injections to maintain blood sugar.

Type 1 diabetics make up about 5 percent of my total diabetic population. The other 95 percent of my diabetic patients are type 2 diabetics.

Defining Type 2 Diabetes Mellitus

Type 2 diabetes is a result of an overproduction of insulin (stage IV insulin resistance that's mentioned in Chapter 4). To understand type 2 diabetes, you really need to understand the five stages of insulin resistance. Once you understand insulin resistance, the progression of diabetes makes much more sense, as do the approaches to treatment and insulin's effect on the diseases of civilization. It becomes intuitive to pursue dietary carbohydrate restriction as an initial approach to treatment.

People with type 2 diabetes make two to twenty times more insulin than necessary. To return to the analogy that insulin is the key that opens the door in every cell in the body, the patient with type 2 diabetes (as well as those in the first three stages of insulin resistance) has a key that is "worn." The insulin doesn't work as efficiently to get the glucose into the cells; it takes an hour, two hours, sometimes five hours for that insulin to open the door and allow access for the glucose to be burned as fuel.

For example, if you give me a donut, my body produces ten times the insulin necessary (because I am very insulin resistant); my body thinks I ate a baker's dozen of donuts, and that insulin lingers in my bloodstream for twelve hours. Therefore, anything that I eat in addition to the donut—be it butter, rib-eye steak, or the sprinkles that came with the donut—are stored for the next twelve hours at ten times the normal rate. That's insulin resistance—overproduction of insulin in response to carbohydrate or excess protein. Type 2 diabetes is the fourth stage of this insulin resistance or insulin overproduction.

The causes of type 2 diabetes are the same as those that cause insulin resistance. We know that there are two abnormalities that lead to insulin resistance: impaired GLUT-2 receptor activation and impairment of the Abca1 transporters. How these receptors and transporters are impaired seems to be associated with the perfect storm of high triglycerides in the presence of diets containing large amounts of fructose, which pretty much sounds like the standard American diet (SAD), doesn't it?

CAN A TYPE 2 DIABETIC BECOME A TYPE 1 DIABETIC?

To be thorough, I want to state that sometimes type 2 diabetics who have been diabetic for many years—which means their pancreases are overworked and underpaid and essentially have been on overdrive for twenty or thirty years—might eventually become type 1 diabetics because their pancreases finally can't keep up, so they give out. When a type 2 diabetic progresses to the type 1 form of diabetes, that's generally what has happened.

THE KETO CURE APPROACH TO TYPE 1 DIABETES

Trying to address type 1 diabetes with the Keto Cure approach is the one area where a ketogenic approach can get squirrely on you. Type 1 diabetics need insulin to survive, but too much insulin leads to weight gain, elevated blood pressure, cardiovascular disease, and increased inflammation. A person who lacks the ability to make his or her own basal level of insulin and follows a ketogenic diet does have the potential to go into a state of ketoacidosis. Therefore, I highly recommend you work very closely with your doctor if you are a type 1 diabetic and you decide to use a ketogenic diet. An appropriate balance is necessary, and the approach can be life-threatening if used incorrectly.

> **⚠ CAUTION!**
> Do not stop or modify your use of insulin without direct consultation with your doctor.

That said, I have several patients who are type 1 diabetics who do tremendously well; in fact, we are able reduce the overall dose of insulin by up to two-thirds when the patient is in a well-controlled state of nutritional ketosis. The patient limits carbohydrates and closely monitors and doses the appropriate amounts of insulin. This is very effective in helping to stabilize blood sugar, weight gain, cholesterol, heart disease risk, and the progression of inflammatory diseases such as gout, psoriasis, and thyroiditis that often occur with type 1 diabetes.

The following sections outline how the principles of the ketogenic approach apply to type 1 diabetes. In the case of Principle 4, Eliminate Problem Medications, please refer to the Part 2 opener for the list of medications that often stimulate insulin production.

JIMMY SAYS

Whenever you make a dietary change, such as switching to a ketogenic diet, having a physician follow your health markers is important, regardless of whether you have a condition like type 1 diabetes. If you're taking any medications, it's critical to let your doctor know what you're doing since keto is such a powerful nutritional therapy.

PRINCIPLE 1
LOWER INSULIN LEVELS WITH DIET

It can be dangerous to treat insulin-dependent diabetes by significantly cutting down carbohydrate intake in someone who has been consuming a large amount of carbohydrate and using a large amount of insulin. I usually start slowly by initially restricting carbohydrate to 20 to 30 grams per meal. This allows a person to back the insulin loads down in a way that won't cause blood sugars to bottom out or to spike.

After you've made initial adjustments, you can lower the carbohydrate even further—to less than 20 grams per day. Eventually many people are able to cut their insulin needs to one-third of the regular dose.

> ⚠️ **CAUTION!**
> **CONSULT WITH A PHYSICIAN**
> Work closely with your doctor to make these changes. Getting the insulin right as you lower carbohydrate intake can be life-changing, but it can also cause severe blood sugar swings if you don't do it cautiously and correctly.

PRINCIPLE 2
AVOID ADDITIVES THAT RAISE INSULIN LEVELS

Many of the sweeteners used in producing "low-carb" or "sugar-free" foods raise insulin without raising blood sugar. In a true type 1 diabetic who doesn't make insulin, this might not be a problem; however, I have a number of patients who have become insulin dependent after many years of uncontrolled type 2 diabetes. Sweeteners can cause havoc in these patients. Read Chapter 16 for more information about those artificial sweeteners that are approved and those that should be avoided.

Insulin is the major medication in the treatment of type 1 diabetes that needs to be lowered to help improve the other diseases of civilization.

Other medications that might need to be lowered, removed, or avoided are the following:

- **BETA-BLOCKERS**, such as Lopressor, Toprol-XL (metoprolol), Tenormin (atenolol), Trandate (labetelol)

- **GLITAZONES**, such as Avandia (rosiglitazone) and Actos (pioglitazone)

INSULIN PUMPS

I have a number of type 1 diabetic patients who use an insulin pump to help modulate the flow of insulin in a more "normal" pattern. I often recommend that patients use an insulin pump where possible. The use of a pump is often effective in providing a basal insulin load that is continuous, and I have found that it makes the use of a ketogenic diet a little easier on the type 1 diabetic patient.

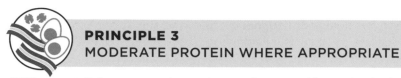

PRINCIPLE 3
MODERATE PROTEIN WHERE APPROPRIATE

With type 1 diabetes, protein can be used as a cushion or brake for the prevention of hypoglycemia. If the blood sugar drops low, protein can be converted into glycogen to prevent hypoglycemia.

Use the protein calculation formula in the Part 2 opener to calculate the ideal protein needs for your body; use this protein calculation as a starting point. I have found that using slightly more protein than the calculated daily need is useful for weaning insulin needs down, and it gives the person a cushion if hypoglycemia occurs from lack of starch and carbohydrate in the diet during the weaning process.

PRINCIPLE 5
ADD MEDICATIONS THAT HELP

There are medications that actually help in the treatment of type 1 diabetes and work synergistically with a ketogenic lifestyle. Work closely with your doctor to identify whether using these medications will be beneficial for you:

- **INSULINS**
  - Long-acting insulins (Levemir, Lantus)
  - Short-acting insulins (Humalin, Novolin)
- **AMYLIN MIMETIC,** such as Symlin

PRINCIPLE 6
CONSIDER APPROPRIATE SUPPLEMENTATION

There are a number of vitamins and herbal supplements that can be beneficial for treatment of type 1 diabetes. Balancing these so that they help without interacting with prescription medications is something you need to coordinate closely with your doctor.

It is important to recognize the normal response of the body when the blood sugar falls. This response can be impaired in the type 1 diabetic patient. For that reason, it's essential that you work closely with your doctor on a ketogenic diet and modification of parameters to achieve nutritional ketosis and monitor for flags that you're progressing to ketoacidosis.

Research has demonstrated that the following supplements help stabilize blood sugar and the inflammatory cascade that commonly occurs in the diabetic patient:

- **MAGNESIUM AND MAGNESIUM RICH FOODS:** Use caution with the overall amount of these foods that are not leafy greens (such as broccoli, almonds, tofu, and pumpkin seeds) because they contain some carbohydrates. Portion control with these foods is the key. Magnesium supplements come in multiple forms (nine prescription formulations and eleven over-the-counter formulations). Most of these formulations have a significant laxative effect. If you're constipated, that won't be a problem. However, to avoid this laxative effect, magnesium glycinate is the formulation least likely to give you gastrointestinal gymnastics.

- **OMEGA-3 FATTY ACIDS:** Increasing the ratio of omega-3s to omega-6s has been shown to suppress appetite and cravings, improve blood sugar control, and reduce blood cholesterol and triglycerides. Fish (specifically mackerel, salmon, sardines, and tuna), grass-fed beef, butter from a grass-fed source, eggs, walnuts, natto, and cod liver oil are the most effective sources of omega-3 fatty acids. Omega-3 can also be added as a supplement if your natural sources in the diet are not available.

- **CHROMIUM:** Chromium helps stabilize the body's use of glucose and has been an effective supplement for diabetes. For my patients, I recommend 1,000 micrograms per day.

- **ALPHA-LIPOIC ACID (ALA):** Alpha-lipoic acid is helpful in the transport of glucose and in preventing its glycosylation (abnormal binding of proteins to glucose that inhibits smooth function). A great starting point is to take 100 milligrams per day. Ketogenic foods containing alpha-lipoic acid include spinach, Brussels sprouts, and organ meats.

- **COENZYME Q10:** Co-Q10, as it is commonly called, is a wonderful antioxidant that plays an effective role in metabolism.

- **BERBERINE:** Berberine is the active ingredient in turmeric and goldenseal. It has been shown to stabilize blood sugar and glucose transport, may have some effect on gluconeogenesis in the liver, and also has anti-inflammatory and antibacterial effects.

JIMMY SAYS

Proper supplementation for balancing blood sugar and inflammation levels is the perfect adjunct to a ketogenic nutritional approach. I personally take most of the supplements Dr. Nally lists on this page, and he and I have a supplement company called Keto Living (www.ketoliving.com) to help meet the unique needs of keto dieters.

HORMONAL COUNTERBALANCE IN A NORMAL PATIENT

In the average human being who doesn't have diabetes, decreases in blood sugar levels trigger changes within the liver to regulate a cascade of hormones. The hormones work together to counterbalance blood sugar much like the instruments in an orchestra perform a wonderful-sounding symphony.

The body attempts to maintain blood sugar between 70 mg/dL (3.9 mmol/L) and 100 mg/dL (5.6 mmol/L).[1] As your body's blood sugar levels change, the following situations result:

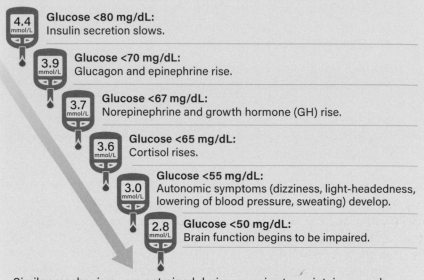

4.4 mmol/L — **Glucose <80 mg/dL:** Insulin secretion slows.

3.9 mmol/L — **Glucose <70 mg/dL:** Glucagon and epinephrine rise.

3.7 mmol/L — **Glucose <67 mg/dL:** Norepinephrine and growth hormone (GH) rise.

3.6 mmol/L — **Glucose <65 mg/dL:** Cortisol rises.

3.0 mmol/L — **Glucose <55 mg/dL:** Autonomic symptoms (dizziness, light-headedness, lowering of blood pressure, sweating) develop.

2.8 mmol/L — **Glucose <50 mg/dL:** Brain function begins to be impaired.

Similar mechanisms are entrained during exercise to maintain normal blood glucose concentrations in the face of elevated glucose disposal into working muscles.[2] At the onset of aerobic exercise, insulin release by the beta cells is reduced, and there are gradual increases in the glucose counter-regulatory hormones (glucagon, catecholamines, GH, and cortisol). This change in hormonal profile increases glucose production and maintains circulating glucose concentrations in a normal range during exercise (approximately 70 to 100 mg/dL [4.0 to 5.5 mmol/L]). As a result of this redundant counter-regulatory system, hypoglycemia rarely occurs during exercise in non-diabetic individuals.[3] If hypoglycemia does occur, then the counter-regulatory hormone response is amplified.[4, 5] During prolonged exercise, the same counter-regulatory hormones help mobilize fuels while limiting peripheral glucose disposal to maintain euglycemia.[6]

Other than being unable to lower insulin secretion at the onset of exercise, those with type 1 diabetes appear to have normal counter-regulatory hormone responses (glucagon, epinephrine, norepinephrine, GH, and cortisol) to both aerobic and anaerobic exercise.[7] However, the counter-regulatory response to developing hypoglycemia during exercise may be impaired.[8] This is why close monitoring of blood sugar and insulin is so important in type 1 diabetic patients.

THE KETO CURE APPROACH TO TYPE 2 DIABETES

Type 2 diabetes is usually treated with diet and oral medications. If you are looking for information about treating type 2 diabetes with insulin, then read the preceding section on type 1 diabetes mellitus.

> ⚠️ **CAUTION!**
> **CONSULT WITH YOUR PHYSICIAN**
> Do not suddenly stop all of your blood sugar/diabetes medications. Work closely with your doctor to wean yourself off of your medications as you begin restricting starch and carbohydrate. With my patients, I frequently cut back carbohydrates and cut oral medications in half. Then I reassess blood sugar in two to four weeks and make further adjustments as necessary.

JIMMY SAYS

Higher insulin levels aren't something that only people with type 2 diabetes have to deal with. Elevated insulin is the first sign of the future development of chronic diseases, and eating keto is the most effective preventative measure you can make to ward this off.

PRINCIPLE 1
LOWER INSULIN LEVELS WITH DIET

I've said it for years: Insulin is the master hormone for causing "weight gain." If you're gaining weight, the number-one hormone responsible is insulin, and you have to identify the excessive insulin production and turn it down. If you haven't turned down insulin production, you're not going to lose the weight, and you're not going to see the diseases of civilization, such as diabetes, improve.

The first step is lowering carbohydrate intake to less than 20 grams per day. This step alone often lowers average blood sugars enough to begin decreasing oral glucose-lowering medications.

After appropriate medication adjustments are made, you can lower carbohydrate intake to less than 20 grams per day. I frequently see people cut their medications in half, or even stop them completely, when carbohydrate is restricted to less than 20 grams per day. Many of my type 2 diabetic patients who became insulin dependent have been able to discontinue the need for any exogenous insulin (insulin injections). Eliminating medication is beneficial to your pocketbook, and insurance companies love the cost savings that this dietary lifestyle provides. Ketogenic carbohydrate restriction is the most powerful treatment approach that reduces the overall costs to both the patient and the insurance provider.

> ⚠️ **CAUTION!**
> **SULFONOUREAS AND SGLT2 INHIBITORS**
> Be advised that medications like the sulfonoureas (glipizide, glimepride, and glyburide) and the SGLT2 inhibitors (canagliflozin, empagliflozin, dapagliflozin, and empagliflozin) can and will cause hypoglycemia when used with ketogenic-type carbohydrate restriction. Use these medications with great caution when following a carbohydrate-restricted or ketogenic diet. If my patients are on either of these classes of medications, I stop the medications at the time I cut the carbohydrate back; you should consult with your physician about this.

The challenge in today's managed-medical and pay-for-performance environment is that physicians are graded on whether they are using the usual medications that are recommended for a diagnosis of diabetes. The physician gets "dinged" on future reimbursements if a specific percentage of his or her patients are not using XYZ drug with XYZ diagnosis. If you experience pushback from your physician about reducing your use of medication for treating diabetes, this may be one of the reasons. Re-education of the third-party insurance payers will foreseeably need to occur with regard to the treatment of insulin resistance, pre-diabetes, and type 2 diabetes.

Adequate carbohydrate restriction can be assessed by three measures:

- You start seeing your waist circumference shrink. My average patient loses up to an inch off the waist every month.

- I recommend you check your blood sugar every morning before breakfast. Fasting blood sugars (blood-sugar testing done first thing in the morning before a meal) will decrease to the normal range between 70 and 120 mg/dL. Yes, I know that 70 to 100 mg/dL is normal, but don't freak out. It takes eighteen to twenty-four months for the insulin resistance to improve. You may see blood sugars of 90 to 110 mg/dL that persist for a year and a half or two years. This is physiologic glucose sparing that often occurs when a body is using ketones as its primary fuel for longer than five to six months.

- Blood ketones can be measured at any time throughout the day and should fall between 0.5 and 4.0 mmol/L if you are staying in adequate nutritional ketosis.

THE KETOGENIC DIET AND EXOGENOUS INSULIN

If you are using exogenous insulin as a type 2 patient, I highly recommend you check your blood sugar before every meal for the first two to four weeks that you're following the ketogenic diet so that you can closely monitor your response to carbohydrate restriction.

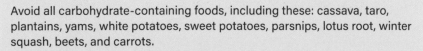

ARE ANY CARBS OKAY?

The Paleo and/or ancestral diets advocate for the use of "dense carbs." I find that this practice inhibits nutritional ketosis and dramatically slows the healing process for insulin resistance. If you are using "low-glycemic carbohydrates" or "dense carbohydrates," you are not letting your pancreas heal. JUST STOP IT!

Avoid all carbohydrate-containing foods, including these: cassava, taro, plantains, yams, white potatoes, sweet potatoes, parsnips, lotus root, winter squash, beets, and carrots.

The following carb-containing foods (less than 10 grams of carbohydrate per 100-gram serving) can be consumed; however, portion control is essential: onions, butternut squash, rutabaga, jicama, kohlrabi, spaghetti squash, turnips, and pumpkin.

PRINCIPLE 2
AVOID ADDITIVES THAT RAISE INSULIN LEVELS

Additives can be sugar-controlling medications that specifically raise insulin or other foods that inadvertently raise insulin without raising blood sugar.

Insulin is the major medication in the treatment of type 2 diabetes that needs to be lowered or removed to help eliminate the other diseases of civilization. In addition to the medications listed in the opening to this part of the book, other medications that might need to be lowered, removed, or avoided include sulfonylureas, such as the following:

- Amaryl (glimepride)

- DiaBeta (glyburide)

- Glucotrol, Glucotrol XL (glipizide)

- Chlorpropamide

- Tolazamide

- Tolbutamide

As mentioned earlier, many of the sweeteners used to produce "low-carb" or "sugar-free" foods raise insulin without raising blood sugar. Sweeteners and artificial sweeteners can wreak havoc in some patients. Avoid the following like the plague:

JIMMY SAYS

Many people justify their indiscriminate use of sugar alternatives because the artificial sweeteners are devoid of calories. However, as shared earlier, the hormonal impact of a food trumps its calorie count, and any ingredient that raises insulin levels is one you shouldn't be including in your diet. Finding those sweeteners that don't raise insulin is the key to making keto work for you.

SWEETENERS	ARTIFICIAL SWEETENERS
Corn syrup	Mannitol
High-fructose corn syrup	Xylitol
Agave	Maltitol
Honey	Isomalt
Monk fruit	Acesulfame potassium
	Dextrose
	Maltodextrin
	Aspartame

You can find the comprehensive analysis of artificial sweeteners that are approved and those that should be avoided in Chapter 16.

PRINCIPLE 3
MODERATE PROTEIN WHERE APPROPRIATE

With type 2 diabetes, protein can be used as a cushion or brake to prevent hypoglycemia. If the blood sugar drops too low, protein can be converted into glycogen to prevent hypoglycemia. Use the protein calculation formula in the Part 2 opener to calculate the ideal protein needs for your body; use this protein calculation as a starting point. I have found that consuming slightly more protein than the calculated daily need is useful for weaning insulin needs down and gives the person a cushion if hypoglycemia occurs from lack of starch and carbohydrate in the diet during the weaning process.

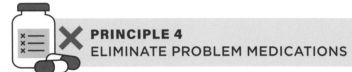

PRINCIPLE 4
ELIMINATE PROBLEM MEDICATIONS

Aside from the list of medications in the opening pages of this part, SGLT2 inhibitors can stimulate insulin production either primarily or secondarily. These medications also can be administered in combination with medications that help insulin resistance (such as metformin, DPP4 inhibitors, and GLP-1 agonists). I won't go into the mechanisms here because it is outside the scope of this text, but I'm providing a list of SGLT2 inhibitors so that you can discuss these with your doctor to identify alternatives where necessary:

- Farxiga (dapagliflozin)
- Invokana (canagliflozin)
- Jardiance (empagliflozin)

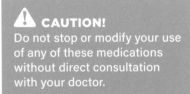

⚠ CAUTION!
Do not stop or modify your use of any of these medications without direct consultation with your doctor.

PRINCIPLE 5
ADD MEDICATIONS THAT HELP

There are medications that actually help with type 2 diabetes and work synergistically with a ketogenic lifestyle. Work closely with your doctor to identify whether using these medications will be beneficial for you:

- **BIGUANIDE**
  - Metformin (Glucophage)

- **DPP4 INHIBITORS**
  - Januvia (sitagliptin)
  - Onglyza (saxagliptin)
  - Tradjenta (linagliptin)
  - Nesina (alogliptin)
  - Galvus (vildagliptin)

- **GLP-1 INHIBITORS**
  - Byetta (exenatide)
  - Bydureon (exenatide ER)
  - Tanzeum (albiglutide)
  - Trulicity (dulaglutide)
  - Victoza (liraglutide)

- **AMYLIN MIMETICS**
  - Symlin (pramlintide)

PRINCIPLE 6
CONSIDER APPROPRIATE SUPPLEMENTATION

A number of vitamins and herbal supplements can be beneficial for the treatment of diabetes as a disease. Balancing these supplements so that they help without interacting with other prescription medications is something you need to coordinate closely with your doctor.

It is important to recognize the normal response of the body when blood sugar falls. This response can be impaired in a type 2 diabetic patient. For that reason, it's essential to work closely with your doctor on a ketogenic diet and modification of parameters to achieve nutritional ketosis and monitor for flags that you're progressing to ketoacidosis.

Research has shown that the following supplements can help stabilize blood sugar and the inflammatory cascade that commonly occurs in type 2 diabetic patients:

- **MAGNESIUM AND MAGNESIUM RICH FOODS:** Use caution with the portions or amount of foods like spinach, broccoli, almonds, tofu, and pumpkin seeds. They do contain some carbohydrate, and when these foods are cooked the carbohydrate content accessible to your gut doubles. Portion control with these foods is the key.

- **OMEGA-3 FATTY ACIDS:** Increasing the ratio of omega-3s to omega-6s has been shown to stabilize and reduce appetite, improve blood sugar control, and reduce blood cholesterol and triglycerides. Fish (specifically mackerel, salmon, sardines, and tuna), grass-fed beef, butter from a grass-fed source, eggs, walnuts, natto, and cod liver oil are the most effective sources of omega-3 fatty acids. Omega-3 can also be added as a supplement if natural sources in the diet are not available.

- **CHROMIUM:** Chromium helps stabilize the body's use of glucose and has been an effective supplement for diabetes. For my patients, I recommend 1000 micrograms per day.

- **ALPHA-LIPOIC ACID (ALA):** Alpha-lipoic acid is helpful in the transport of glucose and in preventing its glycosylation (abnormal binding of proteins to glucose that inhibits smooth function). A good starting point is 100 milligrams per day. Ketogenic foods containing alpha-lipoic acid include spinach, Brussels sprouts, and organ meats.

- **COENZYME Q10:** Co-Q10, as it is commonly called, is a wonderful antioxidant that plays an effective role in the metabolism.

- **BERBERINE:** Berberine is the active ingredient in turmeric and goldenseal. It has been shown to stabilize blood sugar and glucose transport, may have some effect on gluconeogenesis in the liver, and also has anti-inflammatory and antibacterial effects.

BERBERINE AND METFORMIN

Berberine acts in the liver the same way metformin does, and it's not effective if you're using metformin at the same time. If you are using metformin, there is no need to use berberine.

CHAPTER 6

HYPERTENSION

Hypertension is elevated blood pressure while you are sitting at rest during the squeezing phase of the heart (systolic pressure) or the relaxed phase of the heart (diastolic pressure). Systolic blood pressure that's greater than 140 mmHg and/or diastolic pressure that's greater than 90 mmHg is the classic definition of hypertension. Uncontrolled hypertension increases risk for coronary artery disease, heart attack, stroke, vascular disease (such as aneurysms), and heart failure. Uncontrolled hypertension also increases the risk for kidney failure, brain bleeding, and retinal damage. That's a lot of potential damage resulting from one controllable factor!

WHAT IS HYPERTENSION?

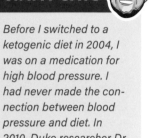

Before I switched to a ketogenic diet in 2004, I was on a medication for high blood pressure. I had never made the connection between blood pressure and diet. In 2010, Duke researcher Dr. William Yancy published a forty-eight-week study in Archives of Internal Medicine *that found nearly half of the participants following a low-carb, ketogenic diet were able to come off of their blood pressure medications. Amazing!*

 **CAUTION!**
Because there can be other consequences associated with changing blood pressure medications, please work closely with your doctor before stopping or changing any of your prescription medications.

Blood pressure reacts to a number of environmental changes to maintain needed blood perfusion to the organs of the body. The primary players in this perfusion orchestra are the sympathetic nervous system, the renin-angiotensin-aldosterone system, and the plasma volume (which is usually controlled by the kidneys). Blood pressure medications focus on modifying one or more of these three systems. Amazingly, insulin has a dramatic effect on all three systems as well. That's why a ketogenic lifestyle is so effective in controlling blood pressure.

Where should your blood pressure be while you're sitting in your chair? The following are the criteria that determine whether your blood pressure is normal or you're in a state of hypertension:

- **NORMAL BLOOD PRESSURE:**
  Systolic < 120 mmHg and diastolic < 80 mmHg

- **PRE-HYPERTENSION:**
  Systolic 120 to 139 mmHg or diastolic 80 to 89 mmHg

- **HYPERTENSION:**
  - **Stage 1:** Systolic 140 to 159 mmHg or diastolic 90 to 99 mmHg
  - **Stage 2:** Systolic > 160 mmHg or diastolic > 100 mmHg[1, 2]

These stages may be identified by your doctor; however, for simplicity we can consider hypertension to be having elevated blood pressure on two separate occasions where the systolic measurement (the top number) is greater than 140 or the diastolic measurement (the bottom number) is greater than 90.

Hypertension is a disease of civilization. Although you might have been told that you have it because there is too much salt in your diet or it's genetic, this is actually a gross misrepresentation of the metabolism and genetics. Primary (essential) hypertension is due to elevated insulin levels. If you lower your insulin load, your blood pressure will normalize.

How do I know this? Because I've seen it happen over and over for more than twelve years. Within one to two weeks of cutting carbohydrate intake to less than 20 grams per day, blood pressure usually normalizes. The exciting part is that blood pressure medications can usually be cut in half or discontinued altogether.

APPLYING THE KETO CURE APPROACH

The following sections describe how to apply the principles of the Keto Cure approach to addressing hypertension. For Principle 3, there are no concerns specific to hypertension. Refer to the first few pages of Part 2 for general information about that principle.

PRINCIPLE 1
LOWER INSULIN LEVELS WITH DIET

Two key players in the Standard American Diet (SAD) raise blood pressure. First, sugar is made up of a glucose molecule and a fructose molecule. Most of the glucose is processed in the cells of the body when insulin rises, and glucose enters the cell as fuel. However, 100 percent of the fructose is metabolized in the liver along the same pathway that alcohol is processed. The figure below illustrates this pathway.

JIMMY SAYS

Prior to finding a low-carb, ketogenic diet, I used to drink sixteen cans of Coca-Cola a day. That's 45 grams of sugar from high-fructose corn syrup per can. You do that math—it's shocking! How I survived having sustained high blood pressure over years of eating this way is a miracle. Keto turned it all around for me.

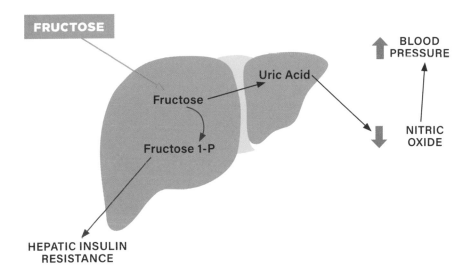

The problem with eating any food that contains fructose (like table sugar, high-fructose corn syrup, or fructose alone) is that fructose lowers nitric oxide, which causes a rise in blood pressure by vascular constriction. Fructose metabolism also stimulates increased glucose production and increased hepatic insulin resistance due to inflammatory pathway stimulation.

Another issue is that insulin directly increases activity of the epithelial sodium channel in the kidney, which activates Na-K-ATPase—the electrolyte transporter in the kidney.[3] As a result, more sodium is retained in the blood, which contributes to hypertension and, over time, edema and worsening congestive heart failure. The more insulin produced (as in those people who have insulin resistance and overproduce insulin; see Chapter 4 for more information), the more sodium we retain and the higher our blood pressure creeps. I've seen many patients with insulin resistance who experience a rise in blood pressure that occurs fifteen to twenty years before abnormal blood sugar levels are ever detected.

Limiting carbohydrate intake both eliminates the fructose effect on the liver and blood vessels and dampers down the insulin effect on sodium retention. It never fails to amaze me when a patient changes his or her diet and blood pressure naturally returns to normal by dropping up to 40 mmHg.

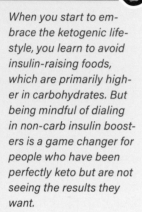

JIMMY SAYS

When you start to embrace the ketogenic lifestyle, you learn to avoid insulin-raising foods, which are primarily higher in carbohydrates. But being mindful of dialing in non-carb insulin boosters is a game changer for people who have been perfectly keto but are not seeing the results they want.

PRINCIPLE 2
AVOID ADDITIVES THAT RAISE INSULIN LEVELS

Caffeine raises blood pressure, and recently I've noticed that the insulin stimulus from black tea, oolong tea, and even some forms of green tea have an insulin-stimulating effect up to fifteen times greater than normal. If you're a tea drinker and you've changed your diet, but your blood pressure is still high, eliminate your tea consumption.[4]

In addition to avoiding sweeteners (see Chapter 16) and caffeine, try to avoid or minimize your consumption of the following:

- Non-dairy creamers and soy milk

- Alcohol; drinking more than two drinks per day notably increases incidence of hypertension[5, 6]

PRINCIPLE 3
MODERATE PROTEIN WHERE APPROPRIATE

A number of proteins stimulate a variable insulin response. These include arginine, lysine, and leucine to some degree.

The following high-protein foods have high arginine and lysine counts. You should limit your consumption of these foods if you are having trouble controlling your blood pressure:

- Sea lion liver
- Soy protein isolate
- Crab
- Shrimp

- Sesame flour
- Pork loin
- Chicken
- Pumpkin seeds

- Peanuts
- Spirulina

PRINCIPLE 4
ELIMINATE PROBLEM MEDICATIONS

Beta-blockers, which are blood-pressure-lowering medications, top the list of medications that can cause issues (refer to page 49 for the complete list). I love how effective beta-blockers are at lowering blood pressure and improving heart contractility in the long run, but you have to weigh the risk-to-benefit ratio of these medications. One thing to note is that beta-blockers don't actually stimulate insulin as much as they slow metabolism and increase hunger cravings. If you are using a beta-blocker for reasons other than hypertension, work with your doctor to find possible alternatives.

Aside from the medications listed at the beginning of Part 2, the following drugs can also create issues for those people who have hypertension:

- **ORAL CONTRACEPTIVES WITH HIGHER ESTROGEN DOSES**

- **NSAIDS**
  - Celebrex, Mobic
  - Motrin, Advil, ibuprofen, naproxen

- **DECONGESTANTS**
  - Sudafed and other pseudoephedrine products

- **WEIGHT LOSS/APPETITE SUPPRESSANTS**
  - Adipex-P; Lomaira (phentermine)
  - diethylpropion

- **IMMUNOSUPPRESSANTS**
  - Neoral, Sandimmune, Gengraf, Restasis (cyclosporine)

- **STIMULANTS**
  - Adderall (dextroamphetamine)
  - Concerta (methylphenidate)
  - Vyvanse (lisdexamfetamine)

- **ILLICIT DRUGS**
  - Amphetamines
  - Cocaine

PRINCIPLE 5
ADD MEDICATIONS THAT HELP

There are medications that help various diseases and work synergistically with a ketogenic lifestyle. Work closely with your doctor to identify whether using these medications will augment your nutritional ketosis. In cases where ketogenic dietary changes have been instituted, discuss the use of the following classes of medications with your doctor:

- Thiazide diuretics

- Angiotensin-converting enzyme (ACE) inhibitors

- Angiotensin II receptor blockers (ARBs)

- Calcium channel blockers

PRINCIPLE 6
CONSIDER APPROPRIATE SUPPLEMENTATION

The following is a list of supplements that might be beneficial in managing hypertension:

- **ALLIUM SATIVUM (garlic):** Garlic has long been used for treating both high cholesterol and blood pressure. It is thought to increase nitric oxide production in the liver, which leads to smooth-muscle relaxation.[7]

- **ANNONA MURICATA (prickly custard apple):** This fruit is found in the Caribbean and Central America. The leaf extract has been reported to decrease blood pressure by lowering vascular resistance.[8]

- **APIUM GRAVEOLENS (celery):** Celery has long been recognized by the Chinese as an effective dietary treatment for hypertension.

- **BLOND PSYLLIUM (Indian plantago):** A daily dose of 15 grams has been shown to modestly lower blood pressure.[9]

- **CRATAEGUS PINNATIFIDA (Chinese hawthorn):** The two components that contribute to hawthorn's effects on the heart are flavonoids and oligomeric procyanidins, which are potent antioxidant agents.

- **RHYNCHOPHYLLINE (cat's claw):** This alkaloid in cat's claw has the ability to inhibit platelet aggregation and thrombosis, which suggests that it might be useful in preventing strokes and reducing the risk of heart attack by lowering blood pressure, increasing circulation, and inhibiting both the formation of plaque on arterial walls and the formation of blood clots in the brain, heart, and arteries.[10]

- **LYCOPERSICON ESCULENTUM (tomato):** Tomato contains lycopene, which lowers blood pressure. Although tomatoes contain some carbohydrate, they do have an effect on lowering blood pressure.[11]

- **OCIMUM BASILICUM (basil):** Dose-dependent blood pressure improvement has been demonstrated with crude extracts of basil. However, the effect is short term. It appears to work by short blockade of calcium channels in the cardiovascular system.

- **PINUS PINASTER (maritime pine):** Pycnogenol is a French extract from maritime pine bark. Clinical research shows that 200 milligrams per day can have a modest blood pressure effect by inhibiting the angiotensin-converting enzymes.[12]

- **RAUWOLFIA SERPENTINA (rauwolfia):** This plant is considered to be the one that has the strongest hypotensive effect. Reserpine, a purified alkaloid of the plant, was the first widely used long-term anti-hypertensive. However, an unfortunate side effect is nasal congestion.[13]

- **THEOBROMA CACAO (chocolate, cocoa bean, cocoa butter):** Flavonoids, which are in chocolate, stimulate formation of nitric oxide, increasing vasodilatation, lowering blood pressure, and reducing endothelial dysfunction. The challenge with using these options to lower blood pressure is avoiding sweetened forms of cocoa.[14]

- **UNCARIA RHYNCHOPHYLLA (cat's claw):** This is a traditional Asian medicine used for blood pressure. The hypotensive effect has been attributed to an indole alkaloid called hirsutine, which acts at the Ca2+ channels to lower blood pressure.[15]

- **ZINGIBER OFFICINALE (ginger):** Ginger root has been a common ingredient in Asian cooking. It has been shown to improve circulation by relaxing smooth muscles surrounding the blood vessel wall. Ginger works through calcium channel blockade, similarly to the way the medication verapamil works. In rats it has been shown to reduce hypertension caused by fructose, but the results aren't nearly as effective in human studies.[16, 17]

CHAPTER 7

ABNORMAL CHOLESTEROL (DYSLIPIDEMIA)

At least three or four times a day I'm asked, "What will happen to my cholesterol if I lower my carbohydrates and eat more fat?" The answer: Your cholesterol will improve!

Yes, you read that right: Cholesterol will improve.

There's always a follow-up question of disbelief: "Cholesterol improves when you eat fat?!" Based on all we've been taught over the years, that's pretty surprising, huh? It surprised me, too.

How do I know that lowering carbohydrate intake in your food improves cholesterol? I'm an obesity specialist. I specialize in fat (or lipids, to put it in kinder, more scientific terms). To specialize in fat, one must know where it came from, what it's made of, and where it's going.

I've been closely monitoring cholesterol over the last fifteen years with low-carbohydrate and ketogenic diets. (As a family doctor, looking at patients' cholesterol levels is one of the things I've been doing five to ten times per day for almost two decades.) Dyslipidemia, or abnormal cholesterol, is one of the most challenging things that internists, family physicians, and cardiologists work on daily. It is challenging because we've been told that if we eat less fat (as we are told to do when we have a high-carbohydrate, low-fat diet), our cholesterol will go down. However, what I've seen is that the bad cholesterol always gets worse, which increases the risk for heart disease, stroke, and vascular disease. So, we must prescribe a cholesterol pill.

Over time, I started seeing a different result that really shocked me: Cardiovascular risk, including improvement in the significant cholesterol markers, gets better when we cut out carbohydrates rather than fat. This has happened in every single patient with whom I have used this dietary change for the last twelve years—myself included.

This concept can be a difficult one to grasp. Here are the main points:

- Cutting out only fat doesn't work. Cholesterol stays elevated.

- Cutting out fat and carbohydrate usually doesn't work, either. You must eat more lean protein to feel full and satiated, but lean protein is high in arginine and tyrosine, which are two amino acids that cause insulin to rise. Cholesterol still stays elevated in many people. ("You just have bad cholesterol genes" is what I started hearing people say when this method didn't work.)

- What works is cutting out carbohydrate, maintaining adequate protein, and increasing fat to the point that you feel full.

For more than fifty years, we've been taught that putting any form of fat (especially saturated fat) into our mouths will cause our cholesterol to rise. This dogma is so ingrained into our minds and cultures that many patients have emotional reactions to the thought of eating more butter or bacon. Even the mention of using lard (pure animal fat) when we discuss meals and meal plans in the exam room makes people turn up their noses. I am amazed at how many people claim they "don't like the taste of fat." When we begin to discuss why they don't like it and when in life they formed this opinion, they realize it is directly tied to an image of a heart attack or stroke.

Even when reassured that eating fat improves cholesterol, there is a disconnect in people's minds that fat still can't be good for the heart. Patients say to me at least three or four times a day, "But wait! What about my heart? All that fat can't be good for my heart?!"

 JIMMY SAYS

It's so difficult for people to wrap their heads around how a low-carb, high-fat diet can be healthy for their cholesterol when all they hear from mainstream health "experts" is that it puts you at a greater risk of heart disease. But increasing your dietary fat intake while cutting carbs improves every relevant marker on your cholesterol panel. Read my book Cholesterol Clarity *to learn more about how we were lied to about cholesterol.*

SOME HISTORY ABOUT CHOLESTEROL

The measurement of cholesterol, specifically total cholesterol, started in the 1950s. When Ancel Keys published his Diet-Heart Hypothesis in 1952, he found a very weak correlation between heart disease and fat. From his observational work he concluded that "the results of a fatty diet are hypercholesterolemia [elevated cholesterol]." A number of studies showed that increasing fat in the diet increased total cholesterol; however, no link to heart disease was ever proven.[1]

Studies published by E. H. Ahrens, Jr., showed the cholesterol increased because of carbohydrate intake, not fat alone.[2] This question and known effective cholesterol-reducing dietary approaches were ignored in 1984 by the National Institutes of Health (NIH) Consensus Development Conference on Lowering Cholesterol to Prevent Heart Disease, a report that was based heavily on epidemiological data rather than clinically reproducible science.[3] Despite scientific evidence that refuted the Diet-Heart Hypothesis, the decisions by the NIH were based on the politics and massive publicity campaigns of 1984.

Since that time, multiple fat- and cholesterol-containing foods have been demonized. One of those is eggs—specifically, egg yolks. Interestingly, there is actually no data association between whole-egg consumption and heart disease. The science simply does not exist.

Further, the Diet-Heart Hypothesis does not explain what is known as the European or French Paradox. The French prefer cooking in butter rather than vegetable oil. In fact, the French eat 40 percent fat in their diet, and more than 15 percent of that is saturated fat. Interestingly, the French and those who eat the most cheese, butter, and whole eggs have the lowest rate of coronary vessel calcification and heart disease. Articles have been published as attempts to explain away this phenomenon as epidemiological error or interactions between macronutrients of a specific diet, but none of those studies clarify why the paradox occurs.[4] According to the Diet-Heart Hypothesis, eating a diet that's 40 percent fat should place France on the map as the heart disease capital of the world, yet the French have the lowest rates of heart disease in the world.

A second paradoxical problem with the Diet-Heart Hypothesis is that of life span. According to the Diet-Heart Hypothesis, people with familial hypercholesterolemia should have much shorter life spans and are at increased risk of early mortality or death. However, there is actually no scientific evidence of this. In fact, the Honolulu Heart Program study revealed that people with low cholesterol are the ones at risk of early mortality or death.[5] The *British Medical Journal* also published a cohort review of nineteen studies involving more than 68,000 elderly individuals. The study showed that low LDL-C actually increases risk of mortality and that those with high total cholesterol live longer.[6]

So, why have physicians been pushing the use of statin medications to reduce the risk of coronary heart disease? It started with the Lipid Research Clinics Coronary Primary Prevention Trial (LRC-CPPT), a study of 480,000 men treated with a cholesterol-lowering medication called cholestyramine.[7] There was a very slight absolute reduction in coronary heart disease risk, but no reduction in the risk of death. Overall, cholestyramine (such as Prevalite, Questran, and Questran Light) reduced heart disease in 8 of the 480,000 men.

When the LRC-CPPT study results were run through the statistical reporting of relative risk, it looked like cholesterol-lowering medication reduced the risk by 19 to 24 percent. A layperson would assume that this is absolute risk, not relative risk. However, there was an increased risk of death by all causes in the group that used cholestyramine (a fact that was never really emphasized, just as relative risk was not emphasized).

This relative risk reduction drove the statin era we've been living through. Atorvastatin (such as Lipitor) reduced actual heart disease risk by only 1 percent in those in the study group who took it compared with those who didn't. However, when you use the "relative risk reduction" term that's often emphasized in advertisements, it appears that the risk is reduced by 36 percent. Rosuvastatin (such as Crestor) was shown to have an absolute risk reduction in heart disease of 1.2 percent, but when run through the relative risk reduction statistic, the manufacturer can claim a relative risk reduction of 44 percent.

WHAT DO CHOLESTEROL NUMBERS MEAN?

Now that you know there's science that contradicts the bad press cholesterol has gotten over the years, how do you know what your cholesterol numbers mean?

Cholesterol metabolism is a very complex system that has many lever points. However, one way to understand this complex system is to think of cholesterol particles as buses for triglycerides, which are called lipoproteins. The buses are spheres of phospholipids with protein and cholesterol esters in the walls. Inside these buses are triglycerides (glycerol and fatty acids). High-density lipoproteins (HDL), intermediate-density lipoproteins (IDL), low-density lipoproteins (LDL), and very low-density lipoproteins (VLDL) are all essential triglyceride and cholesterol ester transporters. There are

ABSOLUTE RISK VERSUS RELATIVE RISK

Absolute risk is your risk of developing a disease over a period of time. For example, if you had a one in ten chance of developing an allergic reaction to a medication, you could say that you have a 10 percent risk. This can also be described in decimals as a 0.1 risk.

Relative risk is used to compare two different groups of people—for example, those who use a drug and those who don't. Statistics can be made to look more impressive by showing the percent increase from the group that takes the medication in comparison with the group that doesn't.

"cholesterol buses" that move fat from the gut to the fat cells, buses that move fat from the fat cells to the liver, brain, and muscles, and buses that move the fat back to the fat cells again if it wasn't used elsewhere in the body.

I'm not going to take much space to delve into the science of all these particles—whole textbooks have been written about them. The important thing here is to identify some basics about how carbohydrate restriction affects these lipoprotein molecules.

Let's start with the contents of the standard cholesterol panel, or Lipid Panel. For the last twenty to thirty years, the following four numbers have been regarded as the holy grail of heart disease risk:

- Total cholesterol
- HDL (the measured number for "good" cholesterol)
- LDL-C (the calculated number for "bad" cholesterol)
- VLDL-C (the calculated number for very low-density cholesterol)
- Triglycerides

The first problem with this panel is that it makes you believe there are four different forms of cholesterol. NOT TRUE! Actually, cholesterol is a molecule that can be esterified or non-esterified, and it either makes up a part of the lipoprotein molecule or is transported with the triglycerides as a passenger. The lipoproteins are actually not that different other than their passenger load (causing increased or decreased density) and the proteins contained within the wall of the lipoprotein. Here, size does matter; size determines the function of the molecule at a given moment.

The cholesterol-particle buses, big and small, carry passengers. The triglycerides and cholesterol are actually the passengers inside the bus. But the presence of triglycerides in the system seems to change the density of the lipoproteins. Now picture big, medium, and small buses that equate to the HDL, IDL, and LDL. The density of a bus gets lower as triglyceride levels rise and fewer cholesterol esters and proteins are bound. As HDL goes up, LDL-C goes down.[8]

The second problem is that the VLDL-C and LDL-C are calculated numbers that don't reflect the true presence of the lipoprotein particles as the triglyceride number rises. For the accountants, mathematicians, and engineers reading this, that calculation is called the Friedwald Equation and is as follows:

$$\text{LDL-C (mmol/L)} = \text{Total Cholesterol (mmol/L)} - \text{HDL-C (mmol/L)} - \text{TG (mmol/L) / 2.2}$$

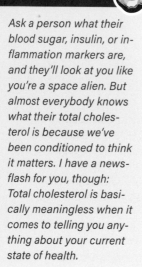

- This equation falls apart when the triglyceride level is greater than 400 mg/dL (4.52 mmol/L), which is a patient with hyperinsulinemia.

The third problem is that the Lipid Panel doesn't tell you that the lipoprotein categories (HDL, LDL, IDL, and VLDL) have three to four individual subtypes or subparticles that are further differentiated by weight and size (see the illustration). It is the smallest and most dense particles (small-dense LDL) that place us at risk for heart disease and stroke.

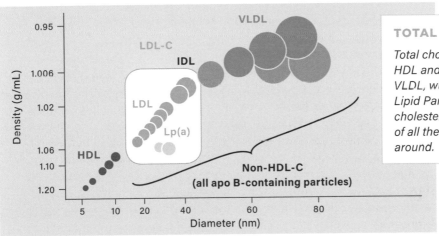

TOTAL CHOLESTEROL

Total cholesterol is the sum of HDL and LDL, as well as IDL and VLDL, which aren't reported in the Lipid Panel. In other words, total cholesterol is basically the sum of all the buses you have driving around.

Knowing the LDL-C doesn't really give you a clear idea of heart disease risk. It becomes essential to know which type of LDL lipoprotein particle is the atherogenic or heart disease–causing particle. To date, research points to the small-dense LDL particle.[9, 10]

The actual number of LDL particles (LDL-P) can be measured with four different assays, and these measurements have identified that there are specifically three LDL subtypes:

- "Big fluffy" or large-dense LDL

- Medium-dense LDL

- Small-dense LDL

Research has identified that increased numbers of small-dense LDL correlates closely with risk for inflammation, heart disease, and vascular disease.[11] According to this research the LDL-C that we've been brainwashed into thinking is the problem isn't the culprit. (Yes! I used the word *brainwashed*—but that's a subject for another book.)

JIMMY SAYS

If your doctor is concerned about your "high" cholesterol, ask him or her to run an advanced lipid panel called the NMR Lipoprofile test from the LipoScience lab (U.S. only); it can be ordered through LabCorp. This test reveals the total number of LDL particles as well as the breakdown of the small LDL particles that are the most atherogenic. The LDL-C on your standard cholesterol panel doesn't show you this breakdown, which is important to determine whether your LDL is unhealthy or benign.

Those of us using ketogenic diets know that LDL-C commonly rises with increased saturated fat intake. This is to be expected because LDL-C comprises the three different LDL subparticles (big fluffy, medium, and small-dense). We've known for the last twenty years that increased intake of saturated fat in one's diet causes a shift in these particles to bigger, "fluffier" particles.[12]

We also know that the small-dense LDL particles are the atherogenic/inflammatory particles participating in the formation of vascular disease (arterial blockage), and their presence in the blood is directly correlated with the level of triglyceride. The big, "fluffy" particles reduce the risk of vascular disease.[13]

Those of us following ketogenic lifestyles and treating disease with these protocols also know that triglyceride levels are increased directly by increasing levels of insulin. Therefore, anything you eat that raises insulin (like carbohydrate or starches) raises your triglycerides. When triglycerides go up, the number of small-dense LDL subparticles goes up, shifting the density of the LDL and changing the cholesterol and protein mix of the individual molecule, which increases risk for heart disease.

The 2015 *British Medical Journal* published a study reviewing the relevant nineteen peer-reviewed medical articles that included more than 68,000 participants. This review showed that there is no association of high LDL-C (a calculated value of all the LDL subparticles) with mortality (meaning that an elevated LDL-C *does not lead* to an increased risk of death from heart disease).[14] In stark contrast to this landmark review, The American Heart Association's (AHA) Presidential Advisory published in the June 20, 2017 issue of *Circulation* states that saturated fat is the cause of increased LDL-C, and elevated LDL-C is associated with an increase in death by cardiovascular disease. This claim is based on a single, four-year (2009 to 2013) literature review completed by the World Health Organization with a mere 2,353 participants. Most of these studies lasted only three to five weeks (which is not nearly long enough to see fully effective cholesterol changes), and none of which had any focus on carbohydrate intake, insulin levels, or LDL subparticle measurement.[15]

From this single study, the AHA concludes that elevated LDL-C is an indicator of increased cardiovascular mortality. That's the equivalent of saying, "You know cars drive on the roads and encounter potholes. Potholes are caused by heavy vehicles like SUVs and large trucks. We must all STOP driving large SUVs and trucks because it is causing our freeway system to have increased potholes." In truth, we know that potholes are caused by water in the cracks and crevices of the road that freezes during winter; the ice expands, which breaks out pieces of the road. Cars, SUVs, and trucks hit these potholes and widen them over time. The underlying cause of potholes is ice in the road—not large trucks. The underlying cause of heart disease is high insulin response to carbohydrates, which leads to blood vessel wall damage, inflammation, and blockage; the cause is not the presence of one form of cholesterol.

You can't extrapolate mortality risk based on a single small study that doesn't actually identify correlation or causation. But the AHA did exactly that in 1961 with the E.H. Ahrens, Jr., study I mention at the beginning of this chapter, and they are trying to do it again today.

The Multiple Risk Factor Intervention Trial for the Prevention of Coronary Heart Disease (MRFIT) is a study that started in 1972 and finished in 1998. It's the largest study ever completed that examines the result of using dietary fat reduction to reduce heart failure risk.[16] It is frequently quoted in medical circles as the study that demonstrates that a reduction in LDL-C cholesterol leads to reduction in risk for cardiovascular disease.

However, this trial was a failure and did not demonstrate improved risk by lowering cholesterol. In fact, the director of the study, Dr. William Castelli, stated "...the more saturated fat one ate, the more cholesterol one ate, the more calories one ate, the lower people's serum cholesterol..." was. "We found that the people who ate the most cholesterol, ate the most saturated fat, ate the most calories weighed the least, and were the most physically active," he said.

Isn't that interesting?

JIMMY SAYS

Someday in the not-too-distant future, historians will look back on this age of cholesterol testing and shake their heads in bewilderment that we ever made a connection between a high-fat diet and heart health. What Dr. Nally and other keto-friendly physicians are realizing is the critical importance of controlling inflammation levels rather than worrying about LDL or total cholesterol in their patients. And consuming a ketogenic diet is one of the most anti-inflammatory actions you could ever take.

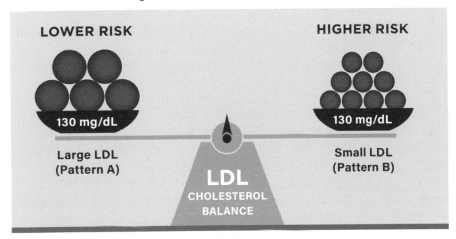

If you've been a follower of my blog (DocMuscles.com) for a while, you've seen the illustration of the LDL Cholesterol Balance. This picture illustrates why the calculated LDL-C can be misleading. Both sides of the scale reflect an LDL-C of 130 mg/dL. However, the left side is made up of only a few large, fluffy LDL particles (this is the person with reduced risk for heart disease and the lowest insulin level), which is called Pattern A. Even though the LDL-C is elevated above the recommended level of 100 mg/dL, the patient on the left has much less risk for vascular disease. (This is why you can't trust LDL-C as a risk factor.)

The right side of the scale shows that the same 130 mg/dL of LDL-C is made up of many more small-dense LDL particles (called "sd LDL-P"), which is called Pattern B type. This type is at increased risk for heart or vascular disease. This patient's triglycerides are usually greater than

100 mg/dL, and he or she has an insulin level somewhere between stage 2 and stage 4. This is where the standard Lipid Panel mentioned earlier fails to identify heart disease and its progression.

Research tells us that the small-dense LDL particle levels increase as the triglycerides increase. We also know that triglyceride levels increase in the presence of higher levels of insulin, which leads to a cascade of inflammatory changes. Insulin is directly increased by the ingestion of simple and complex carbohydrates. Insulin also increases with the ingestion of too much protein. That's why you'll occasionally see a marathon runner with blocked arteries. He or she lives on a diet of chicken and turkey (low in fat, but high in the amino acid arginine that stimulates insulin without raising blood sugar). That chicken salad or the oatmeal you ate, thinking it was good for you, actually just raised your cholesterol. If you are insulin resistant, your cholesterol increased by two to ten times the normal level.

So now maybe you're saying, "Okay, Dr. Nally, but there are a few different companies in the market that measure these fractional forms of cholesterol. Which one should I choose?" There are four different ways you can check your risk. You need to ask your doctor to order one of these blood tests if you'd like to obtain the results:

THE MOST USEFUL TESTS

With regard to screening for cardiovascular risk, the use of any of the four listed approaches combined with the standard Lipid Panel measurements are more effective than the standard Lipid Panel alone. However, I have found that clinically the NMR Lipo-profile or the Cardio IQ Ion-Mobility tests are the most useful in additionally monitoring insulin resistance, inflammation, and disease progression.

- **APOLIPOPROTEIN LEVELS:** This test measures the proteins within the wall of the lipoprotein specific to LDL or HDL. This can be done through most labs; however, this test doesn't give you additional information on insulin resistance that the other tests can.

- **BERKLEY HEART LAB'S GRADIENT GEL ELECTROPHORESIS:** This test measures the cholesterol weight through a process called electrophoresis. It provides an estimated measurement between Pattern A (good cholesterol) and Pattern B (bad cholesterol).

- **NMR SPECTROSCOPY FROM LIPOSCIENCE:** This test measures the actual number of lipoprotein particles present in the sample, as well as insulin resistance scores. You can also request to have the Lp(a) added to the results. I find the NMR to be the most user-friendly test, and it's most useful clinically in monitoring cholesterol, vascular risk, insulin resistance progression, and control of the inflammation caused by diabetes. This test has the least variation based on collection methods if frozen storage is used.

- **ION-MOBILITY FROM QUEST** (Cardio IQ test): This test also measures the number of lipoprotein particles, but it doesn't include insulin resistance risk or scoring. Because the test is done through a gas-phase electric differential, the reference ranges for normal are slightly different from the NMR.

Over the last twelve years, by using one of the listed tests in conjunction with a standard Lipid Panel measurement, I've found that restricting carbohydrates and following a ketogenic lifestyle have profound effects on vascular and metabolic risk.

APPLYING THE KETO CURE PRINCIPLES

Let's apply the Keto Cure principles to addressing abnormal cholesterol. For Principles 2, 3, and 5, there are no concerns that are specific to managing cholesterol. Refer to the first few pages of Part 2 for general information about those principles.

JIMMY SAYS

When people switch to a ketogenic diet, they may become discouraged in the short term when they see various cholesterol markers get out of whack. This tends to happen as you are losing weight, and I encourage you to stick with your keto plan until you become weight stable and then run those tests again. You'll be surprised at the improvements you'll see in the long run.

PRINCIPLE 1
LOWER INSULIN LEVELS WITH DIET

Remember: Insulin is the master hormone. The first step in addressing many diseases is to get insulin back to its baseline. This is done by restricting dietary carbohydrate intake. The goal is to reduce carbohydrate intake to less than 20 grams per day. When this is done correctly, blood sugar drops into the normal range (60 to 100 mg/dl) and fasting insulin returns (over 12-24 months) to less than 5 mU/mL. I've just been telling you that insulin drives the formation of the atherogenic (heart disease–causing) small-dense LDL subparticles, so it shouldn't seem like rocket science to realize that you can normalize cholesterol by removing carbohydrate from your diet.

When you reduce your carbohydrate intake to less than 20 grams per day, you can watch your cholesterol return to normal. Don't panic if your LDL-C goes up. An increase in LDL-C just means that you have more total LDL in your system at the time of measurement. This isn't a bad thing if your triglycerides are less than 100 mg/dL. We know that when triglycerides are lower than 100 mg/dL, the particle profiles shift from small and dense to big and "fluffy." Big, fluffy LDL is not a risk for heart disease.

When insulin levels are low, triglycerides decrease to less than 100 mg/dL. Insulin is the primary driver in metabolic inflammation. Markers of inflammation—such as C-reactive protein (CRP), apolipoproteins, uric acid, and the secondary inflammatory markers—usually normalize when carbohydrate levels are low enough for insulin to return to baseline.

This really is the key to cholesterol control. Control the insulin, and you control cholesterol.

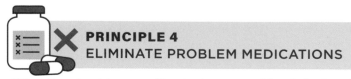

PRINCIPLE 4
ELIMINATE PROBLEM MEDICATIONS

CHAPTER 7:
ABNORMAL
CHOLESTEROL
(DYSLIPIDEMIA)

> ⚠ **CAUTION!**
> Do not stop or modify your use of any medications without direct consultation with your doctor.

NOTE: *Refer to the opening pages of Part 2 for a list of the medications that stimulate insulin, slow your metabolism, or cause cravings.*

JIMMY SAYS

Contrary to popular belief, taking a statin medication isn't a guarantee that you won't have a heart attack. Far too many people assume that's what these drugs do, but there is no evidence that using a pill to artificially lower your cholesterol levels will protect you from a cardiovascular event. And the pharmaceutical companies neglect to tell you that these drugs increase your risk of developing type 2 diabetes, cancer, and even heart disease itself!

What I'm about to say will not win me any friends in the pharmaceutical industry, but here goes: I've stopped more statin medications in patients than I have started in the last five or six years.

Do I just stop patients' statin medications cold turkey? NO! Of course not. The patient and I have a very in-depth discussion about risks and benefits, and, in some cases, we determine that continuation of the statin is the right decision with close monitoring for the potential side effects.

When I decide to stop a patient's statin medication, there are a few very important reasons for my decision:

- Cholesterol is essential for cell metabolism, and limiting your intake increases risk for mental problems, cancer, and reduction in immune function. In one study, 90 percent of 143 users of statin had improved memory when they discontinued the medication.

- As I discussed earlier, there is no real link between eating fat and increased heart disease risk. The risk for heart disease arises when you increase fat and never limit carbohydrate. (Simply put, this is because the high insulin level stimulates inflammation and vascular deposition of small-dense LDL particles.) This effect was originally identified in 1936, and studies in 1984, 2015, and again in 2017 have supported the original finding.

- Third, using a statin drug has been shown to reduce actual heart attack risk only from 2 percent to 1 percent. By using a statistically magic phrase called "relative risk" (see page 75), supporters of this theory can inflate that 1 percent by rephrasing it to be "50 percent improvement." What it really means is that statin medications must be given to one hundred people to decrease the heart attack risk from two people in five years to one person in five years.

My clinical experience demonstrates that approximately 40 percent of the people in my practice have amplified myalgia (muscle aches), memory changes, and risk for liver inflammation, which are all side effects from the statins when used with a ketogenic lifestyle. The *British Medical Journal* showed that the side effect rate for statin medications is around 18 percent to 20 percent.[17] With a benefit ratio of only 1 percent, those are not very good odds—not good enough to convince me that someone needs a statin if he or she instead will agree to cut out the bread, pasta, and oatmeal.

In my clinical experience over the last twelve-plus years, approximately 95 percent of my patients who follow a ketogenic lifestyle have cholesterol return to normal and have no need of pharmaceutical cholesterol treatment.

PRINCIPLE 6
CONSIDER APPROPRIATE SUPPLEMENTATION

The following is a list of supplements that might be beneficial in managing cholesterol:

- **OMEGA-3 FATTY ACIDS:** The research on supplementing with omega-3 fatty acids is mixed. In part, I suspect that those studies didn't address higher insulin levels in those people with insulin resistance.[18, 19] I have found that the addition of omega-3 fatty acids in supplement form has been very helpful in lowering triglycerides if the person is also following a carbohydrate-restricted or ketogenic lifestyle.

- **ZINC:** Literature reviews show that the supplementation of zinc has mild but favorable effects on total cholesterol, LDL, and triglycerides.[20] Further research is needed to see if this has any effect on cholesterol and secondarily the formation of atherosclerosis or mortality due to high small-dense LDL cholesterol.

- **EXOGENOUS KETONES:** The use of exogenous ketones is still in primary evaluation, but preliminary research in animal studies shows that adding them to a ketogenic diet decreased triglycerides while increasing HDL cholesterol.[21]

CHAPTER 8

ATHEROSCLEROSIS

Atherosclerosis, to put it simply, is plaque formation within the arteries of the circulatory system. Blockage in the arteries can lead to heart disease (heart attack), stroke (blockage of blood flow to the brain), or peripheral vascular disease (blockage of blood flow to the tissues of the arms and legs). So, if this chapter had a subtitle, it might be "The Stuff Heart Attacks and Strokes Are Made Of."

For years we've been told that fat is the culprit that causes atherosclerosis. If you've read Chapter 7 about abnormal cholesterol, I hope this myth has been cleared up for you. I explain in that chapter that insulin clogs the pipes. But what does insulin do to actually clog the pipes, and how does the vasculature or the arteries within your body get blocked up by insulin?

Excessive production of insulin drives up the small-dense LDL cholesterol and increases inflammation. This creates the perfect storm for vascular blockage.

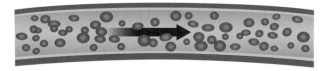

Normal artery

Atherosclerosis

There's a second culprit in the process of atherosclerosis: fructose. Fructose is processed in the liver (just as alcohol is), and the by-product of fructose metabolism is decreased nitric oxide. Lower nitric oxide in the presence of insulin-driven inflammation allows the lining of the blood vessel wall (the endothelium) to "crack" or break. Those cracks allow for the deposition of the smallest LDL particles (small-dense LDL) in the vessel wall. The cracks also allow the inner vessel lining to be exposed to free radicals (which are also present because of increased inflammation), and the small-dense LDL in the cracks becomes oxidized, like metal rusting. These oxidized particles damage the collagen lining of the blood vessel wall. Lp(a), the protein around the small-dense LDL particle, and the collagen in the vessel wall lining are damaged.

Macrophages (the fixer cells of the immune system), monocytes, and smooth muscle cells in the arterial wall attempt to repair the damaged collagen lining. These cells begin the process of fibrous changes in the vessel wall and deposition of cholesterol particulates in the lining. Plaque builds, and it gets bigger and bigger because of the perfect storm of low nitric oxide, high inflammation, high small-dense LDL particles, and activated macrophages. Finally, the fibrous cap breaks, and a thrombus or blood clot forms. This clot can block a heart blood vessel, which causes a heart attack, or it can block a blood vessel to the brain, which causes a stroke.

High insulin levels spur inflammation by increasing a number of inflammatory hormones, including the following:

- C-reactive protein
- Lipoprotein-associated phospholipase (Lp PLA-2)
- Cytokines
- Toll-like receptor gene 4 (TLR4)
- Pregnancy-associated plasma protein–A (PAPP-A)

These hormones call in monocytes and smooth muscle cells to help the macrophages repair and fill the wall with absorbed cholesterol and damaged collagen, which become foam cells. Cytokines are released, causing free radical formation that drives the collagen and smooth muscle cell formation of the fatty streak and later the fibrous cap. The cytokines activate more of the immune system, including T-lymphocytes. TLR4 is a transmembrane protein that helps activate the cytokines. PAPP-A also shows up when the vascular plaque is becoming more unstable. The presence of PAPP-A and Lp PLA-2 are signs that the plaque is unstable and near rupture.[1]

Again, this whole narrative, as far as we understand it, is driven by increased insulin, increased triglycerides, and increased fructose metabolism driven by sugars—not by fat.

If sugars block the pipes, then is there a fuel that cleans the pipes? We know that a diet that lowers insulin also lowers triglycerides. A diet

JIMMY SAYS

I have a family history of atherosclerosis. My father had heart attacks in his late forties followed by bypass surgery in his early fifties, and my brother Kevin experienced three heart attacks at age 32, which eventually contributed to his death at 41. Both men had blockages that were a result of years of poor nutrition and lifestyle choices. I'm bucking this genetic tendency by being proactive about lowering my insulin and inflammation levels through a ketogenic diet.

that decreases the risk of inflammation in the vascular lining decreases the risk of damage to the endothelial lining over the long run.

A ketogenic diet removes sugars, lowers insulin, and eliminates the presence of fructose being metabolized in the liver. Nitric oxide returns to normal, and the inflammatory cascade of hormones doesn't occur.

For the past ten years, I've been doing ultrasound Doppler studies of the carotid arteries and the carotid intimal measurements. I've found that those patients who follow a ketogenic lifestyle seem to see a 10 percent improvement in blockage each year. A few have experienced up to a 20 percent improvement in their blockages. Patients also have seen notable improvements in the thickness of the carotid arterial walls, which makes me think that a ketogenic diet is healing the vascular walls.

A CASE STUDY

Meet "Mrs. Plaque" (her name has been changed to protect her identity). She is a pleasant 78-year-old female with a history of elevated cholesterol, pre-diabetes, peripheral neuropathy, cataracts, and gastro-esophageal reflux; she is post-hysterectomy. She has been my patient for ten years.

Her current medications included Plavix 75 mg, once daily; Premarin Cream, 0.635 mg every other day; Xanax, 0.5 mg at bedtime for anxiety; Lyrica, 50 mg once nightly for neuropathy; vitamin D, 2,000 IU daily; Tums, 750 mg twice daily.

A few years ago, I identified worsening cholesterol and hyperinsulinemia in Mrs. Plaque, and in 2015 she finally decided to go on a ketogenic diet after I noted slightly worsening blood sugar (HbA1c increased to 6.1 percent), worsening cholesterol, and a recent transient ischemic attack (TIA, or "mini stroke"). We identified a 44 percent blockage in her left internal carotid artery and a 21 percent blockage in her right internal carotid artery, which put her at risk for further cerebral ischemic events down the road (such as a stroke and/or other vascular events, like a heart attack). She refused statin therapy because she'd had previous myalgia and side effects as a result of statin use in the past.

Mrs. Plaque's carotid ultrasound and carotid intima-media thickness (CIMT) study was completed on April 1, 2015. In the figure showing the results of her study, you can see that Mrs. Plaque's intima-media thickness is only slightly higher than average for a female (0.851), putting her at the fiftieth percentile for her age.

Mrs. Plaque's husband was diabetic, and Mrs. Plaque had been "partially" restricting sugar in her diet up to this point. However, she had not fully jumped on the ketogenic bandwagon. The "mini stroke" and the CIMT report convinced her that she needed to tighten up her diet.

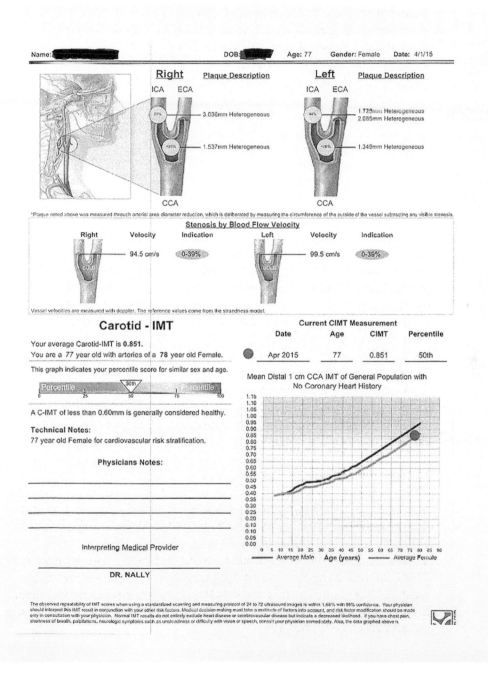

She was placed on a ketogenic diet, which required her to restrict carbohydrates to no more than 20 grams per day and increase total fat to 50 to 60 percent of total calories. Nothing else changed, including her medications. She followed this program for a year; the chart below tracks her bloodwork while following this program.

	4/2/15	8/4/15	11/6/15	5/12/16
HbA1c (%)		6.1	5.8	5.2
Total Cholesterol (mg/dL)	224	156	230	233
HDL (mg/dL)	76	76	87	96
LDL-C (mg/dL)	134	65	128	123
sd LDL-P (nmol/L)	481	150	74	68
Fasting Insulin (uIU/mL)		12		
Glucose (mg/dL)	91	95	92	85

JIMMY SAYS

I have had a CIMT done, and I've had a CT Heart Scan to get my Calcium Score to determine the amount of calcification in my coronary arteries. Since I made the switch to a low-carb ketogenic diet in 2004, I've had three CT Heart Scans, and all three came back as a big fat zero. Over that same time period, my diet has consisted of at least 70 to 80 percent fat daily. Keto isn't artery-clogging at all!

Because she was already partially restricting her sugar intake, her triglycerides and small-dense LDL particle numbers were not bad. However, her average blood sugars were still significantly elevated. Her weight decreased from 127 pounds in April to 119 pounds in August. She admits to a slightly increased protein intake over the holidays, and her weight increased to 125 pounds as of her last visit.

The labs tracked in the chart also demonstrate that total cholesterol and LDL-C don't appear to correlate with the regression of plaque.

We used the same lab to repeat the Doppler ultrasound and CIMT of the carotids for Mrs. Plaque thirteen months after the first report, and you can see the results in the figure of the second report. What is dramatic is that, in one year, she had a more than 10 percent regression in the plaque in both her internal carotid arteries and a return of her carotid intima-medial thickness from the fiftieth percentile for her age to the forty-eighth percentile for her age with a regression of 0.02 millimeters from the previous baseline. This *regression* is dramatic because the average rate of *progression* is up to 0.02 millimeters every two years.[2]

This case study, and many others like it in my office, is consistent with the findings of Iris Shai and group when they did the DIRECT Group study, a two-year comparative dietary intervention study of low-fat, Mediterranean diet, and a ketogenic diet on vessel wall volume and CIMT.[3]

So, does diet reverse vascular disease? Evidence is pointing to the fact that the ketogenic diet does. I return to the statement Hippocrates made more than 2,000 years ago: "Let food be thy medicine, and thy medicine be thy food." (Oh, and pass the bacon.)

APPLYING THE KETO CURE APPROACH

Let's apply the Keto Cure principles to address atherosclerosis. Refer to the first few pages of Part 2 for the general principles of the Keto Cure approach. What's included here are tips that are specific to the treatment of atherosclerosis.

PRINCIPLE 1
LOWER INSULIN LEVELS WITH DIET

In the case study, notice that Mrs. Plaque's fasting insulin was greater than 5 uIU/mL, at 12 uIU/mL. The first step is to get insulin back to its baseline. This is done by restricting dietary carbohydrate intake. The goal is to reduce carbohydrate intake to less than 20 grams per day. When this is done correctly, blood sugar drops into the normal range (60 to 100 mg/dl) and fasting insulin returns to less than 5 mU/mL. In most people, it takes eighteen to twenty-four months for this number to return to normal. In Chapter 7, I explain that insulin drives the formation of atherogenic (heart disease–causing) small-dense LDL subparticles, and continued high insulin stimulates the inflammatory cascade of atherogenesis. So, it shouldn't be too hard to make the leap to the realization that we can, at a minimum, halt the process and possibly reverse it by restricting carbohydrate intake.

Start by reducing your carbohydrate intake to less than 20 grams per day, and your cholesterol should eventually return to normal. Don't panic if your LDL-C goes up. This just means that you have more total LDL in your system at the time of measurement, which isn't a bad thing if your triglycerides are less than 100 mg/dL. When triglycerides are less than 100 mg/dL, the particle profile shifts from small and dense to big and "fluffy." Big, fluffy LDL is not a risk factor for heart disease.

When insulin levels are low, triglycerides decrease to less than 100 mg/dL. Insulin is the primary driver in metabolic inflammation. Markers of inflammation, such as C-reactive protein (CRP), apolipoproteins, uric acid, and the secondary inflammatory markers, usually normalize when carbohydrate levels are low enough for insulin to return to baseline.

JIMMY SAYS

The telltale sign of how well you are doing in your ketogenic diet is triglycerides falling below 100. If they are higher than this, then you need to be more diligent about cutting carbs and moderating protein. When you lower triglycerides to less than 100, you shift the LDL particles to the Pattern A large, fluffy type that are harmless to your cardiovascular health. If your triglycerides are higher than 100, your LDL particles tend to fall into the Pattern B small-dense type that are very dangerous to your heart.

⚠ **CAUTION!**
Do not stop or modify your use of any medications without direct consultation with your doctor.

PRINCIPLE 2
AVOID ADDITIVES THAT RAISE INSULIN LEVELS

If you are a smoker, quit. Quit now. Tobacco use amplifies the progression of atherosclerosis at the endothelial level. Smoking decreases nitric oxide as well. Cigarette smoking increases C-reactive protein (CRP), interleukin-6 (IL-6), and tumor necrosis factor alpha (TNF-α) in men and women. It also decreases platelet sensitivity to nitric oxide, which increases fibrinogen levels and the likelihood that clots and thrombosis will form.

PRINCIPLE 4
ELIMINATE PROBLEM MEDICATIONS

If you have atherosclerosis and documented blockage or CIMT, you need to have a long conversation with your doctor about the actual benefit of continuing a statin medication compared to the side effect risk. Treatment with atorvastatin and rosuvastatin have shown roughly a 5 percent arterial wall thickness regression, from 0.0013 millimeters to 0.038 millimeters per year.[4] So, you must take this into account when deciding to use one of these statins.

PRINCIPLE 5
ADD MEDICATIONS THAT HELP

In cases where atherosclerosis exists, the use of an anti-platelet therapy— such as aspirin or medications like clopidogrel (Plavix) or dipyridamole (Aggrenox)—should be discussed with your doctor. The use of aspirin was shown to reduce stroke within the first year of daily use from 360 to 100 in data of 15,000 people studied.

Please work closely with your doctor to identify whether there are essential medications you should be taking and whether there are any medications that work synergistically with a ketogenic lifestyle.

PRINCIPLE 6
CONSIDER APPROPRIATE SUPPLEMENTATION

The following are some supplements that might help address issues with atherosclerosis:

- **OMEGA-3 FATTY ACIDS:** The research on supplementing with omega-3 fatty acids is mixed. In part, I suspect that the studies didn't address higher insulin levels in those people with insulin resistance.[5, 6] I have found that adding omega-3 fatty acids in supplement form has been very helpful in lowering triglycerides as long as the person is also following a carbohydrate-restricted or ketogenic lifestyle.

- **ALLICIN (found in crushed garlic):** Literature reviews show that supplementing with crushed garlic or allicin has mild but favorable effects on cholesterol, LDL, and triglycerides. It also reduces the formation of reactive oxygen species (free radicals).[7] Further research is needed to see if this has any effect on atherosclerosis or mortality.

- **FLAVANOLS:** Flavanols are found in fruits, vegetables, and cocoa. On a ketogenic diet, you'd find flavanols in leafy greens. Research shows that the use of flavanols improves blood flow and decreases arterial stiffness. Flavanols have also been shown to have an anti-inflammatory effect.[8]

- **BERBERINE:** Berberine has been shown to reduce cholesterol in several studies. It also has been shown to help increase blood flow.[9]

- **CARNOSINE:** Carnosine has been shown to improve insulin resistance, but there has been no observed effect on cholesterol or CRP.[10]

- **EXOGENOUS KETONES:** The use of exogenous ketones is still in primary evaluation, but preliminary research in animal studies shows that adding them to a ketogenic diet decreased triglycerides while increasing HDL cholesterol.[11]

- **CURCUMIN:** Eight weeks of curcumin use was shown to improve flow-mediated dilation in thirty-two post-menopausal women. It also has been shown to decrease arterial stiffness and improve metabolic blood panels.[12]

- **BUTYRATE (fiber in leafy green and fermented food):** Butyrate is a short-chain fatty acid produced during fiber fermentation that has been shown to decrease inflammation, decrease the presence of cytokines, including IL-1β, IL-6, and TNF-α, and improve nitric oxide production. For every 10 grams of fiber (¼ to ½ cup of leafy greens), a reduction in coronary death of up to 27 percent has been shown in six-year outcome trials.[13]

CHAPTER 9

URIC ACID AND GOUT

Gout is a painful swelling that can occur in one of the large joints. This painful swelling of a joint arises when crystals (monosodium urate) from excess uric acid form or precipitate in the fluid inside the joint. Gout usually occurs in a joint of the toe, ankle, or knee; however, I've seen it in hands and elbows as well. The swelling is so painful that it is often disabling. Chronic, recurring gout can actually cause a form of arthritis known as tophaceous gout.

An acute case of gout causes redness, warmth, and notably painful swelling in the joint. The swollen joint is so hypersensitive that even contact with bed sheets can cause severe pain.

IT HURTS!

In case you missed the point that gout is very painful, you should know this: I've seen female patients in the emergency room who were in so much pain that they told me they'd rather deliver twins than have an attack of gout!

When uric acid levels rise and a person gets a little dehydrated, heavy urate crystals form in the synovial fluid of the joint, often a knee or big toe. Uric acid levels rise for a number of reasons: slowing of the removal of uric acid through the kidneys, overproduction of uric acid, and overconsumption of foods that stimulate uric acid in the metabolism.

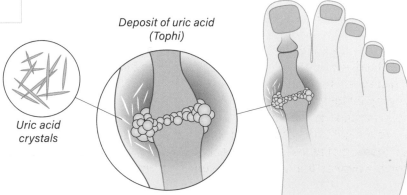

Deposit of uric acid (Tophi)

Uric acid crystals

Here's an analogy: When I was in the first grade, we conducted a science experiment that involved boiling water and then adding salt or sugar to make a superconcentrate (a solution that contains more than a normal amount of salt or sugar). After the salt or sugar had dissolved, we poured the solution into a jar and then suspended a string from a pencil at the top of the jar so that the string dropped into the superconcentrate. Over the next few days, we observed that crystals formed on the string. The excess salt or sugar couldn't remain in a dissolved form as the water evaporated, so it collected on the string.

This crystal-formation process, called precipitation, occurs inside your joint when gout develops. The problem is that these crystals are not square like salt or sugar crystals; they are like double-sided needles, so any movement of the joint feels like someone is sticking a needle into the joint. Once these crystals form, they can last for up to three weeks.

CAUSES OF GOUT

In the past, gout has been attributed to diets rich in pork and alcohol. For many years, the theory was that purines, a form of protein found in pork and alcohol, were metabolized into excessive uric acid. More recently, though, we've found that purines are not solely responsible for the occurrence of gout.

Gout results from a number of modifiable risk factors, including obesity, alcohol consumption, drinking soda and fruit juice, thiazide and loop diuretics, and post-menopausal status. It also occurs in patients who have had organ transplants. The exact reason crystals form in the joint fluid is still unknown. However, we do know that gout crystals form when the body temperature is 98.6°F (37°C) and when the concentration of uric acid is 7 mg/dL.[1, 2]

The warmer the joint, the less likely crystals are to form. Noninflamed joint fluid (synovial fluid) is usually cooler than blood (serum); the joint fluid registers a temperature of around 90°F to 91°F (32°C) in the knee.[3] The lower joint temperature lowers the point at which crystals form, and the concentration of uric acid can be just 6 mg/dL or less.[4]

You might be saying, "But wait, aren't you going to tell me that a ketogenic diet helps? How can eating ham make gout better? Doesn't ham contain purines that will make the uric acid worse?"

JIMMY SAYS

More than a decade ago, noted science journalist Gary Taubes wrote a seminal book about the positive role of low-carb, ketogenic diets in health. Good Calories, Bad Calories laid the groundwork for much of the research and popularity of low-carb, high-fat diets. But a very informative and compelling chapter on gout was cut from the final draft. It's available online on Tim Ferriss' blog: https://tim. blog/2009/10/05/gout.

When I've studied the results in my patients, I've found that no matter how much a person restricts consumption of ham and other foods with a high purine content, gout still reoccurs until the patient decreases the use of foods containing fructose and/or alcohol. (Interestingly, fructose and alcohol are metabolized almost identically in the liver.)

Simple sugar and high-fructose corn syrup have the same effect. Remember, a sugar molecule is one glucose molecule bound to a fructose molecule. High-fructose corn syrup is 45 percent glucose and 55 percent fructose. Yet 100 percent of the fructose in sugar or high-fructose corn syrup is metabolized just like alcohol, and it increases uric acid.

Over the years in my clinic, I've found that when a patient switches to a carbohydrate-restricted (ketogenic) diet—cutting out sugar and fruit and notably limiting alcohol intake—I see a 1.0 to 1.5 mg/dL decrease in uric acid levels in the blood. These people still eat ham and bacon, yet their uric acid levels drop, and they stop having gout attacks.

What's even more fascinating is that the presence of increased ketones decreases inflammation. We've found that the ketones turn down the inflammatory cascade of hormones by blockading an inflammatory molecule called the NLRP3 inflammasome.[5] This means that as a person increases the presence of ketones nutritionally, both the inflammation and the risk of gout crystals forming decrease.

APPLYING THE KETO CURE APPROACH

Let's apply the Keto Cure principles in addressing gout. The information in this section is specific to addressing gout. Any principles that don't require modification related to gout aren't included here; refer to the first few pages of Part 2 for details of those principles.

PRINCIPLE 2
AVOID ADDITIVES THAT RAISE INSULIN LEVELS

Alcohol raises insulin and raises uric acid at the same time. Avoid using alcohol if you are at risk for or have a history of gout. If you ignore this advice, you're playing with fire—the kind that starts in your liver and turns your toe or knee fire-engine red.

PRINCIPLE 5
ADD MEDICATIONS THAT HELP

For the treatment of gout, some physicians advocate the use of glucocorticoids to decrease acute inflammation and reduce swelling. However, using glucocorticoids, such as prednisone, may come at a price if you are following a ketogenic diet. Glucocorticoids may make it more difficult for you to stay in ketosis and can decrease the long-term anti-inflammatory effect of being in ketosis.

The following is a list of medications currently available to treat and prevent gout:

- **NON-STEROIDAL ANTI-INFLAMMATORY DRUGS (NSAIDS)**
  - Aleve (naproxen)
  - Indocin (indomethacin)
- **ANTI-GOUT AGENT,** such as Colcrys (colchicine)
- **GLUCOCORTICOIDS**
  - Prednisone
  - Pediapred (prednisolone)

Be aware that NSAIDs also have the potential to kick you out of nutritional ketosis. In my opinion, it's a good idea to treat the pain and inflammation with an NSAID or colchicine in the short term and then later tighten up the diet to prevent further attacks of gout.

If you have had chronically elevated uric acid levels or reoccurring gout, then a urate-lowering medication may be something you should consider. Many of my patients who fall into this category have been able to lower their uric acid levels with diet alone. However, for a few of them, diet alone has not completely solved the problem, or they've had trouble staying on a ketogenic diet because of work, travel, or other lifestyle issues. In these cases, using one of the following medications might be appropriate:

- **XANTHINE OXIDASE INHIBITOR**
  - Aloprim (allopurinol)
  - Uloric (febuxostat)
- **ANTI-GOUT AGENT,** such as Colcrys (colchicine)
- **URICOSURIC AGENTS**
  - Probenecid
  - Zurampic (lesinurad)

PRINCIPLE 6
CONSIDER APPROPRIATE SUPPLEMENTATION

The following are some supplements to consider for the treatment of gout:

- **CHERRY JUICE:** Cherry juice has a hypouricemic and an anti-inflammatory effect; however, it also contains fructose. The hypouricemic effect of cherries is still unclear. Two studies have shown a lowering of uric acid, but this effect may have been attributable to the fasted state of the subjects the night before the study.[6, 7]

- **VITAMIN C:** One small study revealed that 4 grams of vitamin C lowered uric acid levels. Those people who used 500 milligrams of vitamin C had a decreased risk of gout.[8, 9]

- **ASPIRIN:** Aspirin at doses lower than 3 grams per day causes a retention of uric acid. At doses higher than 3 grams per day, there is a marked lowering of serum uric acid.[10] Regardless of the dose, there is still question about whether aspirin has a beneficial effect.

- **CELERY:** Celery has a diuretic effect and can lower uric acid because it acts as a weak xanthine oxidase inhibitor. It has been shown to provide some help in the prevention of gout, and the literature reveals that celery has some effect on acute cases of gout.[11]

- **EXOGENOUS KETONES:** The use of exogenous ketones is still in primary evaluation, but preliminary research shows that adding them to a ketogenic diet raises ketone levels in the blood. Because of the anti-inflammatory effect of ketones on the NLRP3 inflammasome and the notable lowering of inflammatory pro-cytokines, including IL-1β, IL-6, and IFN-γ (among others), exogenous ketones might be beneficial in the treatment or prevention of gout.[12]

CHAPTER 10

KIDNEY STONES

This chapter is all about the wicked stepchild of gout—kidney stones. There is even a name for them that sounds wicked: *nephrolithiasis*. Let's talk about how a ketogenic lifestyle takes the "wicked" out of your kidneys.

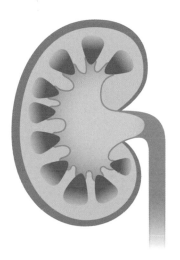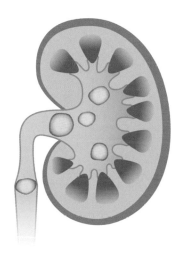

WHAT ARE KIDNEY STONES?

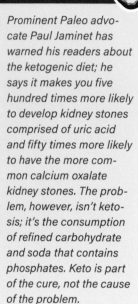

JIMMY SAYS

Prominent Paleo advocate Paul Jaminet has warned his readers about the ketogenic diet; he says it makes you five hundred times more likely to develop kidney stones comprised of uric acid and fifty times more likely to have the more common calcium oxalate kidney stones. The problem, however, isn't ketosis; it's the consumption of refined carbohydrate and soda that contains phosphates. Keto is part of the cure, not the cause of the problem.

A tremendous amount of information about kidney stones and their treatment and prevention has already been published. I'm not going to try to reinvent the wheel and cover all the information that's discussed elsewhere. However, what doesn't exist in the medical or nutrition literature is the effect that fructose and insulin have on kidney stones, so I do want to talk about what carbohydrate restriction does to the formation of kidney stones.

What exactly *is* a kidney stone? It is a formation of hard, sharp, pointed crystals in the collecting system of the kidney. These stones, once formed, travel down the ureter to the bladder. The issue is that the ureter, the tube through which urine travels from the kidney to the bladder, is only 0.3 to 0.5 centimeter wide, whereas kidney stones are often 0.2 to 0.6 centimeter in diameter (and sometimes larger). It's like trying to put a large, square peg in a small, round hole. This is excruciatingly painful and can create significant back pressure on the kidney, with the potential to cause permanent damage to the renal system.

There are actually two types of kidney stones: calcium oxalate stones (the most common) and uric acid stones. Because Chapter 9 was all about uric acid and gout, let's start with the uric acid type of stone.

Just as increased uric acid ups the risk for gout, it can also increase the risk of kidney stones forming. The kidney is responsible for removing uric acid, so, when levels of urate go up, the kidney filters the uric acid into the collecting system of urine to try to protect you from gout. If uric acid goes up, you get dehydrated, and if there is any inflammation or temperature shift in the body, a perfect storm forms within the renal collecting system. Wham! Sharp, needle-like stones form.

If you've had uric acid (urate) stones and you haven't read Chapter 9, stop and read it now. Then come back here and pick up where you left off. Don't worry; I'll wait.

Okay, let's move on.

You've probably heard tales of how painful kidney stones are, so I don't need to spend a lot of time talking about that aspect. However, I had one patient say, "Dr. Nally, I've delivered eight children, and this pain is worse than all eight deliveries put together." If you are one of those people who've had kidney stones and survived, bless you. You are my hero. This chapter is for you. It's my hope that the application of principles herein will prevent you from ever experiencing another kidney stone.

The most common type of kidney stone (75 percent of stones) is made up of a substance called calcium oxalate.[1,2] It is driven by an overproduction of calcium that crystalizes in the renal collecting system. Because of the very complex nature of the system, no one has been able to identify one single mechanism that causes the formation of calcium-based stones.

What's interesting about calcium oxalate and calcium phosphate stones is that they can't form when potassium or magnesium levels (or both) rise in the urine. Potassium and magnesium, two salts commonly excreted at a higher volume when you live a ketogenic lifestyle, prevent the formation or crystallization of calcium stones in the urine. That's why potassium citrate or magnesium citrate is given as a treatment for calcium oxalate stones.

We know that increased glucose and fructose stimulate increased insulin and uric acid formation (as mentioned in Chapter 9). Insulin raises blood pressure, causes the retention of sodium, and slows fluid loss through diuresis. This has a notable effect on raising calcium excretion, which increases the risk for calcium-based stones.[3,4]

Some researchers and physician experts have thought that a high-protein diet would prevent calcium oxalate stones because of the acidic effect of metabolizing sulfur-containing amino acids. Interestingly, it has been found that a high-protein diet does not reduce the risk of calcium excretion or calcium-based stones.[5] What has never been addressed is the increased insulin response from increased amino acids like arginine, lysine, phenylalanine, leucine, and tryptophan.

High-protein diets (those that lower carbohydrates and restrict fat calories) still have significant potential to allow insulin resistance to persist. Conversely, low-carb, high-fat diets that are ketogenic in nature limit insulin production to basal levels through the moderation of protein as one of the primary steps. This allows for a rise in the levels of potassium and magnesium in the urine and lowers the risk of calcium stone formation.

As mentioned in Chapter 9, fructose increases uric acid and the likelihood that urate crystal will form as the kidney filters the uric acid into the urine. A ketogenic lifestyle reduces the formation of uric acid by limiting carbohydrate intake to less than 20 grams per day.

Thus, we can conclude that both calcium-based and uric acid–based stones are driven by glucose and fructose intake. Although the science has not completely clarified the mechanisms in all cases, the ketogenic lifestyle appears to be the only approach that controls kidney stones.

A WORD OF WARNING

Kidney stones are one issue that rears its ugly head in people on a ketogenic lifestyle. But in the years that I've been recommending keto diets to my patients, the only time kidney stones return is when people cheat.

If you have had kidney stones or are at notable risk for them, beware! If you cheat, the stones can return. Often around the end-of-year holidays, people fall back into old eating patterns. If you've been following a ketogenic lifestyle for a while and you fall off the wagon for a few days during the holidays, the kidney stones may return.

The following three tips can minimize your risk:

1. Keep well hydrated.

2. If you're going to cheat, set a limit on sweets and candies.

3. Limit your alcohol intake.

APPLYING THE KETO CURE APPROACH

I started putting people on ketogenic diets around 2005. One of the most prominent outcomes, other than weight loss, was that they stopped developing kidney stones. The following sections describe how to apply the principles of the Keto Cure approach to addressing kidney stones. For Principles 3 and 4, there are no concerns that are specific to kidney stones. Refer to the first few pages of Part 2 for general information about each of the principles.

PRINCIPLE 1
LOWER INSULIN LEVELS WITH DIET

This principle doesn't vary much regardless of which disease you're treating: The first step in addressing many diseases is to get insulin back to its baseline. This is done by restricting dietary carbohydrate intake. The goal is to reduce carbohydrate intake to less than 20 grams per day. When this is done correctly, blood sugar drops into the normal range (60 to 100 mg/dl) and fasting insulin returns (over 12-24 months) to less than 5 mU/mL. In the case of kidney stones (and in the case of gout), you are lowering insulin to allow for greater nutritional ketosis. As insulin falls, more sodium, potassium, and magnesium are excreted in the kidneys, which prevents the formation of calcium-based kidney stones.

PRINCIPLE 2
AVOID ADDITIVES THAT RAISE INSULIN LEVELS

Alcohol raises insulin and, at the same time, raises uric acid. It also is a diuretic; depending on your liver's capacity to detoxify the alcohol, more than one or two drinks can lead to a chronic state of dehydration. Avoid using any alcohol if you are at risk for or have a history of kidney stones. You're playing with fire here—the kind that starts in your liver and feels like someone shoved a hot poker into your flank.

PRINCIPLE 5
ADD MEDICATIONS THAT HELP

Calcium-based kidney stones are treated with increased fluid intake. Your doctor might also recommend the following medications:

- **THIAZIDE DIURETICS TO REDUCE URINARY CALCIUM**
  - Hydrochlorothiazide
  - Chlorthalidone
- **POTASSIUM CITRATE TO LOWER URINE CITRATE**

Any medication that helps control elevated blood sugar or diabetes while limiting insulin also prevents uric acid–based kidney stones. There are a number of medications currently available to treat and prevent kidney stones:

- **ANTI-GOUT/URIC ACID AGENT,** such as Colcrys (colchicine)
- **URINARY ALKALINIZATION AGENTS**
  - Potassium bicarbonate
  - Potassium citrate

If you've had chronically elevated uric acid levels or have suffered from reoccurring gout or kidney stones, then you might want to consider using a urate-lowering medication. Many of my patients who suffer from kidney stones have been able to lower their uric acid levels with diet alone. However, for a few of them, diet has not completely solved the problem, or they've had trouble staying on a ketogenic diet because of work, travel, or other lifestyle issues. In these cases, it might be appropriate to discuss the following medications with your doctor:

- **XANTHINE OXIDASE INHIBITORS**
  - Aloprim (allopurinol)
  - Uloric (febuxostat)
- **URICOSURIC AGENTS**
  - Probenecid
  - Zurampic (lesinurad)

PRINCIPLE 6
CONSIDER APPROPRIATE SUPPLEMENTATION

The following is a list of supplements that might be beneficial in managing kidney stones:

- **CALCIUM CARBONATE (such as Tums):** In people whose calcium stones are oxalate-driven due to high-dose vitamin C, short bowel syndrome from surgery, or increased gastrointestinal absorption of oxalate, the use of calcium carbonate may be considered. Although some calcium is absorbed, the calcium carbonate binds to oxalate in the intestinal lumen and reduces overall absorption.

- **CHERRY JUICE:** Cherry juice has a hypouricemic and an anti-inflammatory effect; however, it also contains fructose. The hypouricemic effect of cherries is still unclear. The two studies available showed a lowering of uric acid, but this effect may be attributable to the fasted state of the subjects the night before the study.[6, 7]

- **CELERY:** Celery has a diuretic effect and can lower uric acid because it acts as a weak xanthine oxidase inhibitor. It has been used with some help in the prevention of kidney stones, and the literature reveals that celery has some effect on acute cases of gout and possibly kidney stones.[8]

- **EXOGENOUS KETONES:** The use of exogenous ketones is still in primary evaluation, but preliminary research shows that adding them to a ketogenic diet raises ketone levels in the blood. Magnesium-based ketone salts may play a role in the prevention of kidney stones. Studies in this area are not yet available.

CHAPTER 11

NON-ALCOHOLIC FATTY LIVER DISEASE

Hepatic steatosis, or non-alcoholic fatty liver disease (NAFLD), is something that affects 22 percent of the population in the United States. As many as 30 percent of Europeans have NAFLD. I am frequently asked about what causes this disease and how to treat it. People are beginning to worry about NAFLD more than forms of hepatitis. In fact, NAFLD is the second-most common topic people ask me about when they find out that I treat obesity and diabetes with a ketogenic lifestyle.

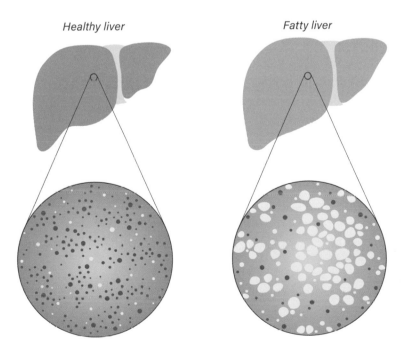

Healthy liver   *Fatty liver*

WHAT IS FATTY LIVER DISEASE?

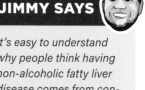

JIMMY SAYS

It's easy to understand why people think having non-alcoholic fatty liver disease comes from consuming fat. It is a "fatty" liver, after all! What they don't realize is that this fat is developed in the liver because of the massive amounts of fructose in the standard American diet, mostly from sugary sodas. Foie gras is made by force-feeding corn to ducks or geese to give them a "fatty liver." The carbs, not the fat, are the culprit.

Fatty liver disease is separated into alcoholic fatty liver disease and non-alcoholic fatty liver disease. The only difference is the absence of alcohol. Both types can progress to cirrhosis and liver failure.

If NAFLD is caught early (before the progression to liver inflammation and fibrosis), the risk of progression to cirrhosis is 1 to 2 percent. However, 10 to 15 percent of patients who have already demonstrated liver inflammation and fibrosis (non-alcoholic steatohepatitis or NASH) will progress to cirrhosis within eight years, and some even progress to hepatic cancer.[1]

Though a few patients complain of fatigue and vague right upper abdominal discomfort, those with NAFLD commonly experience no pain and are asymptomatic. When I started seeing this disease in my practice fifteen years ago, one out of ten people would have mild elevation of liver enzymes (elevated AST and/or ALT levels) in a routine physical exam. An ultrasound of the liver would return results of "fatty liver infiltration" without any other symptoms. These were people who didn't drink—or rarely drank—alcohol, and they had no other risk factors for hepatitis or liver damage. The number of affected people seems to be rising. In the last few years, I've started to see elevated liver enzymes in *two* out of every ten people.

Every one of these patients has features of metabolic syndrome: impaired fasting glucose or type 2 diabetes mellitus, central obesity, elevated cholesterol, and elevated blood pressure. The interesting thing is that all the patients were trying to eat a low-fat, calorie-restricted diet. A few patients I sent to a gastroenterologist for further evaluation were even accused of lying about their diet because "they had to be eating too much fat to get this disease."

Another thing I observed was that every one of these patients had a high insulin response to carbohydrates. As mentioned in Chapter 4 on insulin resistance, a patient with insulin resistance produces two to twenty times the normal amount of insulin in response to carbohydrates or sugars.

WHAT CAUSES THE DISEASE?

Current science demonstrates that NAFLD is a manifestation of triglycerides accumulating in the liver. Remember that insulin directly stimulates triglyceride formation in the liver and the fat cells (adipose tissue). There appears to be a broken or inhibited mechanism in the liver that causes the increased triglycerides that are being formed to be deposited in the liver. It appears that the very low-density lipoproteins (VLDL) can't exit the liver correctly, and triglycerides get deposited there.

Among a number of possible causes of NAFLD, one that seems to play a role is that of adiponectin signaling. Adiponectin is a hormone produced by the fat cells. However, as a fat cell gets bigger and sicker, its production of adiponectin drops due to leptin resistance (leptin is another signaling hormone produced in the fat cells) and insulin resistance.

In mice, the administration of adiponectin actually improved hepatic steatosis and liver enlargement and lowered liver enzymes back to normal.[2] In a study of humans, reduced adiponectin levels correlated with the severity of liver damage in patients with NASH.[3]

Some recent research points to intestinal bacteria playing a role in NAFLD damage. Two specific species of bacteria that are common to our intestines, *bacteroides* and *ruminococcus*, had a significantly increased presence in those people with NAFLD and NASH.[4] The suspicion is that the overgrowth of these bacterial species causes hepatic (liver) injury by producing a bacterial endotoxin that has a structure similar to alcohol and acetaldehyde.[5]

Obstructive sleep apnea is a genetic and structural syndrome that occurs when the back of the pharynx collapses during sleep stages II through IV. This can cause up to forty-five seconds of hypoxia (lack of oxygen to the brain). It is commonly seen in patients who suffer from obesity. Obstructive sleep apnea may also play a role in NAFLD.[6] Those with untreated sleep apnea have increased periods of chronic intermittent

 JIMMY SAYS

What you notice with the development of non-alcoholic fatty liver disease are the ramifications of uncontrolled insulin resistance rearing its ugly head. If you already know you have insulin resistance, then you need to take diligent steps with your diet, such as going keto, to prevent this from happening.

FOIE GRAS

If you're familiar with *foie gras* (French for "fat liver"), you know that this delicacy comes from force-feeing a duck or goose corn, which causes the liver to become "fatty." The bird's fatty liver is enlarged up to ten times its normal size. Fifteen years of medical practice and multiple human studies have demonstrated to me that humans don't get fatty liver disease from eating fat; we get it from eating sugar. The average American diet is 85 percent sugar and starch. The sad part of the comparison between *foie gras* and fatty liver disease in humans is that we humans don't have to be force-fed corn to have fatty livers. Our diet of fish crackers, pretzels, french fries, chicken nuggets, pizza, and soda does the very same thing.

hypoxia (periods during which the oxygen level in the brain drops for up to forty-five seconds) while they're sleeping. Liver damage, inflammation, and fibrosis have been seen due to increased levels of pro-inflammatory cytokines (hormones that start the inflammation cascade) from the periods of poor brain oxygenation.[7]

Also, there is evidence that the effects of fructose metabolism by the liver drive the fatty acid formation and inflammatory changes seen in NAFLD.[8]

In light of all these potential causes, the simple carbohydrate restriction of a ketogenic lifestyle has significant and powerful effects on reversing this disease. I've been quite surprised at the number of my patients whose liver enzymes and ultrasounds have returned to normal within twelve months of making a change to a ketogenic lifestyle. Multiple human studies summarized by Basaranoglu, Basaranoglu, and Bugianesi demonstrated these same results with notable improvement in lipid levels, liver enzymes, and normalization of liver ultrasound.[9]

APPLYING THE KETO CURE APPROACH

So, let's look at how a ketogenic lifestyle can improve NAFLD. The following sections describe how to apply the principles of the Keto Cure approach to addressing NAFLD and NASH. For Principle 3, there are no concerns that are specific to NAFLD and NASH. Refer to the first few pages of Part 2 for general information about each of the principles.

PRINCIPLE 1
LOWER INSULIN LEVELS WITH DIET

In the case of non-alcoholic fatty liver disease, you want to lower insulin to allow for increased nutritional ketosis, turn off the excessive insulin production, and eliminate fructose as a fuel source. Eliminating fructose and lowering insulin actually allows fat cells to reset their production of adiponectin and leptin. Lowering insulin also allows ketones to rise, which suppresses inflammation.

Lowering insulin levels turns down the stimulus of the liver to produce more triglycerides and lowers the VLDL transport out of the liver.

As discussed in previous chapters, start by cutting your carbohydrate intake to less than 20 grams per day.

PRINCIPLE 2
AVOID ADDITIVES THAT RAISE INSULIN LEVELS

It has been found that consuming more than 20 to 30 grams of alcohol on one occasion with the presence of NAFLD increases the risk of fibrosis and liver damage by more than 50 percent.[10] If NAFLD is an issue for you, avoid alcohol. If you don't, you're tempting fate.

PRINCIPLE 4
ELIMINATE PROBLEM MEDICATIONS

If you're using metformin and have been diagnosed with NAFLD or NASH, make sure that your doctor is carefully evaluating your situation. Metformin is metabolized by the liver, and higher doses might cause further liver inflammation. That said, because metformin lowers blood sugar, helps the body use insulin more efficiently, lowers hepatic gluconeogenesis, and increases fatty acid oxidation in the fat cells, it may be a good choice for NAFLD treatment. However, current studies do not show effectiveness in the treatment of NASH.[11]

NAFLD and NASH commonly occur in people who are diabetic. If you are using pioglitazone to treat your diabetes, be aware that in some studies, some improvement in fibrosis of the liver was noted when the pioglitazone was compared with a placebo. However, this must be weighed against adverse effects of using the medication, including weight gain, leg swelling, and risk of heart failure.[12]

PRINCIPLE 5
ADD MEDICATIONS THAT HELP

If you suffer from NASH, a GLP-1 agonist, which helps control blood sugar and promotes more effective insulin use, is something you should discuss with your doctor. In a study conducted over three years, NASH showed improvement in 39 percent of patients treated with the GLP-1 agonist liraglutide.[13]

PRINCIPLE 6
CONSIDER APPROPRIATE SUPPLEMENTATION

The following is a list of supplements that can be beneficial for the treatment of NAFLD and NASH:

- **BERBERINE:** Berberine is the active ingredient in turmeric and goldenseal. It has been shown to stabilize blood sugar and glucose transport, and it may have some effect on gluconeogenesis in the liver. It also has anti-inflammatory and antibacterial effects.

  In animal studies, supplementation with berberine has reduced liver fibrosis. In human studies, it has shown potential to reduce AST and ALT levels in patients with type 2 diabetes and to restore liver function.[14, 15, 16] One human trial demonstrated a greater reduction in hepatic fat content after subjects used berberine compared to subjects who applied only a lifestyle change.[17]

- **OMEGA-3 FATTY ACIDS:** The addition of omega-3 fatty acids to the diet resulted in improvement in liver enzymes and steatosis present on ultrasound.[18]

- **GARLIC:** Whole garlic has been shown to improve the lipid profile through the AMPK pathway. Raw garlic has been shown to improve insulin resistance and oxidative stress as well as enhance lipid metabolism. Garlic contains S-allylmercaptocysteine (SAMC), which has been shown to promote liver regeneration after acute injury.[19, 20]

- **EXOGENOUS KETONES:** The use of exogenous ketones is still in primary evaluation, but preliminary research shows that adding them to a ketogenic diet raises ketone levels in the blood. There is preliminary evidence that supplementing with exogenous ketones in conjunction with a ketogenic diet provides added protection from oxidative stress, one of the factors potentially involved in the process of NASH and NAFLD.[21]

CHAPTER 12

THYROID AND THYROIDITIS

The most common question that I get as I give talks or live stream about ketosis is "What about the thyroid?"

The blunt, sarcastic response in my head is usually, "Well, what about it?"

Buried within that vague question is the real question that is on the minds of thousands of people: "Does ketosis affect my thyroid?"

There's loads of information about the thyroid on the Internet. Seriously. Do a Google search for thyroid, and you'll see thousands of articles, posts, and comments on WebMD, Women's Health, and Wikipedia. But much of that information is garbage.

Everyone, and I mean everyone, seems to have an opinion about the thyroid. Much of the "wikopinion" out there is hearsay, conjecture, and anecdote. It doesn't really give people any foundational understanding of what their thyroids are doing—or more importantly, what their thyroids aren't doing. I'm here to clear up some of the confusion.

THE ROLE OF THE THYROID

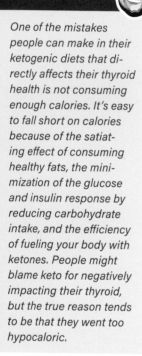

JIMMY SAYS

One of the mistakes people can make in their ketogenic diets that directly affects their thyroid health is not consuming enough calories. It's easy to fall short on calories because of the satiating effect of consuming healthy fats, the minimization of the glucose and insulin response by reducing carbohydrate intake, and the efficiency of fueling your body with ketones. People might blame keto for negatively impacting their thyroid, but the true reason tends to be that they went too hypocaloric.

First, let's define a few things about the thyroid. The thyroid is an endocrine gland that sits just above your Adam's apple in your neck. If it gets enlarged, you can feel it; that's what we refer to as a goiter. Goiters can be caused by low-functioning thyroid tissue that hypertrophies (gets larger) to try to keep up with the work load.

The thyroid gland is essentially the gas pedal for your metabolism. The gland produces T3 and T4 hormones. These hormones go to all the cells in the body and regulate the speed of the metabolism of each cell. The thyroid's function can be assessed by looking at these hormones as well as at TSH, which is a hormone produced by the pituitary gland that controls the speed of thyroid function.

The state of an underfunctioning thyroid gland is referred to as hypothyroidism. This is usually identified by a TSH level that is greater than 4.5 mg/dL. Fatigue, dry skin, hair loss, excessive sleepiness, swelling, and weight gain are all symptoms of an underfunctioning thyroid.

The state of an overfunctioning thyroid gland is referred to as hyperthyroidism. This is usually identified by a TSH level lower than 0.2 mg/dL. Fatigue, insomnia, heart palpitations, and a feeling of anxiety or impending doom are often symptoms of an overfunctioning thyroid gland.

One of the common causes of an abnormal-functioning (either high or low) thyroid gland is something called thyroiditis. Thyroiditis is usually due to an inflammatory autoimmune disease that stimulates a transient overproduction of the thyroid hormone for a period of time. The inflammation causes abnormal elevation in thyroid function. This may stimulate a period of hyperthyroidism.

However, after a few months the thyroid antibodies fade out, the thyroid often becomes underfunctioning, and hypothyroidism ensues. Testing of the thyroid reveals elevated TSH levels and low levels of T3, T4, and so on.

WHAT'S GOING ON WITH THE THYROID?

Thyroid function is a cascade of communicating hormones from the brain to the individual cells. The pituitary gland regulates the thyroid by producing thyroid stimulating hormone (TSH).

Thyroxine (T4) and triiodothyronine (T3) are produced by the thyroid gland and can enter the cells of the body through diffusion or active transport through the cell membrane. T4 can be converted into T3 within the cells of the body. T4 that is not taken up in the cells acts as a feedback to the brain to regulate TSH production.

DOES A KETOGENIC DIET SUPPRESS THYROID FUNCTION?

Of late, the Paleo- and vegetarian-diet thought leaders seem to decry nutritional ketosis because they claim that this dietary approach suppresses thyroid function. This "wiki-theory" (yes, it is just a theory) was extrapolated from a single study in which the T4 level dropped in the first few weeks after subjects entered ketosis. However, just a drop in T4 doesn't mean the diet is suppressing the thyroid.

Using T4 as a screening test alone for assessment of thyroid function is dated thinking. T4 fluctuates with a number of binding proteins, and following this number alone is bad medicine.

In the case of a nutritional ketogenic state, because of a change in the way the nucleus of the cell is handling fuel, a transient lowering of T4 is commonly seen for a number of reasons:

- Excessive leptin production (which occurs in those with leptin resistance) signals increased T4 production. A ketogenic diet allows leptin signaling (and leptin resistance) to improve, and there will be a drop in needed T4.

- T3 signals genetic differentiation (formation signaling) of white and brown fat. Increased conversion of T4 to T3 as the body shifts its regulation of white and brown fat causes a transient drop in T4. Again, this is a normal change.

- Differentiation between primary, secondary, and central hypothyroidism can be completed only by looking at TSH and T4 values together. Without using both, a pituitary mass or other pituitary damage could be missed.

Causes of Hyperthyroidism and Hypothyroidism

One issue that can affect the thyroid gland is iodine deficiency. If you live in the United States and other developed countries, you'll probably never see a true iodine deficiency. That's because iodized salt is common in our cooking and baking. People who live in third-world countries, however, are at risk for not getting enough iodine. Both excessive and low levels of iodine can cause hypothyroidism.

Hypothyroidism also can be caused by a selenium deficiency; it's not uncommon for me to find out this is the reason someone has hypothyroidism. Selenium is a trace metal found in red meat, oysters, pork, and Brazil nuts. Selenium is so common that I put it in the KetoEssentials multivitamin I designed for KetoLiving.com.

Smoking can cause hypothyroidism. Smoking can also drive autoimmune thyroid disease. If you're a smoker, now is a perfect time to quit.

> **HYPOTHYROIDISM AND IODINE DEFICIENCY**
>
> *Sometimes I meet people who have hypothyroidism who are "anti-pill." They come to me and state, "I have hypothyroidism, but I'm not going to take pills. I'm just going to take iodine." I don't recommend this solution because overmedicating with iodine just makes the symptoms worse. There's nothing wrong with checking iodine levels, but in the fifteen years I've been practicing medicine, I've seen only one person in the United States with actual iodine deficiency.*

Obesity and Hypothyroidism and Thyroiditis

How does obesity cause hypothyroidism, hyperthyroidism, and/or thyroiditis? Excessive insulin—the hormone produced when you eat sugar, starch, and some proteins—actually does three things to adversely affect the hormonal balance of the hypothalamic-pituitary axis controlling the thyroid:

- First, and often most problematic, high insulin levels stimulate or seem to play a significant role in increasing thyroid peroxidase antibodies, which can cause or exacerbate thyroiditis.[1] This causes overproduction or underproduction of thyroid hormone, which throws the system out of whack. Thyroiditis is the driver in over- or underfunctioning autoimmune thyroid disease. People with excess insulin gain weight because of the direct influence of insulin (as described in earlier chapters) and because the thyroid often becomes underfunctioning.

- Second, excessive insulin in the presence of thyroiditis also stimulates insulin-like growth factor-1 (IGF-1)—which also amplifies production of thyroid transcription factor (TTF-2). The result of excessive insulin is increased thyroid antibodies, which causes thyroiditis. (Someone who is insulin resistant is notably more susceptible to thyroiditis based on the tight hormonal control of these enzymes.)

  Because 85 percent of the people I see in my office overproduce insulin in response to starches (see Chapter 4 for information on insulin resistance), there is a significant flux in thyroid function due to this pre-diabetic state (insulin overproduction) in those people who are on high-carbohydrate diets.

- Third, insulin resistance leads to leptin resistance. Leptin is the hormone produced by fat cells when they are "full." As a fat cell fills to capacity, it releases leptin, signaling the brain that no more fuel is needed for storage. This is one of the signals of satiation. Leptin tells the brain to stop eating.

Excessive leptin is produced by the fat cells as obesity worsens. As the fat cells "overfill," they overproduce leptin. Some describe the fat cells as being in a "sick state." This leads to another level of hypothalamic-pituitary axis imbalance:

- The higher leptin stimulates the conversion of T4 to T3.[2] It actually can cause subclinical Hashimoto's thyroiditis (overactive thyroid symptoms with elevated TSH and T3 levels).

- At least 40 percent of my obese, insulin-resistant patients are also leptin resistant, meaning they overproduce leptin as well as overproduce insulin. This has a suppressive effect on T4 (by converting it to T3) and is the usual cause of T4 levels being lower when someone initiates a ketogenic diet. This increased T3 level is also the reason some people feel anxious or "activated" or even experience heart palpitations when they first switch to a nutritional ketosis–based diet.

- Leptin resistance also can have the effect of increasing TSH levels, which places people in subclinical states of hypothyroidism while making them feel activated by excess T3. It explains why I see significant fluctuations in TSH, T4, and T3 in many of my patients with insulin resistance.

Leptin resistance is driven by a high level of fructose in the diet and the presence of high triglycerides at the same time. High fructose and high triglycerides inhibit the leptin signal from crossing the blood-brain barrier.[3, 4] As discussed earlier, depending on the abnormal elevation of leptin and abnormal elevation of insulin, either hyper- or hypothyroid symptoms in the presence of varying degrees of thyroiditis can occur. This can be very confusing to a physician who doesn't recognize the effect on the hypothalamus of simultaneous high insulin and high leptin.

As a person follows a ketogenic lifestyle, insulin, leptin, and thyroid function return to normal over a period of three to six months. T4 levels also normalize. Once leptin can cross the blood-brain barrier normally, it can correctly signal to the hypothalamus to produce thyroid-releasing hormone (TRH), which stimulates the pituitary gland to correctly balance the TSH that activates the thyroid gland.

When you follow a DASH, Mediterranean, Paleo, or vegetarian diet, calorie restriction—which is a must for weight loss with these dietary approaches—causes the suppression of other key hormones, such as testosterone and estrogen, as well as the suppression of thyroid function. This leads to worsening T4 suppression over time. So, proponents of calorie-restricted diets can put that in their low-fat vegetarian tacos and smoke it. (Wait…I don't advocate smoking. Smoking can amplify thyroiditis, so, ignore that.) Suppression of testosterone, estrogen, and thyroid function are also reasons I don't advocate frequent, prolonged fasting.

The point is that a ketogenic lifestyle stabilizes thyroid function and improves autoimmune thyroiditis. Nutritional ketosis has a stabilizing effect on the hypothalamic-pituitary-thyroid axis. I've seen it happen clinically since 2005.

Nutritional ketosis dramatically helps stabilize the thirty hormones involved with the diseases of civilization, which include obesity, insulin resistance, thyroid dysfunctional states, and diabetes, as discussed in previous chapters.

APPLYING THE KETO CURE APPROACH

So, let's look at how a ketogenic lifestyle improves thyroid function. For Principles 2, 3, and 4, there are no concerns that are specific to thyroid function. Refer to the first few pages of Part 2 for general information about each of the principles.

PRINCIPLE 1
LOWER INSULIN LEVELS WITH DIET

THYROID REPLACEMENT THERAPY

Because of the complex nature of thyroid replacement, close consultation and monitoring with your physician is recommended to identify the correct replacement when necessary.

In the case of hypothyroidism or hyperthyroidism, you are lowering insulin to allow for increased nutritional ketosis. You are turning off the excessive insulin production and eliminating fructose as a fuel source. Eliminating fructose and lowering insulin allows the fat cells to reset production of adiponectin and leptin, and triglyceride production decreases. Lowering insulin and fructose metabolism allows leptin to cross the blood-brain barrier, improves hypothalamic signaling, and balances thyroid function.

PRINCIPLE 5
ADD MEDICATIONS THAT HELP

In a number of the cases of hypothyroidism that I see in my office, using thyroid medication to ensure that the hypothalamic-pituitary axis is balanced is very important. Our goal is to balance the system, but if the thyroid is notably "underfunctioning" (hypothyroidism), then using thyroid medication to "jump-start" the system and get levels back to where they should be while the adipose cells are healing is critical. This is something you will want to work directly with your doctor to start and closely follow.

In most cases, I've found that people may need the following medications for hypothyroidism:

- **THYROID HORMONE:** Synthroid (levothyroxine)

- **DESICCATED THYROID EXTRACT:**
  - Armor Thyroid
  - Nature-Throid
  - Westhroid (T3/T4 thyroid extract)

In cases where mild hyperthyroidism is an issue, I often find that the ketogenic diet alone is the solution. Lowering insulin turns down the thyroid antibodies, and lowering leptin slows the conversion of T4 to T3. However, moderate or more severe cases might require close monitoring of the thyroid and thyroid hormones and the use of medications to control symptoms such as rapid heart rate, panic attacks, and insomnia. Each case of hyperthyroidism is unique, so the combinations of medications, direction from endocrinology specialists, and/or interventional approaches, including thyroid surgery, are too broad to attempt to summarize here.

⚠️ CAUTION!
ONE SIZE DOESN'T FIT ALL

Because severe cases of hyperthyroidism can be life-threatening, there is not a "one-size-fits-all" approach. If you suffer from symptomatic hyperthyroidism, work closely with your doctor to identify and select the appropriate medical approach that works for you. In most of the cases of hyperthyroidism that I've had experience with, the ketogenic lifestyle provided tremendous value as a baseline to stabilize the other hormones while the doctor and patient decided which additional approach would be most effective.

PRINCIPLE 6
CONSIDER APPROPRIATE SUPPLEMENTATION

The following is a list of supplements that can be beneficial for the treatment of thyroid issues:

- **ESTROGEN REPLACEMENT THERAPY (HRT):** Estrogen increases serum thyroxine-binding globulin (TBG) concentrations, which might increase the need for T4. Thyroid function, including TSH and T4 levels, should be measured twelve weeks after starting estrogen therapy.[5] Low levels of estrogen in women after menopause play a significant role in weight gain. Up to 20 percent of the patients I see who are post-menopausal have trouble with weight loss and energy levels because of the increased TBG concentration effect on T4.

- **SELENIUM:** Selenium is required for deiodinase activity (the deiodinase enzyme is a selenoprotein, which requires selenium for function). Selenium deficiency causes autoimmune thyroid disease. When the thyroid is examined with ultrasound, those with selenium deficiency have a visible destabilization of the thyroid structure.[6]

NEURODEGENERATIVE DISEASES

One of the most exciting and promising effects of a ketogenic diet are the healing changes that occur to the nervous system. When I began using carbohydrate restriction to treat people, I was surprised to see improvement in neuropathies, reduction in the symptoms of multiple sclerosis, and improvement in memory in those with dementia. We've known for almost one hundred years that ketogenic diets stabilize and improve epilepsy, especially in those who've not been responsive to standard medications.

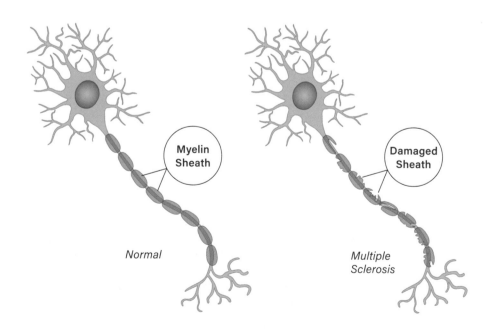

EPILEPSY

Seizures, which are abrupt losses of consciousness that often include rhythmic jerking or repetitive motions of a part or all of the body, are a common occurrence, affecting up to 10 percent of the population.[1, 2] Seizures are the reason for 2 percent of emergency room visits.[3] Seizures often begin in childhood for a number of reasons, and in many cases, they can be life-threatening.

A seizure is a change in behavior caused by electrical hyper-synchronization of the networks of the brain. In layman's terms, the brain attempts to do two or more things at once; it's like an electrical overload of part or all of the brain. This overload can occur due to trauma, infection of the brain (encephalitis), stroke, drug or alcohol withdrawal, or other metabolic electrolyte abnormalities. Seizures can be mimicked by a number of other disorders that I don't have the space to go into here.

Epilepsy is defined when two or more unprovoked seizures occur more than twenty-four hours apart, there is an unprovoked seizure with the likelihood of additional seizures over the next ten years (this is usually seen on electroencephalogram), or a diagnosis of epilepsy syndrome has been made.

The list of causes or triggers of this electrical overload in the brain is long and diverse. There is evidence that the seizures and the conduction of electrical current through the overloaded brain is related to higher levels of glucose. Lowering the glucose level decreases the likelihood of the seizure to occur.[4]

Additionally, a significant commonality in those with epilepsy is an inherited genetic, metabolic, or structural abnormality. These abnormalities might be due to an acquired vascular, degenerative, or even malignant cause. Recent research demonstrates an increased level of glutamate and lowering of gamma-Aminobutyric acid (GABA) increase the seizure risk threshold.[5] However, 60 percent of patients have an unknown cause of epilepsy after a complete head-to-toe evaluation.

Because of the unknown why and the often unknown when, those who suffer from seizures and epilepsy can find it very frustrating, life-altering, and often life-threatening, especially if seizures occur while a person is swimming, bathing, climbing, or driving.

Those who experience seizures should be evaluated and closely followed by their doctors. Because the risk of seizures reoccurring is up to 2.5 times greater in people with epilepsy, anti-seizure medications should be considered and used to prevent reoccurrence and further destabilization of other underlying causes.[6] The challenge arises in that most anti-seizure medications have significant side effects and tolerance issues of their own. To make matters even more complex, up to 33 percent of patients with epilepsy don't respond to any of these medications, and many of the medications have adverse effects when used in children or cannot be used with other genetic diseases that may also be present.

JIMMY SAYS

The treatment of epilepsy is the longest-standing therapeutic use of ketogenic diets in disease management. It was developed by endocrinologist H. Rawle Geyelin in the early 1900s. When anticonvulsant drugs were introduced in the 1940s, the natural keto approach was let go in favor of these prescription medications.

It was this nonresponsive group of epilepsy patients (up to one-third of epilepsy patients) that first brought the ketogenic diet to light almost one hundred years ago. The first reports of using a ketogenic diet were published in the early 1920s.[7]

A ketogenic diet increases the level of ketones, provides increased availability of glucose for the brain to create needed neurotransmitters, and notably decreases inflammation that may play a significant role in the occurrence of seizures. The increased presence of ketones as a fuel and the enhancement of GABA levels reduces neuron excitement. Upon the introduction of a ketogenic diet, up to 50 percent reduction in seizures was noted in refractory epilepsy that had failed drug treatment alone.[8, 9]

JIMMY SAYS

Today, a specifically for-mulated ketogenic diet consisting of upward of 90 percent fat is used by researchers and practitioners in treating children with epilepsy. The leading consumer advocacy group on this subject is The Charlie Foundation (www.charlie-foundation.org).

For those suffering from seizures and epilepsy, a ketogenic lifestyle has reduced seizures by up to 60 percent. Most patients on the ketogenic diet respond with measurable seizure reduction within one to three weeks of switching to the diet.[10, 11] More recently, research demonstrated that seizures were reduced by more than 500 percent when sustained levels of ketones were present through diet and supplementation over those induced by fasting.[12]

The exact mechanism by which epilepsy and seizures are reduced through nutritional ketosis is still unclear. However, the combination of reduction in glucose, increased presence of ketones as a fuel source, reduction in nerve excitement by increased GABA and reduced glutamate, and reduction in the formation of gliosis of the temporal lobe of the brain all seem to provide effective seizure reduction.

In my office, I recommend that serum ketones be kept at or above 1.5 mmol/L to maintain effective seizure control. This can be done with a two-to-one ratio of fat to protein and restriction of carbohydrate to less than 20 grams per day. It can also be achieved by adding exogenous ketones to the diet.

MULTIPLE SCLEROSIS

To understand how the brain and nerves are affected by changing the diet from sugars to fat, let's look at multiple sclerosis. Multiple sclerosis (MS) is a neurological disease caused by demyelination—a breakdown of the myelin coating around the nerve cells.[13] This demyelination is referred to as a neurodegeneration in which the physical structure of the nerve is compromised, much like when the coating around an electrical wire is chipped or stripped away. When that coating is missing, the electrical current can "short-circuit" or trigger other wires that are next to it. The neuron, which acts like a wire that carries electricity, "short-circuits" when its myelin coating has been compromised.

Common symptoms of MS are numbness, tingling, or burning in the extremities or face; loss of vision in one eye; acute weakness of the muscles; diplopia (double vision); disturbance in walking or gait; balance problems; Lhermitte's sign (electric shock–like sensations that run down the back and/or limbs when the neck is flexed); vertigo; bladder problems; loss of control of a limb; and pain. These are all symptoms that occur when a "wire" is missing its coating and "short-circuits."

For many years, the degeneration in MS was thought to occur because of an inflammatory attack on the nerve cells by rogue immune cells crossing the blood-brain barrier. However, treatments focused on modulating the inflammatory attack seemed to have no great effect on the degeneration and demyelination. Thus, the actual definitive cause of this demyelination and neurodegeneration has eluded us since 1868, when Jean-Martin Charcot first described MS as a disease.

Recent studies point to evidence that this demyelination might be due to degeneration or breakdown of the nerve cell's ability to use glucose as a primary fuel.[14, 15] It is now theorized that MS may be due to a combination of degeneration and localized inflammation related to poor glucose uptake, which causes demyelination of the nerve. Demyelination is the classic presentation seen in MS cases.[16, 17, 18]

JIMMY SAYS

Researchers like Dr. Terry Wahls, MD (terrywahls.com), from the University of Iowa, who overcame her MS through a real foods–based, nutrient-dense ketogenic diet, are seeking funding to study this disease and what therapeutic effect a ketogenic approach could have.

With this dual concept in mind, ketogenic diets have demonstrated some promising results when used with neurological diseases. It is becoming apparent that ketogenic diets may play a significant role in the treatment of neurological diseases such as MS because of a two-part effect that occurs when ketones become the primary fuel for the body:

- When a person becomes keto-adapted (fat-adapted) and ketones (rather than glucose) are used as the primary fuel, the body upregulates mitochondria to use ketones for fuel. As the ketone level rises, the need for glucose diminishes. This gives the nerve cell an alternative fuel source if glucose metabolism is impaired. It also decreases the need for and production of insulin, the hormone heavily involved in stimulating inflammation and inflammatory responses.

  In other words, providing an alternative form of fuel for the body allows the damaged nerves to begin to heal. This process can be slow, but I've seen clinically that patients begin to experience improvement and relief from their symptoms over months and years. The effects for an MS patient who switches to a ketogenic diet include elimination or significant reduction in the frequency of symptoms of numbness, tingling, burning, and weakness.[19]

- A ketogenic diet has a favorable effect on inflammation. It has been demonstrated that this diet decreases reactive oxygen species and increases production of superoxide dismutase and catalase, which notably decreases the inflammatory effects of oxidative stress.[20, 21, 22]

Also, a ketogenic diet is well known to raise glutathione levels, another antioxidant that decreases inflammation and oxidative stress.[23, 24, 25]

OTHER DISEASES

CHAPTER 13:
NEURODEGENERATIVE
DISEASES

JIMMY SAYS

The brain thrives on ketone bodies. Since the early 2000s, Alzheimer's disease has been known in research circles as type 3 diabetes. Once you realize that this disease—which we commonly think of as something that naturally happens as people get older—is preventable and reversible (just like type 2 diabetes is), you will take proactive steps to prevent it by making better nutritional choices.

Although the evidence is still somewhat theoretical, studies have pointed to effective dietary treatment and prevention for other degenerative neurological diseases, such as Alzheimer's disease, amyotrophic lateral sclerosis (ALS), Parkinson's disease, and inherited glycogen storage diseases. For example, using ketogenic diets in patients with Alzheimer's dementia has had positive effects on memory and cognition.[26]

Although each of these diseases has different causes and clinical features, common mechanisms among them—including degeneration of the nerves—explain the positive effect of a ketogenic lifestyle.

Alzheimer's Disease

Alzheimer's disease (AD) is the most prevalent neurodegenerative disease we see. There are two types of Alzheimer's dementia: familial Alzheimer's dementia (FAD) and sporadic Alzheimer's dementia. The sporadic form is also referred to as late-onset Alzheimer's disease (LOAD), which is the leading cause of dementia in our aging population.

The FAD form of the disease can be linked to three gene mutations, but the etiology of the LOAD form is still unclear.[27] There is no unified mechanism that explains the deposition of amyloid β-protein and neurofibrillary tangles together with declining mitochondrial function. Both forms are associated with metabolic syndrome and insulin resistance, and some neurologists refer to AD as "type 3 diabetes."[28]

What is fascinating is that research is pointing to the accumulation of advanced glycation end products (AGEs) that are found in both the amyloid plaques and the neurofibrillary tangles. AGEs occur as a matter of course in the aging process, but patients with both forms of AD have notably accelerated formation of the AGEs.[29]

There are several theories as to why this occurs, but one specific theory might explain the success a ketogenic lifestyle has on this disease: The brain's ability to use glucose seems to decline with aging, and as we get older, there is a decreased presence of glucose transporters across the blood-brain barrier. The high insulin load, high ILG-1, and low ability of glucose to enter the brain have been shown to increase amyloid and tau proteins in animal models. This theory is speculative; however, it could explain the abnormal accumulation of amyloid and tau proteins in humans with the disease.[30] It might also explain why changing the fuel source for the brain by shifting to a ketogenic diet is effective in improving cognition without increasing the formation of amyloid proteins.[31]

Amyotrophic Lateral Sclerosis (ALS)

Amyotrophic lateral sclerosis (ALS) is a complex progressive neurodegenerative disorder that causes muscle weakness, debility, and progression to death due to loss of skeletal muscle. It is the most common motor neuron disease currently known. Unfortunately, it is still considered incurable. It is a disease that is diagnosed after the exclusion of all other diseases. It leads to involuntary weight loss, muscle wasting, weakness, and maintained muscle contraction without significant pain. As ALS progresses, muscle strength profoundly weakens, evidence of lower motor neuron damage. However, reflexes remain preserved and some childhood reflexes may return, which points to damage of the upper motor neurons (nerve damage in the brain and cerebral cortex).

Recent research demonstrates that 30 percent of ALS patients have an inherited disorder that affects mitochondrial function. This disorder causes mitochondrial activity in the nerves to die at a more rapid rate. Using a ketogenic diet has been shown to improve neuron survival in ALS patients. It also has been shown to improve motor function in some of these patients.[32]

It is theorized that higher ketone levels provide the ATP that is necessary to preserve nerve and motor function. This research is still preliminary; however, it points to the effect of dietary fat on the preservation of brain function and cognition.[33]

Parkinson's Disease

In Parkinson's disease (PD), mitochondrial function appears to be impaired in the neurons of the brain of the substantia nigra, the area where movement and reward are controlled. Damage in this area leads to the flat emotional personality, shuffling gait, and tremor consistently found in people who have PD.

In animal studies, the use of ketones, specifically β-hydroxybutyrate, protected the neurons of the substantia nigra from degeneration and damage.[34] In humans, a twenty-eight-day ketogenic diet showed notable improvement in subjects' Unified Parkinson's Disease Rating Scale scores.[35]

Inherited Glycogen Storage Diseases

Ketogenic diets also have been shown to improve function and symptoms in people with inherited glycogen storage diseases (GSDs). These are diseases caused by deficiencies in enzymes that are found mainly in the liver and kidneys. These patients have hypoglycemia (low blood sugar) when they're as young as three or four months old. GSDs are identified only through genetic testing. There are eight different types (GSD I through VIII), each of which affects a different enzyme in the pathway of glucose conversion to fuel.

Because of the defective enzymes, the most common symptom of the glycogen storage diseases is hypoglycemia. However, because of the severity of low blood sugar, symptoms can range from simple cognitive changes to seizures and brain damage.

Consequently, a ketogenic lifestyle can make significant improvements in quality of life for those with GSD. In fact, a ketogenic diet has become the gold standard of treatment for GLUT1 deficiency syndrome, which mimics GSDs. For example, ketogenic diets have been very successful in treating McArdle disease (GSD V) and in treating the severe cardiomyopathy that arises in GSD III.[36, 37]

APPLYING THE KETO CURE APPROACH

So, let's look at how a ketogenic lifestyle can be applied to neurodegenerative diseases. For Principles 3 and 4, there are no concerns that are specific to neurodegenerative diseases. Refer to the first few pages of Part 2 for general information about each of the principles.

PRINCIPLE 1
LOWER INSULIN LEVELS WITH DIET

As discussed in previous chapters, start by cutting carbohydrate intake to less than 20 grams per day. In neurodegenerative disease, keeping carbohydrate intake as low as possible should be looked at as the primary lifestyle change. The second component in these disease processes is to provide adequate fat in the form of medium- and long-chain triglycerides. Most of these neurodegenerative diseases have been shown to improve when insulin is lowered and intake of fats such as butter, olive oil, and coconut oil is raised.

A 1971 study found that increasing medium-chain triglycerides to just 60 percent of total caloric intake led to a reduction in seizures in patients with epilepsy by more than 50 percent.[38] Expansion of this study in 1976 showed that seizure reduction correlated with the level of ketones in the blood.[39]

PRINCIPLE 2
AVOID ADDITIVES THAT RAISE INSULIN LEVELS

In the general description of Principle 2, I mentioned that drinking leaf-based teas can sometimes raise insulin. There are studies that show that drinking tea might reduce the risk of Parkinson's disease; however, it appears that this is related to the antioxidant effect of the polyphenol epigallocatechin gallate (EGCG) in the tea.[40] You need to weigh that potential effect against the risk that drinking tea can spike insulin without raising glucose.[41, 42]

> **NOTE**
>
> *I personally avoid tea because of the insulin response and the tannin effect on worsening osteoporosis.[43] Tannins are commonly found in leaf- and plant-bud-based teas and coffee, wine, and the hops in beers. The tannins have a direct stimulus on insulin production without raising blood sugar. Consuming too much of these tannins leads to calcium and iron deficiency in the body and often contributes to osteoporosis and anemia.[44]*

PRINCIPLE 5
ADD MEDICATIONS THAT HELP

Work closely with your physician regarding medications that may be beneficial for the specific neurodegenerative disease you have. A ketogenic diet works well with the medications on the following list. The most common and recommended medications are listed here, but this is not a comprehensive list:

- **CHOLINESTERASE INHIBITORS IN ALZHEIMER'S DISEASE**
  - Aricept (donepezil)
  - Exelon (rivastigmine)
  - Razadyne (galantamine)
- **NDMA RECEPTOR ANTAGONIST IN ALZHEIMER'S DISEASE,** such as Namenda (memantine)
- **IMMUNOMODULATORY AGENTS IN MULTIPLE SCLEROSIS**
  - Natalizumab
  - Glatiramer acetate
  - Dimethyl fumarate
  - Teriflunomide
  - Fingolimod
- **INTERFERON IN MULTIPLE SCLEROSIS,** such as interferon beta

PRINCIPLE 6
CONSIDER APPROPRIATE SUPPLEMENTATION

The following is a list of supplements that can be beneficial for the treatment of neurodegenerative diseases:

- **VITAMIN B:** In studies of B vitamin supplementation in those with Alzheimer's dementia, it was found that there was no beneficial effect on cognitive measures, and there was no convincing evidence that its use prevents dementia.[45] However, the use of vitamin B in those with elevated homocysteine or low folic acid levels has an inverse relationship with impaired cognition.[46]

- **VITAMIN E:** High-dose vitamin E actually increased mortality in studies, especially in heart failure and cardiovascular disease.[47] However, in a large VA study, doses of less than 2,000 IU showed a mild reduction in the degree of dementia compared with a placebo.[48]

- **ELDEPRYL (SELEGILINE):** Selegiline is now available without a prescription. Studies of the use of selegiline reveal a mild delay in the progression of dementia and death with only some beneficial effect in the cognitive benefits of behavior and mood.[49]

- **OMEGA-3 FATTY ACIDS:** Observational studies suggest an association between dietary omega-3 and a lower risk of dementia. However, clinical trials have not supported supplementation in the treatment of Alzheimer's disease.[50]

- **EXOGENOUS KETONES:** The addition of ketones to the diet has been studied in both animals and humans. The nerve cells of the body benefit from reduced free radical production in the mitochondria.[51, 52] Exogenous ketones have also been shown to reduce the risk of movement disorders and stabilize the dopamine center of the brain in early development.[53]

  Lastly, increasing ketones improves resistance to seizures, nerve reactivity, and nerve repair by shifting the formation of glutamate down and increasing the formation of GABA.[54]

CHAPTER 14

TESTOSTERONE & NUTRITIONAL KETOSIS

If you've ever watched TV in the wee hours of the morning, I'm sure you've seen the commercials for treatments of "low-T," or low testosterone. Everyone seems to have an answer with their "latest and greatest supplement." Here's the thing: When so many offer a treatment, you can be sure that there is no great treatment available that solves the problem. (And certainly not one that you can buy from an infomercial.)

Low testosterone is an issue that occurs more and more commonly in men over the age of fifty. My clients ask me about low testosterone at least three to five times each week. Recently, I've started seeing very low testosterone levels that affect men who are as young as their early thirties.

Insulin resistance is one of the major causes of testosterone levels falling below normal in men and one of the primary causes of rising testosterone in women (leading to polycystic ovary syndrome [or PCOS] in women and infertility in both men and women).[1, 2, 3] (Read Chapter 15 for more information about PCOS.)

TESTOSTERONE BASICS

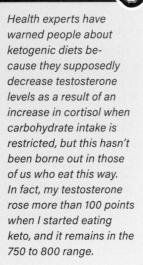

JIMMY SAYS

Health experts have warned people about ketogenic diets because they supposedly decrease testosterone levels as a result of an increase in cortisol when carbohydrate intake is restricted, but this hasn't been borne out in those of us who eat this way. In fact, my testosterone rose more than 100 points when I started eating keto, and it remains in the 750 to 800 range.

We know that testosterone normally goes into a mild decline as we age—usually starting sometime after we turn thirty. (The period when testosterone starts to decline is sometimes referred to as *andropause*.) However, the decrease is only minimal, and many men are not symptomatic. We know that a much more significant testosterone decrease occurs in men who are insulin resistant, diabetic, and/or obese because of a very complex change in the hypothalamic-pituitary-testicular (HPT) axis. In these cases, multiple factors play a contributing role to the decline of testosterone.[4]

DECLINING TESTOSTERONE AND ED

Many men assume, and advertisements on TV imply, that erectile dysfunction (ED) is due to a decline in testosterone. However, this is rarely the case. ED is usually due to atherogenesis (vascular plaque) in the pelvic and genital blood supply. Ninety percent of the men who visit my office and complain of ED have normal testosterone. Their ED is usually due to vascular disease, medication side effects, and/or psychological stress related to relationships (but that's a topic for another book).

Because each person is different with regard to genetics, age, and degree of insulin resistance, the changes in testosterone I see clinically vary significantly from one individual to the next. As a result, it's difficult to identify a common, broadly effective treatment approach for "low T."

Symptoms of Low Testosterone

Symptoms of low testosterone can vary, but often include one or more of the following:

- Low sex drive

- Significant loss of muscle mass

- Increased body fat (especially around the middle)

- Gynecomastia (enlargement of the breasts)

- Fatigue or lack of energy

- Dysthymic mood (lack of general enthusiasm for things that were previously enjoyable)

- Frequent or continuous irritability

- Feeling depressed
- Low semen volume
- Hair loss
- Testicular shrinkage
- Erectile dysfunction

I see the listed symptoms in at least one-third of the men in my clinic who have some degree of insulin resistance. It is actually quite alarming!

> **PRIMARY VERSUS SECONDARY HYPOGONADISM**
>
> *Low testosterone can be caused by acquired or developmental damage to the testicles. This is referred to as* primary hypogonadism, *and it occurs because of congenital birth defects or direct trauma or damage to the blood flow to the testicular area. Although primary hypogonadism is very common, for the purposes of this book, I'm discussing* secondary hypogonadism, *which is defined as low testosterone caused by metabolic disease of the hypothalamus and/or the pituitary gland. Although congenital genetic deficiencies can cause secondary hypogonadism, the most common cause of secondary hypogonadism that I see in the office is caused by systemic disorders of the metabolism.*

JIMMY SAYS

Like with the thyroid issues that are typically blamed on ketosis, your testosterone also requires sufficient calories to stay at the proper level when you are eating keto. Going too low in calories on a ketogenic diet is what has the most profound negative effect on testosterone levels. Eat more bacon!

Causes of Lower Testosterone

Calorie restriction is one cause of lower testosterone levels. We've known since the late 1970s that restricting calories decreases testosterone production by up to 50 percent.[5, 6, 7] This is why I am not a fan of frequent or prolonged fasting. It's also the reason why bodybuilders struggle with muscle gain when they calorie restrict (testosterone helps stabilize building muscle) and why they eat so frequently (as many as six or eight times a day).

It's also the reason why men who have typically tried losing weight with a calorie-restricted diet might find that they suffer from low testosterone. In fact, the more a man restricts calories, the more his testosterone falls.[8] The more the testosterone falls, the more fatigued and hungry you get. In my clinical experience, many people, especially men, fall off the wagon with a calorie-restricted diet for this specific reason.

The second reason that testosterone decreases is excessive exercise without adequate recovery time. If you don't give yourself 24 to 48 hours to rest a muscle group, you will see testosterone fall. What this means is that if you do the same repetitive exercise every day without giving your body time to rest from that exercise type, the muscles fatigue and testosterone tanks.

The third issue is that chronic stress plays a significant role in lowering testosterone. Testosterone and cortisol have an inverse relationship. When cortisol is low, testosterone is dominant. When cortisol is high, testosterone drops, and the effects of testosterone are reversed.[9] This change can be caused by something as simple as experiencing social rejection or being defeated in a competition. This means that repetitive social rejection or competitive failures can lead to chronically low testosterone.

The fourth reason for testosterone decline, and the one that plays the largest role in my practice, is high levels of insulin due to insulin resistance. To understand the complex mechanism by which this works, it is important to understand how testosterone is stimulated in the human male.

The hypothalamus of the brain releases gonadotropin-releasing hormone (GnRH), which stimulates the anterior pituitary gland to release follicle-stimulating hormone (FSH) and luteinizing hormone (LH). FSH stimulates the Sertoli cells of the testes to mature the developing sperm, and LH stimulates the Leydig cells within the testes to produce and release testosterone. Testosterone acts as a negative feedback on the hypothalamus and the anterior pituitary gland.

In the case of insulin resistance, excess insulin production stimulates increased calcitonin gene-related peptide (CGRP), which has a suppressive effect on both LH and FSH. This both suppresses testosterone production and stops sperm maturation in the testes. However, there's more. As mentioned in other chapters, excess insulin hinders the ability of leptin (the hormone produced by the fat cells) to cross the blood-brain barrier effectively. Decreased leptin signaling in the brain causes a decrease in kisspeptin (metastin) and thereby suppresses GnRN production at the hypothalamus.[10] As you can see in the figure below, this also decreases FSH and LH and secondarily decreases testosterone production.[11, 12]

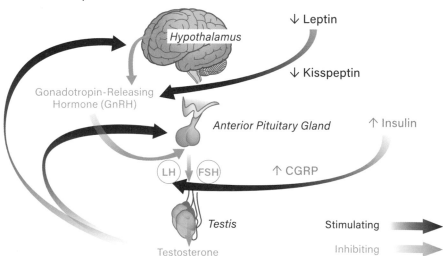

To make matters even worse, as our fat cells get "fatter," they become sicker. We call this *adiposity,* and an additional consequence is a lowering of another hormone called adiponectin. Adiponectin is produced by the fat cells to signal to the brain that you are full. However, fat cells that are "sick" produce less adiponectin.

When adiponectin falls, sex-hormone binding globulin (SHBG) levels fall. Lower SHBG also directly lowers testosterone levels available to the cells of the body.[13]

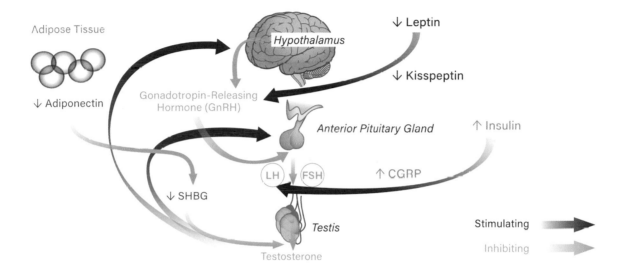

To summarize, weight gain and insulin resistance directly suppress testosterone by affecting the HPG axis at multiple levels.

HOW DOES TESTOSTERONE AFFECT WEIGHT LOSS?

Testosterone stimulates the upregulation of alpha- and beta-adrenergic receptors in the walls of the fat cells. These receptors more efficiently allow catecholamines (like epinephrine and norepinephrine) and adrenaline to more effectively release fat into the bloodstream to be used as fuel (turned into ketones), which decreases weight. Therefore, any process that decreases normal production of testosterone in a man causes weight gain.

APPLYING THE KETO CURE APPROACH

First, do me a favor and turn off the late-night TV so you don't see any more of those "low T" infomercials. Now, let's look at how to effectively raise testosterone via your diet. Please refer to the first few pages of Part 2 for general instructions on the use of the principles that follow.

PRINCIPLE 1
LOWER INSULIN LEVELS WITH DIET

As always, step one is to lower carbohydrate intake to less than 20 grams per day. This simple step corrects the high overproduction of insulin and allows leptin to cross the blood-brain barrier more effectively and signal to the brain regarding the production of GnRH. Over time, adiponectin increases to a normal level, increasing the presence of SHBG and allowing testosterone production to return to normal. Shifting the metabolism to the use of fat as the primary fuel has been shown to correct adiponectin production in the fat cells and increase testosterone.

Clinically, it seems to take about three months to see these changes take full effect. Whether that is the speed with which the ketogenic lifestyle aids healing of the adipose (fat) cells or the balance between the pancreas and liver regulation of insulin and glucose is corrected is still to be determined.

PRINCIPLE 2
AVOID ADDITIVES THAT RAISE INSULIN LEVELS

As insulin excess seems to play a major role in hypogonadism and lowering of testosterone levels, it should be clear that artificial sweeteners, leaf-based tea, or other insulin-stimulating substances should be avoided.

Leptin resistance is driven by fructose and alcohol use. If you have low testosterone, eliminating fructose and alcohol from your diet is essential.

PRINCIPLE 3
MODERATE PROTEIN WHERE APPROPRIATE

Testosterone is essential for stabilizing muscle mass. Anything that improves the level of ketosis will allow for the preservation of testosterone and a more efficient use of protein. Using the calculator in the opening pages of Part 2, calculate your protein needs. Exercise increases the need for protein, especially for preserving testosterone.

PRINCIPLE 4
ELIMINATE PROBLEM MEDICATIONS

Medications that elevate insulin or slow the metabolism have been discussed in previous chapters. Regarding testosterone, the biggest concern is medications that suppress this hormone.

If you are taking any of the following medications, speak with your doctor about whether there are alternatives that might work for your situation:

- **ANTI-ANDROGENS**
  - Casodex (bicalutamide)
  - Xtandi (enzalutamide)
  - Eulexin (flutamide)
  - Nilandron (nilutamide)
- **AZOLES**
  - Clotrimazole
  - Itraconazole
  - Ketoconazole
  - Miconazole
  - Fluconazole
  - Voriconazole
  - Posaconazole

> ⚠ **CAUTION!**
> **CONSULT YOUR DOCTOR**
> If you have prostate cancer, do not stop taking any anti-androgen medication without consulting your oncologist.

Because these medications are inhibitors of the cytochrome P450 enzymes, they can inhibit the formation of testosterone, as well as other adrenal glucocorticoids (sterols essential in forming cholesterol and converting progesterone to 17α-hydroxyprogesterone).

PRINCIPLE 5
ADD MEDICATIONS THAT HELP

The goal is to have serum testosterone between 450 and 1,000 ng/dL, which is essentially back to the normal range. You can usually achieve this level by switching to a ketogenic lifestyle, but about 30 percent of the time, I find that supplementation is necessary. If you're following a ketogenic lifestyle, you should see 100 to 150 points of improvement in your testosterone after the first two to three months. Testosterone can be satisfactorily replaced whether the deficiency is primary or secondary.

> ⚠️ **CAUTION!**
> **SUPPLEMENT ONLY WHEN NECESSARY**
> Supplementing testosterone when it's not needed or to higher levels than normal can result in acne, prostate enlargement, sleep apnea, erythrocytosis, and blood clots.

Testosterone supplements come in several forms: oral, topical, injectable serum, and subcutaneous (implantable) pellets. Oral supplements are associated with side effects to the liver, and most people who try them do not see a full resolution of their symptoms. I recommend that you consult with your doctor about the type of testosterone that is appropriate for you and the frequency of use. Also plan to have regular follow-up testing (at least every two to three months) while you're taking testosterone supplements.

The following are some options for testosterone supplements:

- **ORAL ANDROGEN REPLACEMENT PREPARATIONS**
  - Android (methyltestosterone)
  - Oxandrolone

- **TRANSDERMAL GEL/CREAM**
  - Axiron, AndroGel, Fortesta, Testim (testosterone transdermal gels)
  - Androderm (transdermal patch)

- **INJECTABLES**
  - Testosterone cypionate
  - Testosterone enanthate
  - Testosterone undecanoate (not available in the U.S.)

- **SUBCUTANEOUS PELLETS:** Testopel

PRINCIPLE 6
CONSIDER APPROPRIATE SUPPLEMENTATION

The Leydig cells of the testicles need cholesterol to make testosterone, which is why a ketogenic lifestyle is so effective for testosterone production. Leafy greens (such as cabbage and kale) as well as broccoli and cauliflower help lower estrogen to stabilize testosterone.

Eggs are the perfect food for stabilizing testosterone. One egg contains 7 grams of protein and 7 grams of fat, including cholesterol.

The following are some more ways to supplement to improve testosterone levels:

- **EXERCISE:** Exercise, specifically resistance training (weight lifting, yoga, Pilates, and so on), has been shown to increase testosterone acutely. People who participated in more than two years of regular exercise have consistently been shown to have notable elevated levels of testosterone.[14, 15]

- **VITAMIN D:** Supplementation with vitamin D has been shown to increase testosterone in humans.[16, 17]

- **ZINC:** Zinc deficiency has been associated with low testosterone. Adding zinc as a supplement has doubled testosterone levels in those who were deficient.[18]

- **HERBAL AGENTS:** Over the centuries, various herbal products have been touted as having testosterone-raising properties. These include astralagus root, Chinese yam, fenugreek, tribulus terrestris, and ginkgo biloba. All of them had some positive effect in animal studies; however, there was no significant improvement when these herbal agents were tested in humans.[19]

  There is some small evidence that the flavonoid chrysin, one of the passion flower species, has some weak aromatase activity in humans. It is claimed that chrysin inhibits the conversion of testosterone to estrogen. This result can be amplified by using an extract of black pepper called piperine that increases flavonoid absorption in the intestine.[20, 21, 22]

  Longjack root extract has been studied recently and was found to increase testosterone to normal levels in 90 percent of the seventy-six human subjects evaluated with its use.[23] Another study found that it stabilized lean body mass with a 5 percent increase in overall muscle mass.[24, 25]

CHAPTER 15

POLYCYSTIC OVARY SYNDROME

I write this chapter with my sweet wife in mind. She lived with the symptoms described in this chapter for quite some time. My heart goes out to any woman reading these pages who has experienced polycystic ovary syndrome (PCOS).

PCOS was originally described in the late 1980s as functional ovarian hyperandrogenism (FOH) due to abnormal over-secretion of sex hormones.[1] However, this definition didn't always match what was seen clinically.

Symptoms of PCOS are hard to miss. However, they don't always occur simultaneously and can often be confusing for both the patient and her physician. Some women have all of the symptoms, and others have only a few. As a result, many women and their doctors haven't really known what to make of, or how to treat, this discouraging condition. Many women have struggled with weight gain, difficult menstrual cycles, fertility issues, and severe cramping related to the cysts and the irregularity of their menses.

The most common symptoms are

- ▶ Irregular periods
- ▶ Facial hair growth
- ▶ Acne
- ▶ Obesity

These symptoms are often accompanied by the following:

- ▶ Skin tags
- ▶ Infertility
- ▶ Acanthosis nigricans
- ▶ Multiple cysts on the ovaries (visible via ultrasound)

PCOS was originally defined as laboratory and clinical evidence of elevated androgens (testosterone and/or DHEA-S) with evidence on ultrasound of multiple ovarian cysts.[2, 3] These symptoms were often associated with either absent or abnormal menstrual cycles, hirsutism (facial hair growth), infertility, and obesity.

For those who like to geek out on a little scientific definition, PCOS has since been defined in four different phenotypes:

- **Phenotype 1** (classic PCOS)

  1 Clinical or lab evidence of hyperandrogenism (elevated testosterone, DHEA-S, hirsutism, inflammatory acne, and so on)

  2 Evidence of abnormal menstrual cycling/ovulation

  3 Ultrasound evidence of a polycystic ovary (ovary with multiple cysts)

- **Phenotype 2** (NIH criteria)

  1 Clinical or lab evidence of hyperandrogenism (elevated testosterone, DHEA-S, hirsutism, and so on)

  2 Evidence of abnormal menstrual cycling/ovulation

- **Phenotype 3** (ovulatory PCOS)

  1 Clinical or lab evidence of hyperandrogenism (elevated testosterone, DHEA-S, hirsutism, and so on)

  2 Ultrasound evidence of a polycystic ovary (an ovary with multiple cysts)

- **Phenotype 4** (nonhyperandrogenic PCOS)

  1 Evidence of abnormal menstrual cycling/ovulation

  2 Ultrasound evidence of a polycystic ovary (an ovary with multiple cysts)[4]

JIMMY SAYS

One of the most eye-opening discoveries for women with PCOS is the realization that this condition is a telltale sign that they have insulin resistance and is the primary reason they may be struggling with infertility. A 2005 pilot study by Dr. Eric Westman confirms that a low-carb, ketogenic approach is the perfect remedy for PCOS.[5]

What is interesting is that a significant number of patients with PCOS (around 50 percent) also have impaired glucose tolerance. These patients show up in my office with any number of the symptoms, including weight gain, abnormal or absent menstrual cycles, infertility, facial hair growth, and a history of cysts on the ovaries. One hundred percent of the patients with PCOS who have presented in my clinic have had evidence of insulin resistance when we looked for it.[6, 7]

In other words, excessive production of insulin in the insulin-resistant patient plays a big role, if not the leading role, in the development of PCOS. As of the writing of this text, there are a number of hypotheses about the cause of PCOS, but the exact physiologic cause still eludes us. It is not my intention to answer that complex question in this chapter, but I want to cover a few things that might help you understand how the ketogenic lifestyle may benefit you if you suffer from PCOS.

THE RELATIONSHIP BETWEEN PCOS AND INSULIN

The ovary is made up of two types of cells: theca cells and granulosa cells. The theca cells are responsible for the conversion of cholesterol into the seven key steroid hormones necessary for function, including progesterone and testosterone.

We know that excess insulin (the common denominator in insulin resistance) drives the cholesterol within the theca cell to convert to progesterone, which then converts to 17α-hydroxyprogesterone, which eventually converts to testosterone. (This chain of conversion is the reason many women with PCOS have measured high in testosterone.)

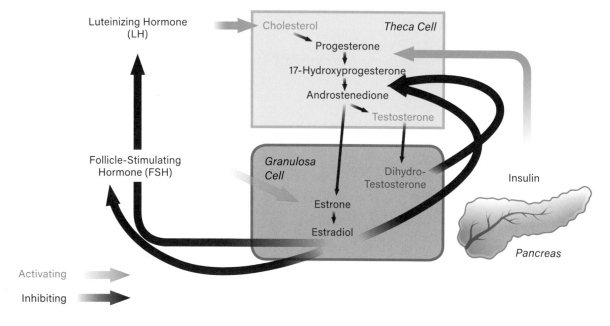

Luteinizing hormone (LH) normally is produced by the pituitary gland as estradiol rises. It stimulates the conversion of estradiol to estrogen, which quickly escalates the menstrual cycle. This rise in estrogen causes maturation of the follicle within the ovary, and an egg is released. Tissue within the egg, the corpus luteum, makes and secretes more progesterone. The increased progesterone and its conversion to 17α-hydroxyprogesterone and then androstenedione drives production of estrone and estradiol in the granulosa cells. This has an inhibiting effect on follicle-stimulating hormone (FSH).

FSH is also produced in the pituitary gland, and its job is to stimulate growth of the follicle within the ovary.[8] LH helps the follicle mature and be released as an egg into the fallopian tube.

However, insulin suppresses LH production in the pituitary gland. Higher levels of insulin (present at up to twenty times that of normal levels) can have a powerful suppressive effect on the production of the egg within the follicle of the ovary. This may be the cause of the variable number of cysts (which are immature follicles in a constant state of growth). LH should cause the maturation and release of the egg into the fallopian tube, but if LH is suppressed, this process and the normal menses will not occur correctly.

Excess testosterone, which exists in the presence of excess insulin, drives the facial hair growth (hirsutism) seen in many women, and it also contributes to acne and obesity.

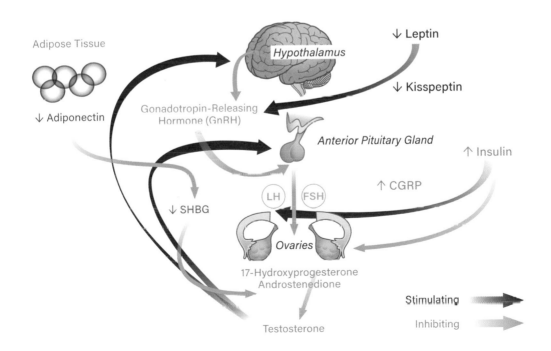

Women may also have leptin resistance, which has a suppressive effect on gonadotropin-releasing hormone (GnRH) and can cause variability in the production of FSH and LH. This situation can contribute to the symptoms of PCOS, and it is why we see notable changes with increases or decreases in dietary carbohydrate intake.

Lastly, when the adipose (fat) cells become larger, which often happens in those people who are insulin resistant, they become sicker and produce less adiponectin. This lowers the presence of sex-hormone binding globulin (SHBG) and may have a suppressive effect on testosterone (again adding to the variability of the presence of testosterone).

For many years, the use of metformin (Glucophage) has been used to treat PCOS. This has been effective because of metformin's modulating control on insulin release and the counterbalance effect it has on the liver's regulation of blood glucose. However, for those women who have PCOS, the most effective treatment I have found is dietary carbohydrate restriction.

We still have much to learn about PCOS, but to state it simply, stabilizing insulin release and the effects it has on FSH, LH, and testosterone plays a huge role in helping women with PCOS return to more normal physiologic function.

THE KETOGENIC LIFESTYLE AND PREGNANCY

One of the most rewarding days of my practice was after I had been treating a wonderful woman who had suffered from PCOS, obesity, and hirsutism for years. She had been to two infertility physicians who had tried every available medication to treat her symptoms. When she came to me, the medication had resulted in partial improvement in her menses, but she could not lose weight and hadn't been able to conceive. After years of trying, she had given up hope of becoming pregnant and stopped her medication.

This woman had come to me for obesity treatment, not PCOS treatment. We restricted her carbohydrate intake to less than 20 grams per day and increased her fat intake. She was to follow up with me in a month or two.

She returned three months later and apologized for not seeing me sooner. Instead of coming to see me after two months, she had to see her obstetrician. During the second month of her ketogenic diet, she had gotten pregnant!

Has carbohydrate restriction fixed every case of infertility I've seen in patients with PCOS? No. But it has been effective with enough of my patients for me to consider it a basis for nutritional change when addressing PCOS and infertility.

APPLYING THE KETO CURE APPROACH

Are you ready to dive into applying the Keto Cure principles to address your symptoms? It really isn't that difficult—nowhere near as difficult as dealing with years of PCOS symptoms. I assure you that the benefit you will see will be tremendous. I seem to get the most smiles and hugs from patients who have treated their PCOS with a ketogenic lifestyle. In fact, on the day I wrote this chapter, a thirty-year-old woman gave me a huge hug and said, "This ketogenic lifestyle has given me my life back!" So what are you waiting for?

Make sure to read the information in the first few pages of Part 2 for information about Principle 3.

PRINCIPLE 1
LOWER INSULIN LEVELS WITH DIET

Step number one is to lower your carbohydrate intake to less than 20 grams per day. This simple step corrects the high overproduction of insulin, allows for the normalization of LH and FSH production, corrects the overproduction of testosterone, and allows leptin to cross the blood-brain barrier more effectively. This helps stimulate normal production of GnRH from the brain.

As women restrict carbohydrates and weight loss occurs, over time adiponectin increases to a normal level, which increases the presence of SHBG and allows testosterone production to return to normal. Shifting the female metabolism to the use of fat as the primary fuel has been shown to correct adiponectin production in the fat cells and normalize testosterone production.[9]

Clinically, it takes roughly three to six months for these changes to become fully effective. So, be patient with the process of nutritional healing.

PRINCIPLE 2
AVOID ADDITIVES THAT RAISE INSULIN LEVELS

As excess insulin seems to play the role of antagonist in PCOS, it should be clear that you should avoid artificial sweeteners, leaf-based tea, and other insulin-stimulating substances.

Leptin resistance is driven by fructose and alcohol use. If you have PCOS, eliminating fructose and alcohol from your diet is essential.

PRINCIPLE 4
ELIMINATE PROBLEM MEDICATIONS

Aside from the medications listed on the opening pages of Part 2, medications that are of concern for people who have PCOS are the azoles, such as the following:

- Clotrimazole
- Fluconazole
- Itraconazole
- Ketoconazole
- Miconazole
- Posaconazole
- Voriconazole

Because these medications are inhibitors of the cytochrome P450 enzymes, they can inhibit the formation of testosterone as well as other adrenal glucocorticoids (sterols essential in forming cholesterol and converting progesterone to 17α-hydroxyprogesterone).

PRINCIPLE 5
ADD MEDICATIONS THAT HELP

If you are already following a ketogenic lifestyle, you will probably see a normal testosterone level as a female, but if you still have issues, you should talk to your physician about the possibility of including the following medications in your regimen:

- **BIGUANIDE:** metformin (Glucophage)
  Glucophage use has been very effective in my practice in helping to modulate insulin in those who are in the third and fourth stages of insulin resistance and type 2 diabetes. Glucophage works by reducing liver glucose output, which allows for lower insulin needs.[10] If you are following a ketogenic lifestyle and your fasting glucose levels are still elevated to more than 100 mg/dL, talk to your doctor about the risks and benefits of Glucophage.

- **ORAL CONTRACEPTIVES**
  Oral contraceptives are the mainstay of pharmacologic treatment of PCOS because of the menstrual dysfunction and hyperandrogenism. However, the risk of venous thromboembolism (blood clot) is present, especially in women who are obese.

Because women with PCOS are at an increased risk of endometrial hyperplasia and endometrial cancer (due to a lack of ovulation), oral contraceptives offer endometrial protection and help with the hirsutism (facial hair growth) that often accompanies PCOS.

Talk to your doctor about the risks and benefits of oral contraceptive use if your menstrual irregularities do not improve after you've been on a ketogenic lifestyle for some time.

- **ANTI-ANDROGENS**
Medications such as Aldactone and CaroSpir (spironolactone) can be useful in treating hirsutism and acne. Note, however, that this is an off-label use of these medications.

PRINCIPLE 6
CONSIDER APPROPRIATE SUPPLEMENTATION

The following is a list of lifestyle modifications and supplements that can be beneficial for the treatment of PCOS:

- **OBSTRUCTIVE SLEEP APNEA (OSA):** OSA is quite common among women with PCOS. Continuous positive airway pressure (CPAP) has been shown to improve insulin sensitivity and reduce diastolic blood pressure in women with PCOS.[11] If you snore and/or stop breathing for short periods while you're sleeping (which are called *apneic episodes*), you should consider a sleep study and treatment with CPAP.

- **EXERCISE:** Exercise, specifically resistance training (weight lifting, yoga, Pilates, and so on), has been shown to improve insulin sensitivity, blood sugar, lipids, and weight within three months of starting moderate-intensity progressive training.[12]

> **HERBAL AGENTS**
>
> *Over the centuries, some herbal products have been used as natural remedies for PCOS. Studies of these supplements have been small. Cautiously consider trying these supplements, and always consult with your physician before doing so.*

- **LICORICE:** A small study of nine women with PCOS showed a measurable reduction in testosterone over a two-month period when the women consumed 3.5 grams of commercial licorice on a daily basis. Licorice was shown to slow the enzymes that convert progesterone to testosterone. I realize that this is a small study and further research is necessary; however, possible adjuvant therapy for licorice may be considered in the future.[13]

- **ALOE VERA:** Restoration of menses, glucose sensitivity, and steroid activity occurred with a 1-milliliter oral dose of aloe vera gel in an animal study. It is suspected that the phyto-component of the aloe vera extract is the active ingredient.[14]

I don't recommend that you run out and start chewing on aloe vera leaves; consuming aloe vera can cause notable abdominal cramps and diarrhea. However, we may see further study into the use of aloe extracts to restore normal menses in women with PCOS in the future.

- **ASTRAGALUS POLYSACCHARIDES:** Astragalus was found to reduce testosterone and lipids. It improved insulin levels in thirty-two women with PCOS who were treated over a three-month period.[15]

- **N-ACETYL CYSTEINE (NAC):** A combination of clomiphene citrate with NAC significantly improved ovulation and pregnancy rates in women with PCOS.[16]

- **D-CHIRO-INOSITOL:** This phytic acid found in vegetables and fruits was given to forty-four women over a period of eight weeks. Notable improvements in testosterone, triglycerides, and blood pressure were found in nineteen of the twenty-two patients within the treatment arm.[17]

- **CHASTEBERRY:** In a three-month study of fifty-three women who used a daily supplement of tincture of dried berry, seventeen of the women had normalized menstrual cycles and had conceived by six months. In the placebo group, no menstrual changes occurred, and only four women out of forty conceived.[18]

CHAPTER 16

SWEETENERS: THE GOOD, THE BAD, AND THE UGLY

Many people in this fast-paced world we live in are so busy that cooking "the old-fashioned way" doesn't even cross their minds. However, as you begin following a ketogenic lifestyle, being able to make a meal from scratch with "real food" ingredients becomes a priority. This naturally leads to the question of which sweeteners are okay or "safe" for use in a low-carbohydrate or ketogenic kitchen. If you've spent any time in the baking aisle at your local grocery store, you know that there are lots of sweeteners and sugar substitutes available. However, many of them are not appropriate for use on a low-carbohydrate, ketogenic diet.

As discussed in the early chapters of this book, weight gain and weight loss are controlled by thirty different known hormones. Insulin, of course, is the master hormone, and glucose (a carbohydrate in its simplest form) stimulates the release of insulin. A low-carbohydrate diet like the ketogenic diet is effective because restricting the amount of carbohydrate you take in significantly lowers your insulin levels throughout the day.

On traditional diets that focus on taking in fewer calories than you expend, any sugar substitute that has zero calories might be considered suitable. The problem, though, is that many of these sweeteners, even though they are "zero calorie," still stimulate an insulin response at a hormonal level, which leads to weight gain and inflammation. Many of these products trigger a hormone response like sugar does, only without raising the blood sugar or having any caloric value. So, how do you know which sweeteners are okay and which are off-limits?

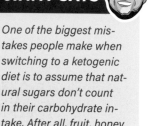

JIMMY SAYS

One of the biggest mistakes people make when switching to a ketogenic diet is to assume that natural sugars don't count in their carbohydrate intake. After all, fruit, honey, and maple syrup are real foods and thus can't possibly be bad for you, right? Please don't fall into that trap. Understand this loud and clear: Sugar is sugar is sugar, no matter whether it's natural or created in a laboratory.

DON'T BE FOOLED BY FRUCTOSE

Fructose is sometimes promoted as a suitable sweetener for patients with diabetes or people who want to follow a low-carb diet; however, even though fructose doesn't cause a significant insulin rise, it's rapidly absorbed by the liver and converted to glycerol, which leads to an increase in insulin a few hours later. It also raises triglyceride and cholesterol levels.

Even though fructose occurs naturally in fruits and some vegetables, it is usually present in those foods in small amounts, and the fiber in the fruits and vegetables balances out the fructose content. Today, a highly refined, purified form of fructose called high-fructose corn syrup is added commercially to many foods. Be careful—this form of fructose is found in soft drinks, iced teas, fruit drinks, jams, jellies, desserts, baked goods, and even many baby foods. Fructose stimulates an extremely powerful response in the liver to form triglycerides and leads to fatty liver disease, a form of non-alcoholic cirrhosis (read more about NAFLD in Chapter 11).[1]

The first step is to understand how these carbohydrates or sugars are labeled or named so that you can identify them in the food products you purchase and eat. Many sugars are labeled with the ending "–ose," so when you read ingredients lists, look for things like sucrose, fructose, glucose, dextrose, lactose, and maltose. These sugars stimulate a significant insulin rise and lead to weight gain and elevations in cholesterol and triglycerides.

Also keep an eye out for these other common names for sugar: white and brown sugar, sucanat, corn syrup, high-fructose corn syrup, honey, malt syrup, cane juice, cane syrup, rice syrup, barley syrup, maple syrup, molasses, turbinado, agave, monk fruit, and fruit juice concentrate. Beware of products labeled as "no added sugar" because they often contain sugar concentrates in the form of concentrated grape or apple juice.

Most artificial sweeteners are classified as "non-nutritive," meaning that they have no nutrient value to the human body. They provide a sweet taste without raising blood sugar. These sweeteners can be useful in cooking and in maintaining blood sugar levels; however, it is essential to realize that many of them still stimulate an insulin response. The following sections provide more detail about some of these sweeteners.

ASPARTAME

The most popular artificial sweetener in use today is aspartame, sold under the brand names NutraSweet and Equal. Aspartame is calorie- and carbohydrate-free. It is produced in liquid form, and in its liquid state, it tastes sweet. It's used as a sweetener in many diet products, including diet soda. However, aspartame is not ideal for cooking because of its chemical instability. When heated, it breaks down into its chemical constituents— namely phenylalanine and aspartic acid—which results in a very sour, almost metallic taste. Aspartame has also been found to break down as it ages. Because of its tendency to break down when heated or as it's stored over long periods, aspartame is unsuitable for use in any cooking and problematic for food that will be stored for more than a few days or weeks.

To make aspartame a crystal, it is usually bound to dextrose or maltodextrin, which are sugars that spike insulin. Some products, such as some forms of Equal, have added acesulfame potassium, which is covered later in this chapter. These additives spike insulin, cause weight gain and inflammation, and increase the risk of diabetes.

Mixed reports in the past few years have made aspartame controversial. In a number of studies, results show weight loss, decreased caloric intake, and improved insulin response in tests that use the liquid form of aspartame.[2, 3, 4] Other studies, which look specifically at the diet sodas that include aspartame in the form of NutraSweet, Equal, or a combination of aspartame with other sweeteners, demonstrate an increased risk of weight gain, metabolic syndrome. and diabetes.[5, 6, 7]

The manufacturer of aspartame maintains that the product's safety profile has not changed. Even though most people enjoy its use without any problems, a few might experience side effects, including headache, stomach upset, migraine, and exacerbation of depression.[8, 9]

To further add to the confusion about this sweetener, a recent animal study that examined aspartame in the liquid form demonstrated weight loss, reduced caloric intake, and no rise in insulin response. This was especially true in animals that were fed a high-fat diet. However, in the animals, there seemed to be a persisting insulin resistance that resulted in mild hyperglycemia. Whether this is due to changes in the gut bacteria or the effect on the liver is still to be determined.[10]

There is an additional animal study that shows brain cellular death because of damage to the mitochondria of brain cells with prolonged exposure to a by-product of aspartame metabolism.[11] This may have an effect of chronic stress on the body and be the reason that some people experience adverse effects from using aspartame.

Many diet soda manufacturers have stopped using this sweetener because of bad press about non-nutritive sweeteners in general and

JIMMY SAYS

I often refer to aspartame as "nastytame" because, in my opinion, it's one of the more egregious artificial sweeteners on the market, and it's in almost everything sugar-free and low-carb. One of the problems with this fake sugar is that it isn't meant to be heated to high temperatures, and it can be especially harmful when it is.

because of the difficulty with storing products that include it for more than a few months; however, aspartame remains the only sweetener in diet soda that does not raise insulin levels in human studies.

Experts still disagree on the use of aspartame in a ketogenic lifestyle. It should be noted that among obesity experts, nutritionists, and the authors of this text there is disagreement on the use of aspartame.

Because aspartame in the liquid form has been shown to help with obesity and does not appear to affect ketosis, during the past twelve years I had been comfortable with weight-loss patients using the liquid form, such as in diet sodas. In my clinical obesity practice I have found that bridging the dietary changes from a traditional diet to a ketogenic diet are enhanced by allowing the use of selected diet sodas.

However, because of the new information we have on the effect of aspartame on the gut microbiome, possible effects on insulin resistance, and the effect of aspartame on the mitochondria, the use of diet sodas should be considered with great caution and avoided as much as possible.

Furthermore, I do not recommend using Equal or NutraSweet packets. They contain dextrose and/or maltodextrin, which cause a rise in insulin and lead to weight gain and metabolic syndrome. You should not use aspartame in cooking or meal preparation, nor should you use products that contain aspartame and are past their expiration date.

ACESULFAME POTASSIUM

Another sweetener that food and beverage companies use is acesulfame potassium (sold under the brand names Ace-K and Sunette). This sweetener is not fully absorbed by the gut, yields no calories, and doesn't raise blood sugar. It also contains no carbohydrates. To many palates, it has a slightly bitter flavor, so it is often combined with aspartame to eliminate the bitter aftertaste. The problem with acesulfame potassium is that a number of studies reveal that it significantly increases insulin response without raising blood sugar. This is exactly what you're trying to avoid when you're working to lose weight. Studies show that the insulin response is as remarkable as if a person had ingested an equivalent amount of glucose.[12] It appears that acesulfame potassium works directly on the pancreas to stimulate insulin release.[13]

This product is currently one of the most popular artificial sweeteners used in several low-carb/ketogenic products. It can be found in many of the protein bars and protein shakes on the market. It is also found in Coca-Cola Zero Sugar and some other diet sodas.

I have found in my private medical practice that acesulfame potassium significantly limits weight loss and raises both triglycerides and small-dense LDL particles (the ones that cause atherosclerosis and vascular disease). I don't recommend using this sweetener at all.

SUCRALOSE

Sucralose (sold under the brand name Splenda) is a liquid that's derived from regular sugar in such a way that the body doesn't recognize it, and it is not absorbed. When sucralose is bound to dextrose or maltodextrin, crystals form. In its pure form, sucralose contributes no calories or carbohydrates to the body. Amazingly, it remains stable in heat, which makes it ideal for cooking and baking. Splenda is available as a bulk sweetener and measures equivalently to table sugar.

The down side is that sucralose is not carbohydrate-free. Because of the maltodextrin used to make it bulk or crystallized for cooking, it contains about 0.5 gram of carbohydrate per teaspoon, or about one-eighth of the carbohydrate of sugar. So, if you're cooking with Splenda, 1 cup is equivalent to 2 tablespoons of sugar, which means there's 12 to 15 grams of carbohydrate in 1 cup.

Also, sucralose does cause insulin release. Research substantiates the effects that I often see clinically, which is that Splenda frequently causes weight gain or difficulty with weight loss when used in excess.[14]

JIMMY SAYS

There are several liquid forms of sucralose that eliminate the maltodextrin fillers used in the powdered forms, including EZ Sweetz, Sweetzfree, FiberFit, and Splenda Zero.

SACCHARINE

Saccharine (sold under the brand names Sweet'N Low and SugarTwin) is another unstable chemical when heated; however, it does not react chemically with other food ingredients and thereby stores well. It was one of the original artificial sweeteners, and it was used for quite some time in many products. As other sweeteners have been developed, its use has become less frequent. It is often combined with other sweeteners to preserve the food product shelf life.

Saccharine doesn't increase glucose or blood sugar, but it does stimulate an insulin response. Because of this, it is problematic for weight loss, and I don't recommend its use.[15]

CYCLAMATE

Cyclamate (sold under the brand names SugarTwin and Sucaryl) is a sweetener available in Canada that is often combined with saccharine and is similar to sucralose. However, there is some controversy over this substance because it is known to cause bladder cancer in rats. However, there has been no human occurrence of similar results in thirty years of study.[16] This product is currently banned in the United States because of the notable potential for cancer. Cyclamate is heat-stable and therefore is an alternative for cooking and baking.

STEVIA

JIMMY SAYS

Not all stevia sweeteners are created equal. Watch out for popular brands that use GMO corn erythritol (Truvia is an example); instead, choose liquid stevia whenever possible. Avoid products that add dextrose or maltodextrin as a bulking agent.

Stevia in its liquid form is a non-caloric natural sweetener that contains no carbohydrate. It is derived from a South American shrub called *Stevia rebaudiana* that has very sweet-tasting leaves. The leaves are processed to form a liquid extract or a white powder. You can purchase stevia as an extract, powder, or powdered green herbal leaf. It has an intense sweet taste that actually has the potential to be slightly bitter.

Stevia has two faults:

- It is so sweet that it is hard to know just how much to use in cooking.

- It often has a slightly bitter taste despite its extreme sweetness.

To counteract the bitterness, stevia is often combined with fructooligosaccharide (FOS; see the later section). FOS is a sugar, but it is such a large molecule that the human gut can't break it down and absorb it. Because of this, it doesn't raise blood sugar or stimulate insulin release. Similarly, stevia doesn't increase blood sugar, and it appears to improve insulin sensitivity in the pancreas.[17] FOS is only half as sweet as table sugar; therefore, it makes a perfect partner for stevia.

However, be aware that because of its popularity, some manufacturers have combined stevia with dextrose or maltodextrin to add bulk for use in cooking. Be cautious with these forms of stevia because the dextrose and maltodextrin raise insulin and blood sugar levels.

MONK FRUIT (MOGROSIDE V)

Mogroside V (luo han guo) is one of the newer sweeteners on the market and is more commonly known as monk fruit or Buddha fruit. Mogroside V is an extract from a melon-like gourd found in Asia. It gets its name from the monks who cultivated it years ago and used it as a folk remedy to treat coughing, constipation, and some metabolic deficiencies. It is two hundred to five hundred times sweeter than regular sugar.

Monk fruit is now found in a number of different brands. It has been used in "low-carb" foods because it doesn't raise blood sugar. It also has great popularity because of the ease with which it can be used in cooking.

Studies show that monk fruit does not raise blood sugar; however, it does stimulate insulin secretion.[18] Even though it contains no calories and does not raise blood sugar, my clinical experience is that it halts weight loss and shifts some people who use it out of ketosis. For example, when I test my ketones, I have found that monk fruit knocks me out of ketosis; my wife, on the other hand, can use it without a problem. I am notably more insulin resistant than she is, and I suspect that is why she can tolerate it and I cannot. About 50 percent of the patients in my clinic have had problems using monk fruit, so my recommendation is to use it with great caution.

OLIGOFRUCTANS

Fructooligosaccharides (FOS) are often called oligofructans. They are short-chain fibers derived from inulin. Oligofructans exhibit a sweetness between 30 and 50 percent of sugar and have been used commercially since the 1980s. Common sources are chicory root, bananas, onions, garlic, and blue agave. Because of their configuration, they resist breakdown by intestinal digestive enzymes and instead are broken down through fermentation in the colon by anaerobic bacteria. Consequently, eating larger amounts of FOS can lead to gastrointestinal "gymnastics."

FOS combine well with other, more intense sweeteners to improve the overall sensation of sweetness and diminish any aftertaste. FOS don't raise blood sugar and have not been shown to affect insulin. Therefore, they are a good sweetener to use with a low-carbohydrate or ketogenic diet.[19]

A great option that I recommend for use in cooking is a product called Swerve, which is a combination of FOS and erythritol (see the next section).

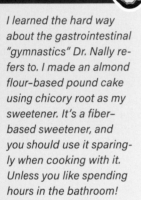

JIMMY SAYS

I learned the hard way about the gastrointestinal "gymnastics" Dr. Nally refers to. I made an almond flour-based pound cake using chicory root as my sweetener. It's a fiber-based sweetener, and you should use it sparingly when cooking with it. Unless you like spending hours in the bathroom!

SUGAR ALCOHOLS

Sugar alcohols are also called polyols. These are a class of long-chain carbohydrates that are neither sugar nor actual alcohol. Included in this group are maltitol, sorbitol, mannitol, xylitol, erythritol, lactitol, and hydrolyzed starch hydrolysates (HSH). These long-chain carbohydrates give the texture and sweetness of sugar to corn syrup and can be used to make crunchy toffee, chewy jelly beans, slick hard candies, moist brownies, and creamy chocolate. They are partially, but incompletely, absorbed by the human intestine, which causes side effects that can include gas, bloating, and diarrhea for a significant portion of people.

The other challenge with sugar alcohols is that there seems to be notable variability in people's ability to absorb these long-chain carbohydrates. In other words, these sweeteners affect people differently and increase blood sugar and insulin release in varying degrees among individuals.

Maltitol, sorbitol, and xylitol seem to be worse offenders in this class of artificial sweeteners. They cause an insulin response of about half that of sugar.[20] Maltitol and sorbitol have also been shown to increase cholesterol.[21]

The exception is erythritol, which is absorbed and excreted unchanged. It appears to have no insulin response.[22] Erythritol also seems to have an inhibiting effect on fructose absorption.[23]

Truvia is a sweetener made from a combination of stevia and erythritol. In clinical use of Truvia, insulin and blood sugar appear to remain stable; however, the erythritol in the product can cause gastrointestinal distress when used in excess! Be aware that the manufacturer of Truvia Baking Blend recently added maltodextrin to its ingredient list, so use the Baking Blend with extreme caution, if at all.

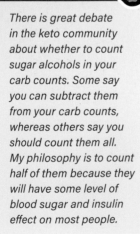

JIMMY SAYS

There is great debate in the keto community about whether to count sugar alcohols in your carb counts. Some say you can subtract them from your carb counts, whereas others say you should count them all. My philosophy is to count half of them because they will have some level of blood sugar and insulin effect on most people.

ALLULOSE

Allulose, also known as D-psicose and D-allulose, is a new sweetener on the market. It has been approved by the FDA and is available under the brand name All-u-Lose. (It is not currently available in Europe.)

Allulose is a unique, rare, and naturally occurring molecule found in wheat, figs, and raisins. Like glucose, it is a single molecular sugar structure—a monosaccharide. It has a similar taste and texture to sugar but is notably lower in calories. Studies preliminarily demonstrate that allulose is safe and does not necessarily raise glucose or insulin levels in animals.[24] No negative side effects were noted in doses up to 3 teaspoons (15 grams) per day in human studies.[25, 26]

JIMMY SAYS

Maria Emmerich highly recommends using Swerve because it's the perfect combination of erythritol and oligosaccharides for baking and any other sweetening needs.

In fact, studies have shown that allulose improves blood sugar control, reduces the risk of progression to diabetes, and slows weight gain, especially in the presence of diabetes. Animal studies of allulose have even shown it to be protective to the beta cells of the pancreas.[27]

However, some recent research on allulose reveals that an insulin spike occurs fifteen minutes after ingestion.[28] This same study found that the blood sugar and limitation in weight gain with D-allulose use is due to hormonal stimulation of gut GLP-1 that lasts up to two hours, causing appetite suppression in the vagal afferent pathways of the brain (feeding center regulation). Preliminarily, this is quite exciting.

There are still some questions to be answered before this sweetener can be given the "all clear" for regular, long-term use. Inhibition of weight gain has been demonstrated; however, because of the insulin spike, will long-term use inhibit weight loss? At this point, we don't have enough information to know. In addition, allulose is quite expensive; as of this writing, it costs twice as much as erythritol alone or in a blended sweetener like Swerve.

MY RECOMMENDATION

Since I started using ketogenic diets in 2005, I have found both personally and clinically that combinations of stevia, FOS, and erythritol seem to give baked goods adequate texture and remove any aftertaste that the individual sweeteners have. These combinations don't impede weight loss, result in weight regain, or cause adverse metabolic changes when used as part of a keto lifestyle. The other sweeteners listed in this chapter can limit your ability to lose weight and lead to a significant insulin response.

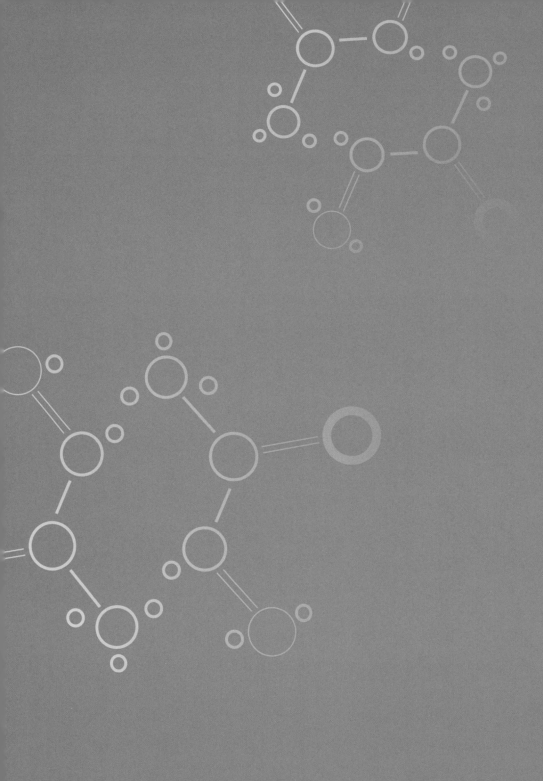

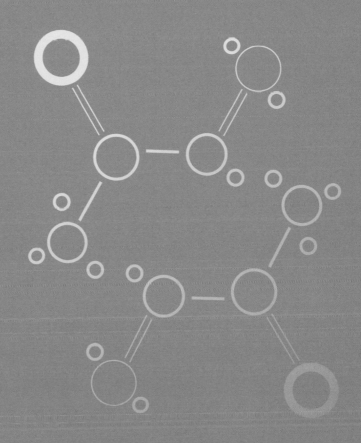

PART 3

THE RECIPES

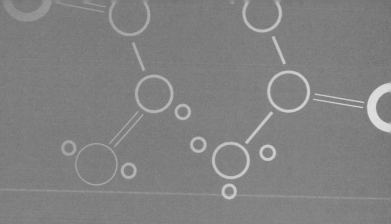

BREAKFAST

CHORIZO BREAKFAST ASPARAGUS

YIELD: 1 serving   **PREP TIME:** 5 minutes   **COOK TIME:** 10 minutes

6 spears asparagus

1½ teaspoons ghee, lard, or coconut oil

2 ounces Mexican-style fresh (raw) chorizo, removed from casing

2 large eggs

¼ teaspoon fine sea salt

⅛ teaspoon ground black pepper

1½ teaspoons chopped fresh cilantro, for garnish

1 Trim the asparagus and discard the woody stems.

2 Melt the ghee in a cast-iron skillet over medium heat. Add the chorizo and cook for 4 minutes or until cooked through, breaking up the sausage with a spoon as it cooks. Use a slotted spoon to remove the chorizo from the skillet, leaving the drippings in the pan.

3 Add the asparagus to the hot skillet with the sausage drippings and cook until crisp-tender, about 5 minutes, depending on how thick the asparagus is.

4 Crack the eggs into the pan, on either side of the asparagus. Sprinkle with the salt and pepper. Reduce the heat to medium-low and cook the eggs, sunny-side-up, until the whites are set but the yolks are still runny. To ensure that the tops of the eggs cook evenly, baste them with the fat in the pan or place a lid on the pan.

5 Place the asparagus and eggs on a plate and add the chorizo. Garnish with the cilantro.

NUTRITIONAL INFORMATION		
per serving	393 calories	31 g fat
21 g protein	5 g carbs	1 g fiber

GREEK FRITTATA

OPTION   OPTION

YIELD: 2 servings   **PREP TIME:** 5 minutes   **COOK TIME:** 7 minutes

5 large eggs

1 cup pitted Greek olives (Kalamata olives or mixed olives), left whole or chopped, plus more for garnish

¼ cup crumbled feta cheese, plus more for garnish (omit for dairy-free)

¼ cup unsweetened, unflavored cashew milk (or heavy cream if not dairy-sensitive)

½ teaspoon fine sea salt

½ teaspoon dried basil

¼ teaspoon dried oregano leaves

⅛ teaspoon ground black pepper

1 clove garlic, minced

Sliced fresh basil, for garnish

1 Preheat the oven to 375°F.

2 Heat a greased cast-iron skillet over medium-low heat.

3 In a large bowl, whisk together the eggs, olives, feta, cashew milk, salt, dried basil, oregano, pepper, and garlic. Pour the egg mixture into the hot skillet. Cook, while stirring, for 1 minute.

4 Place the skillet in the oven and cook for 6 minutes or until the eggs are just set and cooked through. Garnish with the fresh basil and additional olives and feta.

5 This dish is best served fresh, but if you have leftovers, you can store them in an airtight container in the refrigerator for up to 3 days. Reheat in a greased skillet over medium heat for a few minutes, until warmed to your liking.

NUTRITIONAL INFORMATION		
per serving	531 calories	45 g fat
27 g protein	9 g carbs	6 g fiber

MUSHROOM ROSTI

OPTION

YIELD: 2 servings **PREP TIME:** 5 minutes **COOK TIME:** 12 minutes

A client from Santa Monica, California, told me about her favorite restaurant, Rosti. It not only has amazing food but also has the cutest little outdoor patio, which is decorated with white decorative lights that twinkle in the trees above. She said they serve the most amazing brunch, including fantastic egg and mushroom dishes similar to this one.

3 tablespoons unsalted butter or ghee (or avocado oil if dairy-free), plus more for drizzling

1 cup sliced mushrooms

¼ cup thinly sliced onions

¾ teaspoon fine sea salt, divided

¾ teaspoon ground black pepper, divided

6 large eggs

2 ounces goat cheese, crumbled (omit for dairy-free)

¼ cup chopped fresh chives, for garnish

1 Melt the butter in a 9-inch nonstick skillet over medium heat. Add the mushrooms, onions, and ¼ teaspoon each of the salt and pepper. Sauté, stirring often, until the mushrooms are golden brown and the onions are translucent, about 6 minutes.

2 In a medium bowl, beat the eggs with the remaining ½ teaspoon each of salt and pepper. Add the goat cheese to the skillet, then pour the eggs over the goat cheese mixture. Cook until the edges are set but the center is not yet fully cooked, about 5 minutes. Place a large, flat plate on top of the skillet and then carefully turn the skillet over to flip the rosti onto the plate. Slide the uncooked side of the rosti into the skillet and cook until the center is set, about 1 minute more.

3 Slide the rosti onto a serving plate. Drizzle with melted butter or ghee and garnish with the chopped chives.

4 Store leftovers in an airtight container in the refrigerator for up to 3 days. Reheat in a greased skillet over medium heat for a few minutes, until warmed to your liking.

NUTRITIONAL INFORMATION		
per serving	463 calories	38 g fat
26 g protein	6 g carbs	1 g fiber

BUFFALO CHICKEN MINI QUICHES

YIELD: 24 mini quiches (3 per serving) **PREP TIME:** 10 minutes (not including time to cook chicken)
COOK TIME: 10 minutes

Coconut oil, for the pan

2 dozen large eggs

1 cup shredded cooked chicken (see Note)

½ cup crumbled blue cheese (about 2 ounces) (omit for dairy-free), divided

2 tablespoons medium-hot hot sauce, plus more for drizzling

2 tablespoons chopped fresh chives, plus more for garnish

1 teaspoon fine sea salt

1 teaspoon ground black pepper

6 yellow cherry tomatoes, quartered, for garnish (optional)

1 Preheat the oven to 325°F. Grease a 24-well mini-muffin pan.

2 In a large bowl, whisk the eggs. Add the chicken, most of the cheese (reserve a little for garnish), hot sauce, chives, salt, and pepper and stir to combine.

3 Pour the egg mixture into the greased muffin pan, filling each well about three-quarters full.

4 Bake until the center of each quiche is firm, about 10 minutes. Let cool for 5 minutes and then run a sharp knife around the edge of each quiche to loosen before turning them out of the pan.

5 If you're using cherry tomatoes, use a toothpick to secure a tomato quarter to the top of each quiche. Drizzle the quiches with hot sauce and garnish with chopped chives and the reserved blue cheese crumbles. Serve warm.

6 Store leftovers in an airtight container in the refrigerator for up to 3 days. Reheat on a rimmed baking sheet in a preheated 325°F oven for a few minutes, until warmed to your liking.

NOTE: If you don't have leftover cooked chicken on hand, you can purchase an organic rotisserie chicken from your local market. Use the meat for this dish, and use the bones to make bone broth!

NUTRITIONAL INFORMATION		
per serving	333 calories	21 g fat
31 g protein	2 g carbs	0.3 g fiber

COWBOY SCRAMBLED EGGS

OPTION

YIELD: 1 serving **PREP TIME:** 5 minutes **COOK TIME:** 8 minutes

1 tablespoon unsalted butter or ghee (or lard if dairy-free)

¼ cup diced red and green bell peppers

2 tablespoons diced onions

3 large eggs, beaten

2 tablespoons water

½ teaspoon fine sea salt

⅛ teaspoon ground black pepper

2 tablespoons shredded sharp cheddar cheese (omit for dairy-free)

FOR GARNISH:

Salsa

Sour cream (omit for dairy-free)

Chopped fresh cilantro leaves

1 Melt the butter in a cast-iron skillet over medium heat. Add the peppers and onions and sauté for 5 minutes, or until the onions are soft.

2 Meanwhile, place the eggs, water, salt, and pepper in a bowl; whisk well to combine. Pour the egg mixture into the skillet.

3 Scramble the eggs until they're almost set. Add the cheese and heat until the cheese has melted and the eggs are cooked to your liking. Garnish with salsa, sour cream, and chopped cilantro.

NUTRITIONAL INFORMATION		
per serving	432 calories	34 g fat
23 g protein	6 g carbs	1 g fiber

BAKED EGGS

YIELD: 4 servings **PREP TIME:** 5 minutes **COOK TIME:** 15 minutes

OPTION

4 teaspoons ghee or unsalted butter (or lard if dairy-free), melted, divided, plus more for the ramekins

8 large eggs

2 tablespoons chopped fresh chives

1 teaspoon fine sea salt

1 teaspoon ground black pepper

1   Preheat the oven to 350°F. Grease four 4-ounce ramekins with ghee.

2   Gently crack 2 eggs into each ramekin without breaking the yolks. Season the eggs evenly with the chives, salt, and pepper. Drizzle the contents of each ramekin with 1 teaspoon of the melted ghee, and arrange the ramekins on a rimmed baking sheet.

3   Place the baking sheet in the oven and bake until the egg whites are opaque and the yolks have firm edges but are still soft in the center, about 15 minutes. Serve immediately.

4   Store leftover eggs in the ramekins in an airtight container in the refrigerator for up to 3 days. To reheat, place the ramekins in a preheated 350°F oven or toaster oven for a few minutes, until the eggs are warmed to your liking.

NUTRITIONAL INFORMATION		
per serving	195 calories	15 g fat
13 g protein	1 g carbs	0.2 g fiber

PEACHES AND CREAM SHAKE

OPTION

YIELD: 2 servings   **PREP TIME:** 15 minutes

1 cup heavy cream (or full-fat coconut milk if dairy-free)

1 cup strong-brewed peach tea, chilled

2 ounces cream cheese (¼ cup) (or Kite Hill brand cream cheese–style spread if dairy-free)

3 tablespoons Swerve confectioners'-style sweetener or equivalent amount of liquid or powdered sweetener

1 teaspoon peach extract

¼ teaspoon peach-flavored liquid stevia (optional)

¼ teaspoon fine sea salt

1 cup crushed ice

1 Place all the ingredients in a blender and blend until smooth. Pour into two 8-ounce glasses and serve.

2 If you won't be consuming the entire shake right away, combine all the ingredients except the crushed ice. Blend the portion you'll be consuming immediately with ice and store the rest without the ice to keep it from getting too watery. Store the remaining portion in an airtight container in the refrigerator for up to 3 days, then blend it with ice immediately before serving.

NUTRITIONAL INFORMATION		
per serving	280 calories	27 g fat
4 g protein	3 g carbs	0 g fiber

HAM 'N' CHEESE EGG BAKE

YIELD: 8 servings   **PREP TIME:** 5 minutes   **COOK TIME:** 40 minutes

6 large eggs

1 cup sour cream

¾ cup heavy cream (or unsweetened, unflavored cashew milk if not nut-sensitive)

½ teaspoon fine sea salt

¼ teaspoon ground black pepper

¼ teaspoon ground nutmeg

2 cups chopped ham

1 cup shredded sharp cheddar cheese, plus more for topping, if desired

2 teaspoons dried chives

1 Preheat the oven to 325°F and grease a 13 by 9-inch casserole dish.

2 In a large bowl, whisk together the eggs, sour cream, heavy cream, salt, pepper, and nutmeg. Stir in the ham and cheese. Pour the mixture into the greased baking dish and top with the dried chives. Sprinkle with extra cheese, if desired.

3 Bake for 40 minutes, or until the middle is set and doesn't jiggle when shaken. Let cool for 10 minutes before cutting.

4 Store leftovers in an airtight container in the refrigerator for up to 3 days. Reheat on a rimmed baking sheet in a preheated 350°F oven for a few minutes, until warmed to your liking.

NUTRITIONAL INFORMATION		
per serving	252 calories	18 g fat
21 g protein	1 g carbs	0.1 g fiber

CHOCOLATE ALMOND CEREAL

OPTION

YIELD: 4 servings   **PREP TIME:** 5 minutes   **COOK TIME:** 7 minutes

½ cup vanilla whey protein powder (or egg white protein powder if not egg-sensitive)

¾ cup blanched almond flour

¼ cup unsweetened cocoa powder

¼ cup Swerve confectioners'-style sweetener or equivalent amount of liquid or powdered sweetener

¼ teaspoon baking powder

¼ teaspoon fine sea salt

¼ cup unsweetened natural almond butter

2 teaspoons almond extract

2 tablespoons water (just enough to hold the dough together)

Unsweetened cashew milk, for serving

1   Preheat the oven to 400°F and line a rimmed baking sheet with parchment paper.

2   In a medium bowl, stir together the whey protein powder, flour, cocoa powder, sweetener, baking soda, and salt.

3   Use a pastry blender or your fingers to cut the almond butter into the dry mixture until the lumps are pea-sized or smaller.

4   Add the almond extract and water and mix well until crumbs form.

5   Spread the mixture on the lined baking sheet until it's about ¼ inch thick. Bake for 7 to 10 minutes, until the edges are lightly browned. Remove the pan from the oven and allow the cereal to cool. Break into small pieces.

6   Serve the cereal with unsweetened cashew milk.

7   Store leftovers in an airtight container in the refrigerator for up to 5 days, or freeze for up to a month.

NUTRITIONAL INFORMATION		
per serving	252 calories	21 g fat
13 g protein	5 g carbs	2 g fiber

EGGS IN A NEST

YIELD: 6 servings (2 nests per serving)   **PREP TIME:** 10 minutes   **COOK TIME:** 30 minutes

4 cups shredded red or green cabbage

2½ tablespoons melted ghee or unsalted butter, plus more for greasing pan

2½ teaspoons fine sea salt

1 teaspoon ground black pepper

⅔ cup shredded cheddar cheese, plus ¼ cup more for topping the nests

12 large eggs

8 slices ham, chopped, or 8 strips cooked and crumbled bacon

Chopped fresh chives or green onions for garnish

1   Preheat the oven to 350°F. Grease the wells of a 12-well standard-size muffin pan.

2   Combine the cabbage, ghee, salt, pepper, and ⅔ cup of the shredded cheddar cheese in a bowl. Divide the mixture among the prepared muffin wells and use your fingers to shape the mixture into nests with hollows in the middle.

3   Bake until the nests are browned on the edges and the cheese has melted, 15 to 18 minutes. Remove the pan from the oven.

4   Whisk the eggs in a bowl; season with a pinch each of salt and pepper. Pour an equal amount of the egg mixture into each nest, then sprinkle evenly with the ham or bacon crumbles. Top each with 1 teaspoon of the remaining cheddar cheese.

5   Bake until the eggs are set and the whites are opaque, 13 to 16 minutes. Let the nests cool slightly before removing them from the pan. Enjoy warm.

6   Store leftovers in an airtight container in the refrigerator for up to 4 days. Reheat on a rimmed baking sheet in a preheated 350°F oven for 5 minutes or until warmed through.

NUTRITIONAL INFORMATION

per serving	257 calories	18 g fat
19 g protein	5 g carbs	1 g fiber

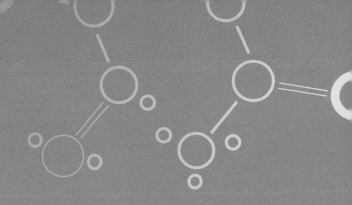

APPETIZERS & SNACKS

SIMPLE CEVICHE WITH AVOCADO

YIELD: 8 servings **PREP TIME:** 5 minutes, plus 2 hours to marinate

1 pound firm white fish fillets, such as snapper or halibut, cut into ½-inch pieces

½ cup freshly squeezed lime juice

1 green bell pepper, diced

1 tomato, diced

¼ cup diced red onions

¼ cup chopped fresh cilantro leaves

1 to 3 tablespoons seeded and minced jalapeño pepper, to desired heat

3 cloves garlic, minced

¾ teaspoon fine sea salt

½ teaspoon ground black pepper

4 drops of orange oil (optional)

2 avocados

Pork rinds, for serving (optional)

Lime wedges, for serving (optional)

1 Place the pieces of fish in an 8-inch square casserole dish and pour the lime juice over them. Stir well to coat. Add the bell pepper, tomato, red onions, cilantro, jalapeño, garlic, salt, black pepper, and orange oil, if using. Cover and refrigerate for 2 to 3 hours, until the fish is no longer pink and translucent; it should be white and opaque.

2 Just before serving, slice the avocados in half, remove the pits, and cut the flesh into ½-inch pieces. Remove the ceviche from the refrigerator and gently fold in the avocado. Serve with pork rinds and lime wedges, if desired.

VARIATION: Ceviche in Avocado Boats.
To turn this into a meal serving four people, serve the ceviche in avocado boats. To make, complete Step 1, and then, instead of dicing the avocados and folding them into the ceviche, simply cut the avocados in half and remove the pits. Slice a very small amount off the bottom of each avocado half to create a flat surface (to keep the "boats" from rocking). Sprinkle the insides of each avocado boat with lime juice and salt; then divide the ceviche among the boats. Note that the calories, fat, protein, carbs, and fiber will double per serving.

NUTRITIONAL INFORMATION		
per serving	164 calories	9 g fat
14 g protein	8 g carbs	4 g fiber

TUNA SALAD ZUCCHINI BITES

OPTION

YIELD: 4 servings   **PREP TIME:** 5 minutes   **COOK TIME:** 15 minutes

1 medium zucchini (about 12 inches long)

1 (7-ounce) can tuna packed in water, drained

3 tablespoons mayonnaise

Fine sea salt and ground black pepper

½ cup shredded sharp cheddar or Monterey Jack cheese (omit for dairy-free)

FOR GARNISH:

Freshly ground black pepper

Fresh herbs of choice

1 Preheat the oven to 375°F.

2 For a pretty presentation (optional), peel the zucchini in alternating strips, leaving strips of green every ¼ inch.

3 Cut the zucchini crosswise into ½-inch rounds. Use a small spoon to scoop out the seeds in the center of each slice.

4 In a bowl, mix together the tuna and mayonnaise, then season with salt and pepper to taste.

5 Place the zucchini slices with the scooped-out sides facing up on a rimmed baking sheet. Fill the divots with the tuna salad and top with the cheese. Bake for 15 minutes, or until the zucchini is fork-tender and the cheese has melted.

6 Remove the zucchini bites from the oven and garnish with freshly ground black pepper and the herbs of your choice.

7 Store leftovers in an airtight container for up to 3 days. Reheat on a rimmed baking sheet in a preheated 350°F oven for a few minutes, until warmed to your liking.

NUTRITIONAL INFORMATION		
per serving 228 calories	16 g fat	
19 g protein	2 g carbs	1 g fiber

BACON-WRAPPED SCALLOPS

OPTION

YIELD: 4 servings   **PREP TIME:** 5 minutes, plus 30 minutes to marinate   **COOK TIME:** 20 minutes

Red Lobster has an amazing appetizer: delicious scallops that are marinated in lots of butter and then wrapped in smoky bacon. What's not to love? This is my keto-friendly version of that dish.

½ cup melted unsalted butter or ghee (or avocado oil if dairy-free)

3 tablespoons freshly squeezed lemon juice

½ teaspoon paprika

½ teaspoon fine sea salt

½ pound scallops

⅓ pound bacon, cut in half crosswise

Chopped fresh chives, for garnish (optional)

Lime slices or wedges, for serving (optional)

1 In a shallow dish, combine the melted butter, lemon juice, paprika, and salt. Add the scallops and toss well to coat; cover and place in the refrigerator to marinate for at least 30 minutes.

2 Preheat the oven to 400°F.

3 Remove the scallops from the marinade and wrap a half-slice of bacon around each scallop. Secure the ends of the bacon with a toothpick. Place the scallops on a rimmed baking sheet and bake for 10 minutes.

4 Flip the scallops and cook for another 8 to 10 minutes, until the bacon is cooked through and the scallops are no longer translucent. Garnish with chives and serve with lime slices, if desired.

5 Store leftovers in an airtight container in the refrigerator for up to 3 days. Reheat on a rimmed baking sheet in a preheated 400°F oven for a few minutes, until warmed to your liking.

NUTRITIONAL INFORMATION		
per serving	429 calories	42 g fat
13 g protein	1 g carbs	0.1 g fiber

SALMON LOG

 YIELD: 12 servings **PREP TIME:** 20 minutes, plus time to chill **COOK TIME:** 35 minutes

½ cup diced onions

½ cup diced red bell peppers

Juice of 1 lemon or lime

1 clove garlic, smashed to a paste

¼ teaspoon paprika, plus more for sprinkling

¼ teaspoon dried thyme leaves

¼ teaspoon cayenne pepper

2 large eggs

¼ cup horseradish mustard

1 tablespoon mayonnaise

1 cup powdered Parmesan cheese (see below)

1 (14.75-ounce) can salmon, drained (see Note)

Fresh herbs, such as cilantro or parsley, for garnish

1 to 2 red bell peppers, cut into cracker-sized pieces, and/or 1 batch Keto Crackers (page 182), for serving

1 Preheat the oven to 350°F.

2 Place the onions, bell peppers, lemon juice, garlic, spices, eggs, horseradish mustard, mayonnaise, and powdered Parmesan cheese in a medium bowl. Stir well to combine. Add the salmon and stir well.

3 Place the salmon mixture on a piece of parchment paper and roll into a 3-inch log. Sprinkle paprika all over the log. Fold the ends of the paper so they're securely closed around the log, tucking in the ends, and place the log on a rimmed baking sheet.

4 Bake for 35 minutes, until the salmon log is firm. Remove from the oven, allow to cool to room temperature, and then place in the refrigerator until chilled, at least 30 minutes. Garnish with fresh herbs and serve with red bell pepper pieces and/or keto crackers.

5 Store leftovers in an airtight container in the refrigerator for up to 3 days.

> **NOTE:** This log is just as delicious made with canned tuna. If using tuna, be sure to buy tuna packed in water to avoid inferior oils.

> **TIP: How to Make Powdered Parmesan Cheese.**
> Powdered Parmesan is simply Parmesan cheese that has been grated to the point of being light, fluffy, and powdery. Fresh pregrated Parmesan cheese available at supermarket cheese counters usually has a powdery texture and can be a convenient option in recipes that call for powdered Parmesan. To make powdered Parmesan at home, place grated Parmesan in a food processor or spice grinder and pulse until it's fluffy and powdery.

NUTRITIONAL INFORMATION		
per serving	99 calories	5 g fat
11 g protein	2 g carbs	1 g fiber

KETO CRACKERS

 YIELD: 12 servings   **PREP TIME:** 8 minutes   **COOK TIME:** 25 minutes

1½ cups grated hard cheese, such as aged Gouda or Parmesan

1½ cups blanched almond flour

¼ teaspoon fine sea salt

3 tablespoons beef broth or water

¼ cup fresh rosemary leaves, roughly chopped (optional)

1   Preheat the oven to 350°F.

2   Place the cheese, almond flour, and salt in a food processor and pulse until well combined.

3   Add 1 tablespoon of broth to the flour mixture and pulse to combine. Add more broth, a tablespoon at a time, and pulse until the ingredients form a firm ball of dough that holds together. (You should not need more than 2 additional tablespoons of broth.)

4   Place the dough on a greased piece of parchment paper and top with another greased piece of parchment. Roll the dough into a thin square, about ⅛ inch thick. Remove the top sheet of parchment. If you're using rosemary leaves, sprinkle them on top of the dough and use the palms of your hands to press them into the dough.

5   Use a pizza cutter or knife to cut the dough into squares, about 1¼ inches, and transfer the parchment with the crackers to a baking sheet.

6   Bake for 25 minutes, or until the crackers are lightly browned. If the crackers are still soft, break them apart along the cut lines and spread them out on the baking sheet, making sure that there's space between the crackers. Bake for an additional 5 minutes.

7   Store leftover crackers in an airtight container in the refrigerator for up to 1 week.

> **VARIATION: Sweet Cinnamon Keto Crackers.**
> To make these crackers sweet, add 1 teaspoon of ground cinnamon to the flour mixture in Step 2, and use water instead of broth when forming the dough in Step 3. Sweeten the dough by adding ¼ cup of Swerve confectioners'-style sweetener or an equivalent amount of powdered sweetener to the dry mixture in Step 2, or use an equivalent amount of liquid sweetener and add it to the dough in Step 3. Omit the rosemary topping.

NUTRITIONAL INFORMATION

per serving	121 calories	10 g fat
7 g protein	3 g carbs	2 g fiber

PICKLE DIP

YIELD: 12 servings   **PREP TIME:** 5 minutes

2 (8-ounce) packages cream cheese, softened

½ pound pastrami, chopped

1 cup diced dill pickles

2 tablespoons dill pickle juice from jar

Fine sea salt and ground black pepper

SERVING SUGGESTIONS:

Sliced bell peppers or cucumbers

Cornichons

Corned beef or pastrami slices, for wrapping

1 Place the softened cream cheese in a medium bowl. Add the chopped pastrami, pickles, and pickle juice and stir until well combined. Season with salt and pepper to taste.

2 Serve with the scoopers or wrappers of your choice.

3 Store leftover dip in an airtight container in the refrigerator for up to 3 days.

NUTRITIONAL INFORMATION		
per serving	161 calories	13 g fat
7 g protein	1 g carbs	0 g fiber

KETO HUMMUS

YIELD: 4 servings   **PREP TIME:** 5 minutes

1 (12-inch) zucchini, peeled, seeded, and cut into chunks

½ cup tahini

1 clove garlic, chopped

2 tablespoons avocado oil, macadamia nut oil, or extra-virgin olive oil, plus more for drizzling

2 tablespoons freshly squeezed lime or lemon juice

1 teaspoon ground cumin

1 teaspoon smoked paprika, plus more for garnish

1 teaspoon fine sea salt

Freshly ground black pepper, for garnish

Red pepper flakes, for garnish

Dried chives, for garnish

SERVING SUGGESTIONS:

Pork rinds

Sliced bell peppers

Sliced cucumbers

1 Place all the ingredients in a blender or food processor and purée until smooth. Taste and adjust the seasonings if needed.

2 Place the hummus in a serving dish and garnish with a drizzle of oil, a sprinkle of paprika, freshly ground black pepper, red pepper flakes, and dried chives. Serve with pork rinds, sliced peppers, and cucumbers, if desired.

3 Store leftover hummus in an airtight container in the refrigerator for up to 3 days.

NUTRITIONAL INFORMATION		
per serving	217 calories	19 g fat
8 g protein	10 g carbs	6 g fiber

PUMPKIN PIE HUMMUS

YIELD: 4 servings   **PREP TIME:** 5 minutes

This sweet hummus tastes great with Sweet Cinnamon Keto Crackers (page 182).

1 (12-inch) zucchini, peeled, seeded, and cut into chunks

½ cup tahini

½ cup pumpkin purée

⅓ cup Swerve confectioners'-style sweetener or equivalent amount of liquid or powdered sweetener

2 tablespoons avocado oil, macadamia nut oil, or extra-virgin olive oil, plus more for drizzling

2 teaspoons pumpkin pie spice

Seeds scraped from 2 vanilla beans (about 8 inches long), or 2 teaspoons vanilla extract

½ teaspoon fine sea salt

Ground cinnamon, for garnish

1 Combine all the ingredients in a blender or food processor and purée until smooth. Taste and adjust the seasonings if needed.

2 Place the hummus in a serving dish and garnish with a drizzle of oil and a sprinkle of cinnamon.

3 Store leftover hummus in an airtight container in the refrigerator for up to 3 days.

NUTRITIONAL INFORMATION

per serving	286 calories	24 g fat
8 g protein	14 g carbs	9 g fiber

PIZZA BITES

YIELD: 4 servings   **PREP TIME:** 5 minutes   **COOK TIME:** 8 minutes

1 (8-ounce) package Canadian bacon

1 cup pizza sauce (see Note)

1 cup shredded mozzarella cheese

1   Preheat the oven to 375°F. Line a rimmed baking sheet with parchment paper.

2   Place 8 slices of Canadian bacon on the lined baking sheet. The slices shouldn't overlap, but they can be touching. Place 2 tablespoons of the pizza sauce on each slice of Canadian bacon. Top with 2 tablespoons of the mozzarella cheese.

3   Bake for 8 minutes, or until the cheese has melted. Remove from the oven and enjoy!

4   Store leftovers in an airtight container in the refrigerator for up to 3 days. Reheat on a rimmed baking sheet in a preheated 375°F oven for a few minutes, until warmed to your liking.

NOTE: When purchasing pizza sauce, check the ingredient list for added sugar and unhealthy oils, such as soybean, canola, or vegetable oil.

NUTRITIONAL INFORMATION		
per serving	167 calories	10 g fat
16 g protein	3 g carbs	1 g fiber

PIZZA DEVILED EGGS

 YIELD: 24 deviled eggs (3 per serving)   **PREP TIME:** 5 minutes   **COOK TIME:** 11 minutes

12 large eggs

1 cup mayonnaise

1 teaspoon pizza sauce

2 teaspoons Italian seasoning, plus more for garnish

½ teaspoon red pepper flakes, plus more for garnish

½ teaspoon fine sea salt

Mini pepperoni slices, for garnish

1   Place the eggs in a large saucepan and cover with cold water. Bring the water to a boil, then immediately cover the pan and remove from the heat. Allow the eggs to cook in the hot water for 11 minutes. Drain the eggs and rinse with very cold water for 1 to 2 minutes to stop the cooking.

2   Peel the boiled eggs and cut them in half lengthwise. Remove the yolks and place them in a food processor. Pulse the yolks until they are the texture of very fine crumbles.

3   Add the mayonnaise, pizza sauce, Italian seasoning, red pepper flakes, and salt and pulse until smooth. Fill the egg white halves with the yolk mixture. Garnish each egg with mini pepperoni slices, Italian seasoning, and red pepper flakes.

4   Store leftovers in an airtight container in the refrigerator for up to 3 days.

> **BUSY FAMILY TIP:** I keep a dozen hard-boiled eggs in my refrigerator at all times. My little boys love to help me in the kitchen. Peeling eggs is one of the things they can do without requiring constant attention, which means I can prepare other food.

NUTRITIONAL INFORMATION		
per serving	291 calories	27 g fat
9 g protein	0.5 g carbs	0 g fiber

GREEK FAT BOMBS

YIELD: 16 fat bombs (2 per serving)   **PREP TIME:** 5 minutes, plus time to chill overnight

1 (8-ounce) package cream cheese, softened

1 cup chopped black olives

¼ cup crumbled feta cheese

3 tablespoons Greek salad dressing, plus more for serving (optional) (see Note)

1 teaspoon Greek seasoning

1 cup finely chopped salami

Cucumber slices, for serving (optional)

1   Place the cream cheese, olives, feta, Greek dressing, and Greek seasoning in a medium bowl and combine until smooth. Cover the bowl with plastic wrap or transfer the mixture to an airtight container and place in the refrigerator to chill overnight.

2   Remove the bowl from the refrigerator. Roll 2 tablespoons of the mixture into a golf ball–sized ball. Roll the ball in the chopped salami and place it on a serving platter. Repeat with the rest of the cream cheese mixture and salami, making a total of 16 fat bombs.

3   Serve the fat bombs with additional Greek dressing and cucumber slices, if desired.

4   Store leftovers in an airtight container in the refrigerator for up to 3 days.

> **NOTE:** When purchasing Greek dressing, make sure that it contains no sugar or soybean oil. My preferred brand is Primal Kitchen.

NUTRITIONAL INFORMATION		
per serving	271 calories	24 g fat
11 g protein	2 g carbs	1 g fiber

TOMATO-BASIL FAT BOMBS

OPTION

YIELD: 16 fat bombs (2 per serving)   **PREP TIME:** 5 minutes, plus time to chill overnight

1 (8-ounce) package cream cheese (or Kite Hill brand cream cheese–style spread if dairy-free), softened

¼ cup powdered Parmesan cheese (see page 180) (or nutritional yeast if dairy-free)

¼ cup marinara sauce (no added sugars)

2 tablespoons chopped fresh basil leaves

Sliced cherry tomatoes, for garnish

Fresh basil leaves, for garnish

1   Place the cream cheese, powdered Parmesan cheese, marinara sauce, and basil in a bowl and combine until smooth. Cover the bowl with plastic wrap or transfer the mixture to an airtight container and place in the refrigerator to chill overnight.

2   Remove the bowl from the refrigerator. Roll 2 tablespoons of the mixture into a golf ball–sized ball and place on a serving platter. Repeat with the rest of the cream cheese mixture, making a total of 16 fat bombs. Garnish with the sliced tomatoes and basil leaves.

3   Store leftovers in an airtight container in the refrigerator for up to 3 days.

NUTRITIONAL INFORMATION		
per serving	116 calories	10 g fat
3 g protein	1 g carbs	0.1 g fiber

SOUPS, SALADS & SIDES

MUSHROOM AND SWISS CHEESEBURGER SOUP

 YIELD: 4 servings **PREP TIME:** 6 minutes **COOK TIME:** 15 minutes

What if I told you when we get a cow from a local farmer we tell the butcher to make it all into ground beef? Even the prize cuts of steak! We love hamburger more than steaks. My kids whine when I make steaks, so why push it? I don't want steaks either. I want hamburgers, sloppy joes, protein noodle lasagna, Keto spaghetti, Paleo chili, easy taco meat . . . you name it. Ground beef and ground venison is how we roll!

2 tablespoons unsalted butter, ghee, or lard

½ cup diced onions

1¼ cups sliced mushrooms

1 pound ground beef (see Note)

1 teaspoon fine sea salt

½ teaspoon ground black pepper

4 ounces cream cheese (½ cup)

½ cup shredded Swiss cheese, plus more for garnish

3 cups beef broth

Melted butter or ghee, for drizzling

Freshly ground black pepper, for garnish

1 Melt the butter in a stockpot over medium heat. Add the onions and mushrooms and sauté for 5 minutes or until the onions are translucent.

2 Add the beef, salt, and pepper. Sauté, breaking up the meat as it cooks, for about 5 minutes, or until the meat is cooked through and no longer pink.

3 Meanwhile place the cream cheese, shredded Swiss cheese, and broth in a blender. Purée until smooth. After the meat has cooked, add the broth mixture to the pot. Heat for 5 minutes or until warm, but do not boil.

4 Divide the soup among bowls and garnish with shredded Swiss cheese, a drizzle of melted ghee, and freshly ground black pepper.

5 Store leftover soup in an airtight container in the refrigerator for up to 3 days. Reheat in a saucepan over medium heat for a few minutes, until warmed to your liking.

> **NOTE:** I am a deer hunter, so along with ground beef, we often have ground venison in our freezer as well. This recipe works great with ground venison, as does any recipe in this book that calls for ground beef. Give it a try!

NUTRITIONAL INFORMATION

per serving	517 calories	42 g fat
28 g protein	5 g carbs	1 g fiber

THE BEST
BROCCOLI SOUP

YIELD: 6 servings   **PREP TIME:** 12 minutes   **COOK TIME:** 15 minutes

2 tablespoons unsalted butter

½ cup diced onions

3 large cloves garlic, minced

6 cups chicken broth

5 cups broccoli florets, plus more for garnish

1 teaspoon fine sea salt

1 avocado, peeled and pitted

¾ cup heavy cream

½ cup sour cream

1 Melt the butter in a stockpot over medium heat. Add the onions and garlic and sauté until softened and translucent, about 3 minutes.

2 Add the chicken broth, broccoli, and salt and bring to a boil. Reduce the heat, cover, and simmer until the broccoli is tender, about 12 minutes.

3 Add the avocado to the soup and use a stick blender to purée the soup. (If using a blender, work in batches: Place one-quarter of the avocado and one-quarter of the soup in the blender and purée until very smooth. Repeat with the remaining avocado and soup, then pour the puréed soup back in the pot.)

4 Stir in the heavy cream and sour cream. Heat on low heat just until warmed. Taste and adjust the seasoning to your liking.

5 Serve with a broccoli floret in the middle of each bowl.

6 Store leftover soup in an airtight container in the refrigerator for up to 3 days. Reheat in a saucepan over medium heat for a few minutes, until warmed to your liking.

NUTRITIONAL INFORMATION		
per serving	331 calories	30 g fat
7 g protein	11 g carbs	5 g fiber

FRENCH DIP SOUP

OPTION

YIELD: 8 servings   **PREP TIME:** 15 minutes   **COOK TIME:** 10 minutes, plus 6 to 8 hours in a slow cooker

¼ cup (½ stick) unsalted butter (or coconut oil if dairy-free)

1 cup chopped onions

3 cloves garlic, minced

2 pounds boneless sirloin steak, cut into 1-inch cubes

1 teaspoon fine sea salt

¾ teaspoon ground black pepper

6 cups beef broth

1 teaspoon fish sauce (optional)

2 cups sliced mushrooms

1 green bell pepper, sliced thin

¼ teaspoon cayenne pepper

1 cup shredded provolone cheese (omit for dairy-free)

1   Heat the butter in a large skillet over medium-high heat. Add the onions and garlic and cook until soft, 3 to 5 minutes. Use a slotted spoon to transfer the onions and garlic to a 4-quart slow cooker, leaving the remaining butter in the skillet.

2   Season the steak on all sides with the salt and pepper. Using the same pan in which you cooked the onions, sear the steak cubes on all sides over medium-high heat until the meat is dark golden brown.

3   Add the steak, broth, fish sauce (if using), mushrooms, green pepper, and cayenne pepper to the slow cooker. Cover and cook on low for 6 to 8 hours, or until the meat is very tender.

4   Just before serving, preheat the oven to 400°F. Ladle the soup into oven-safe bowls, and place the bowls on a rimmed baking sheet. Top each bowl with the shredded provolone cheese and bake for 4 minutes, or until the cheese is bubbly.

5   Store leftover soup in an airtight container in the refrigerator for up to 3 days. Reheat in a saucepan over medium heat for a few minutes, until warmed to your liking.

NUTRITIONAL INFORMATION		
per serving 252 calories		18 g fat
18 g protein	4 g carbs	1 g fiber

SHRIMP AND BACON BISQUE

OPTION

YIELD: 6 servings   **PREP TIME:** 8 minutes   **COOK TIME:** 20 minutes

6 slices bacon, diced

1 cup chopped leeks, white and green parts

1 pound large shrimp, peeled and deveined

1 teaspoon Old Bay seasoning

3 cloves garlic, minced

1 (8-ounce) package cream cheese (or Kite Hill brand cream cheese–style spread if dairy-free)

6 cups chicken or fish broth

¾ cup tomato sauce

1 lime or lemon, cut into 8 wedges

Fine sea salt and ground black pepper

Melted butter or ghee (or extra-virgin olive oil if dairy-free), for drizzling (optional)

1   Heat a stockpot over medium-high heat. Add the diced bacon and sauté, stirring occasionally, until it is slightly crispy, about 3 minutes. Add the leeks and cook for another 4 minutes or until the leeks are tender.

2   Season the shrimp on all sides with the Old Bay seasoning. Add the shrimp and garlic to the pot and sauté until the shrimp has turned pink, about 4 minutes.

3   Place the cream cheese, broth, tomato sauce, and three-quarters of the cooked shrimp in a blender and purée until smooth. Add the purée to the pot and stir well. Simmer on medium-low for 5 minutes.

4   Squeeze one of the lime or lemon wedges into the pot. Taste the bisque and adjust the seasoning to your liking. Ladle into bowls and serve with the remaining lime or lemon wedges. Drizzle with melted butter, if desired.

5   Store leftover soup in an airtight container in the refrigerator for up to 3 days. Reheat in a saucepan over medium heat for 5 minutes, until warmed to your liking.

NUTRITIONAL INFORMATION

per serving	477 calories	36 g fat
30 g protein	8 g carbs	1 g fiber

LEMON PEPPER CHICKEN STEW

OPTION

YIELD: 8 servings   **PREP TIME:** 10 minutes   **COOK TIME:** 12 minutes

8 boneless, skinless chicken thighs, cut into ½-inch pieces

1½ teaspoons fine sea salt

1½ teaspoons ground black pepper

¼ cup ghee or unsalted butter (or coconut oil if dairy-free)

¾ cup diced onions

¾ cup chopped celery

1 (10-inch) zucchini, cut into ½-inch chunks

2½ cups chicken broth

4 ounces cream cheese (½ cup) (or Kite Hill brand cream cheese–style spread if dairy-free)

2 teaspoons grated lemon zest

Juice of 2 lemons

FOR GARNISH:

Melted ghee or butter (or extra-virgin olive oil if dairy-free), for drizzling

Freshly ground black pepper

Lemon wedges

1 Season the chicken pieces on all sides with the salt and pepper.

2 Melt the ghee in a stockpot over medium-high heat. Add the onion, celery, and zucchini and cook, stirring occasionally, for 3 minutes. Add the chicken and cook, stirring occasionally, until the chicken is cooked through and no longer pink inside, about 4 minutes.

3 While the chicken cooks, purée the broth and cream cheese in a blender until smooth.

4 Add the broth mixture, lemon zest, and lemon juice to the stockpot. Simmer over medium heat for 5 minutes. Season to taste with salt, if needed. Ladle into soup bowls and garnish with melted ghee, freshly ground pepper, and lemon wedges.

5 Store leftover stew in an airtight container in the refrigerator for up to 3 days. Reheat in a saucepan over medium heat for a few minutes, until warmed to your liking.

NUTRITIONAL INFORMATION		
per serving	320 calories	23 g fat
25 g protein	3 g carbs	1 g fiber

CREAM OF ASPARAGUS SOUP

YIELD: 6 servings   **PREP TIME:** 5 minutes   **COOK TIME:** 20 minutes

6 tablespoons (¾ stick) unsalted butter

1½ pounds fresh asparagus, tough ends removed and spears cut into 1-inch pieces

1 cup chopped onions

1 teaspoon fine sea salt

½ teaspoon ground white pepper

6 cups chicken or vegetable broth

2 ounces cream cheese (¼ cup)

1 teaspoon dried dill weed

Purple sea salt, pink rock salt, or other rock salt, for garnish (see Note)

1   Melt the butter in a large stockpot over medium heat. Add the asparagus and onions and sauté for 8 minutes, or until the asparagus is softened but not fully cooked. Season with the salt and pepper. Remove the asparagus tips from the pot and set them aside to use as garnish. Add the broth and cook for 8 minutes, or until the asparagus is tender. Remove the pot from the heat and cool slightly.

2   Place the cream cheese in a blender, then pour in the soup, working in batches if needed; purée until very smooth.

3   Return the puréed soup to the pot and add the dill weed. Heat the soup gently; don't boil it. Ladle the soup into bowls and garnish it with the asparagus tips and a sprinkle of purple salt.

4   Store leftover soup in an airtight container in the refrigerator for up to 4 days. Reheat in a saucepan over medium heat for a few minutes, until warmed to your liking.

> **NOTE:** I like to collect different salts when I travel. If you do not have purple salt, any salt will work for garnish.

NUTRITIONAL INFORMATION

per serving	234 calories	21 g fat
6 g protein	6 g carbs	1 g fiber

DECONSTRUCTED COBB SALAD

OPTION

YIELD: 4 servings   **PREP TIME:** 15 minutes, plus 2 hours to chill dressing

To make this salad even easier to prepare, pick up a roasted chicken and some hard-boiled eggs from the grocery!

RANCH DRESSING:

Makes ¾ cup

4 ounces cream cheese (½ cup), softened (or mayonnaise if dairy-free)

¼ cup beef or chicken broth

½ teaspoon dried chives

½ teaspoon dried parsley

½ teaspoon dried dill weed

¼ teaspoon garlic powder

¼ teaspoon onion powder

⅛ teaspoon fine sea salt

⅛ teaspoon ground black pepper

COBB STACK:

2 hard-boiled eggs, diced

¼ cup mayonnaise

Fine sea salt and ground black pepper

1 cup guacamole

1 cup chopped romaine lettuce

1 cup diced cooked chicken thighs

4 strips bacon, diced and fried until crispy

¼ cup blue cheese crumbles (omit for dairy-free)

Snipped fresh chives, for garnish (optional)

1   To make the ranch dressing, place all the ingredients a bowl and stir well until combined. Cover and refrigerate for 2 hours before serving (it will thicken as it rests).

2   In a medium bowl, combine the hard-boiled eggs, mayonnaise, and salt and pepper to taste.

3   To assemble, place ¼ cup of the guacamole in the center of a small serving plate and spread into a thick 3- to 4-inch circle. Top the guacamole with ¼ cup of the chopped romaine, followed by ¼ cup of the diced chicken, one-quarter of the egg salad mixture, one-quarter of the bacon pieces, and a tablespoon of blue cheese crumbles. Repeat with the remaining ingredients to make a total of four stacks. Before serving, drizzle each salad with the dressing. Garnish with a sprinkle of fresh chives, if desired.

4   Store leftovers in an airtight container in the refrigerator for up to 3 days.

BUSY FAMILY TIP: Ranch dressing is a favorite in my family, so it's featured in a few recipes in this book (see pages 232 and 246). To have extra on hand and save prep time later, I recommend you make a double batch. It will keep for up to 6 days in the refrigerator.

NUTRITIONAL INFORMATION

per serving	622 calories	51 g fat
30 g protein	8 g carbs	5 g fiber

CAPRESE SALAD

 YIELD: 4 servings   **PREP TIME:** 5 minutes

2 medium tomatoes, sliced ¼ inch thick

1 pound fresh mozzarella, sliced ¼ inch thick

20 fresh basil leaves

¼ cup avocado oil or extra-virgin olive oil

½ teaspoon fine sea salt

½ teaspoon ground black pepper

1 On a platter with a defined edge (to contain the oil), layer, at an angle and slightly overlapping, a slice of tomato, a slice of mozzarella, and a basil leaf.

2 Repeat with the remaining slices of tomato, mozzarella, and basil.

3 Drizzle the olive oil over the stacks and season with salt and pepper to taste.

4 Store leftovers in an airtight container in the refrigerator for up to 3 days.

NUTRITIONAL INFORMATION		
per serving 150 calories		11 g fat
13 g protein	4 g carbs	2 g fiber

BLACK-AND-BLUE SALAD

YIELD: 4 servings   **PREP TIME:** 5 minutes, plus 5 minutes for the steak to rest   **COOK TIME:** 4 minutes

1 pound flank steak or skirt steak

Fine sea salt and ground black pepper

2 teaspoons ghee or avocado oil

DRESSING:

3 tablespoons freshly squeezed lime or lemon juice

6 tablespoons avocado oil or extra-virgin olive oil

2 teaspoons Dijon mustard

Fine sea salt and ground black pepper

4 cups chopped romaine lettuce

1 cup cherry tomatoes, halved

¼ red onion, sliced into rings

1 avocado, sliced

4 ounces blue cheese, crumbled

1   Remove the steak from the refrigerator and allow it to come to room temperature. Season all sides generously with salt and pepper.

2   Heat a large cast-iron skillet over medium-high heat; then melt the ghee in the pan.

3   Sear the steak for 2 minutes, then flip it and cook it for another 2 minutes for medium-rare steak (or until done to your liking). Remove the steak from the skillet and place it on a cutting board to rest for 5 minutes.

4   While the steak cooks, make the dressing: Place the lime juice, avocado oil, and Dijon mustard in a small bowl. Whisk to combine; then add salt and pepper to taste.

5   Place the romaine in a large serving bowl. Top with the tomato, red onion, avocado, and blue cheese. Drizzle with the dressing.

6   Cut the steak across the grain into ¼-inch slices and place on the salad.

7   Store leftover salad and steak in separate airtight containers in the refrigerator for up to 3 days.

NUTRITIONAL INFORMATION		
per serving	457 calories	31 g fat
34 g protein	12 g carbs	6 g fiber

SIMPLE SUMMER GREEK SALAD

OPTION

YIELD: 4 servings   **PREP TIME:** 10 minutes

1 small zucchini, cut into ¼-inch pieces

1 yellow bell pepper, cut into ½-inch pieces

1 cup cherry tomatoes, halved

1 cup pitted black olives

1 cup ½-inch-diced salami

2 ounces feta cheese, cut into ¼-inch dice (omit for dairy-free)

Fine sea salt and ground black pepper

¼ cup Greek salad dressing

Fresh oregano, for garnish

1 Place the zucchini, bell pepper, tomatoes, olives, salami, and feta in a large serving bowl. Season well with salt and pepper.

2 Drizzle the salad with the Greek dressing and toss gently to coat. Garnish with fresh oregano.

3 Store leftovers in an airtight container in the refrigerator for up to 3 days.

> **NOTE:** When purchasing Greek dressing, make sure that it contains no sugar or soybean oil. My preferred brand is Primal Kitchen.

NUTRITIONAL INFORMATION		
per serving	386 calories	33 g fat
17 g protein	6 g carbs	1 g fiber

DEVILED EGG SALAD
WITH BACON VINAIGRETTE

 YIELD: 6 servings (4 deviled eggs per serving) **PREP TIME:** 15 minutes **COOK TIME:** 15 minutes

DEVILED EGGS:

12 large eggs

¼ cup mayonnaise

½ small avocado, puréed

2 teaspoons coconut vinegar or red wine vinegar

½ teaspoon fine sea salt

BACON VINAIGRETTE:

4 slices bacon, cut into ¼-inch dice

2 tablespoons diced onions

3 tablespoons plus 2 teaspoons coconut vinegar or red wine vinegar, divided

2 tablespoons Swerve confectioners'-style sweetener or equivalent amount of liquid or powdered sweetener (optional)

1 teaspoon Dijon mustard

3 tablespoons MCT oil or extra-virgin olive oil

Fine sea salt and ground black pepper

FOR THE SALAD:

6 cups mixed greens

1 small tomato, diced

Cooked diced bacon (from above)

4 ounces blue cheese, crumbled (omit for dairy-free)

1 small green onion, sliced

1 tablespoon chopped fresh chives

1 Place the eggs in a large saucepan and cover with cold water. Bring the water to a boil, then immediately cover the pan and remove from the heat. Allow the eggs to cook in the hot water for 11 minutes.

2 Meanwhile, make the vinaigrette: Cook the diced bacon in a skillet over medium heat until crisp, about 5 minutes. Use a slotted spoon to remove the bacon from the skillet and set aside for the salad; leave the drippings in the pan. Add the onions, 3 tablespoons of the vinegar, sweetener (if using), and mustard to the pan. Cook over medium heat until the onions soften, about 2 minutes. Slowly add the oil to the pan, whisking as you add it. Whisk well to combine. Season with salt and pepper to taste. Set the vinaigrette aside.

3 When the eggs have cooked for 11 minutes, drain the hot water and rinse the eggs with very cold water for 1 to 2 minutes to stop the cooking. Peel the boiled eggs and cut them in half lengthwise.

4 Make the deviled eggs: Remove the yolks from the whites and place them in a bowl (or a food processor). Mash or blend the egg yolks with a fork (or pulse in the food processor) until they are the texture of very fine crumbles. To the yolks, add the mayonnaise, 2 teaspoons of vinegar, avocado, and salt; stir to combine. Fill the egg white halves with the yolk mixture.

5 To serve, dress the lettuce with the bacon vinaigrette (see Note) and divide it among 6 plates. Place 4 deviled eggs on each plate. Sprinkle the deviled eggs with the diced tomato, reserved diced bacon, blue cheese, sliced green onion, and chopped chives.

6 Store leftover salad, undressed, in an airtight container in the refrigerator for up to 3 days.

> **NOTE:** If you're not serving the salad immediately, do not dress the lettuce with the vinaigrette until you're ready to serve the dish. You can store the vinaigrette in an airtight jar in the refrigerator for up to 5 days.

BUSY FAMILY TIP: I keep a dozen hard-boiled eggs in my refrigerator at all times. My boys, who are four and six, love to help me in the kitchen, and peeling eggs is one of the things they can do without requiring constant attention, which frees me to prepare other food.

NUTRITIONAL INFORMATION		
per serving	364 calories	30 g fat
17 g protein	6 g carbs	2 g fiber

TURKEY AND BLUE CHEESE SALAD WITH BACON VINAIGRETTE

YIELD: 2 servings   **PREP TIME:** 5 minutes   **COOK TIME:** 5 minutes

One of my favorite salad dressings is Bacon Vinaigrette. I can't get enough of it. I like to use it in this recipe as well as in my Deviled Egg Salad.

1 small head romaine lettuce

2 cups cubed leftover roasted turkey

½ cup quartered cherry tomatoes

4 ounces blue cheese, crumbled

1 batch Bacon Vinaigrette (page 216)

Sliced green onions, for garnish

1   Slice the head of lettuce into quarters, leaving the stem intact to hold the leaves together. Place the lettuce on a serving platter and top with the cubed turkey, tomatoes, and blue cheese. Drizzle with the vinaigrette and garnish with the green onions.

2   Store leftover salad and dressing in separate airtight containers in the refrigerator for up to 3 days.

NUTRITIONAL INFORMATION		
per serving	701 calories	47 g fat
53 g protein	7 g carbs	3 g fiber

BROCCOLI SLAW

OPTION

YIELD: 8 servings   **PREP TIME:** 10 minutes

SIMPLE COLESLAW DRESSING:

1½ cups mayonnaise

2 teaspoons Dijon mustard

2 teaspoons freshly squeezed lemon juice

1 tablespoon plus 1 teaspoon coconut vinegar or apple cider vinegar

¼ cup Swerve confectioners'-style sweetener or equivalent amount of liquid or powdered sweetener (optional)

½ teaspoon fine sea salt

½ teaspoon ground black pepper

½ teaspoon celery seeds

½ teaspoon dried chives

COLESLAW:

1 (1-pound) bag broccoli slaw (about 4 cups)

¼ cup chopped kale

¼ cup chopped radicchio (for lovely purple color)

Fine sea salt and ground black pepper

¼ cup roasted and salted sunflower seeds, for garnish

2 tablespoons slivered almonds, for garnish (omit for nut-free)

1. To make the dressing, place all the ingredients for the dressing in a small bowl and stir well to combine.

2. To make the coleslaw, place the broccoli slaw, kale, and radicchio in a large bowl. Pour the dressing over the slaw and toss gently to coat.

3. Season to taste with salt and pepper and garnish with the sunflower seeds and almonds.

4. Store leftover slaw in an airtight container in the refrigerator for up to 3 days.

NUTRITIONAL INFORMATION		
per serving	292 calories	29 g fat
3 g protein	6 g carbs	2 g fiber

PARMESAN BASIL ASPARAGUS

 YIELD: 4 servings   **PREP TIME:** 4 minutes   **COOK TIME:** 10 to 20 minutes

1 lemon, sliced

1 pound asparagus, tough ends removed

2 tablespoons melted unsalted butter or ghee

½ teaspoon fine sea salt

¼ teaspoon ground black pepper

5 cloves garlic, minced

¼ cup chopped fresh basil leaves, plus more for garnish (optional)

1 cup grated Parmesan cheese

1   Preheat the oven to 400°F.

2   Place the lemon slices in a single layer on a rimmed baking sheet. Top with a single layer of the asparagus, then drizzle the asparagus with the melted butter. Season with the salt and pepper. Top the asparagus with the garlic and basil.

3   Bake for 10 to 20 minutes, until the asparagus is crisp-tender. The time depends on how thick the asparagus is.

4   Remove from the oven and sprinkle the Parmesan on the asparagus. Place back in the oven for 1 minute, or until the cheese is melted. Serve garnished with additional fresh basil, if desired.

5   This dish is best served fresh, but you can store leftovers in an airtight container in the refrigerator for up to 3 days. To reheat, place on a rimmed baking sheet in a 400°F oven for a few minutes, until warmed to your liking.

NUTRITIONAL INFORMATION		
per serving	174 calories	13 g fat
9 g protein	5 g carbs	1 g fiber

CAULIFLOWER AREPAS

YIELD: 2 servings   **PREP TIME:** 4 minutes   **COOK TIME:** 10 minutes

Have you ever had an arepa? If not, you are in for a real treat! Arepas are a common staple in Colombia and Venezuela. You can eat them as a side, alongside a meal, or split them and stuff them with fillings such as cheese or avocado. I love scrambled eggs, chili, and salsa in mine!

Not only are these low-carb cauliflower arepas super easy to make, but they taste amazing as leftovers! I suggest making a double or triple batch and storing them in the refrigerator for easy sandwiches.

1½ cups riced cauliflower

1 large egg

2 cups grated Parmesan or other hard cheese

Butter, ghee, or lard, for the pan

Fillings of choice (optional)

1   Preheat the oven to 425°F. Grease a cookie sheet.

2   In a food processor, blend the cauliflower, egg, and cheese until a thick dough forms.

3   Form the dough into 6 discs about ½ inch thick and 2½ inches in diameter.

4   Place the discs on the greased cookie sheet and bake for 10 to 12 minutes, until the edges are brown. Remove from the oven. If they flattened a little during baking, just cup them with your hands while still warm to reform them into 2½-inch discs. Before the cheese hardens, the arepas are very flexible. Let cool before slicing.

5   Just before serving, slice the discs in half. Melt a tablespoon of butter in a cast-iron skillet over medium-high heat and place the arepa halves cut side down in the skillet. Fry for 2 minutes, then flip and fry for another 2 minutes, or until golden brown. Stuff with the fillings of your choice, if desired.

6   Store leftovers in an airtight container in the refrigerator for up to 4 days.

NUTRITIONAL INFORMATION		
per serving	398 calories	25 g fat
35 g protein	8 g carbs	3 g fiber

KETO GRITS

YIELD: 2 servings   **PREP TIME:** 2 minutes   **COOK TIME:** 4 minutes

If you own some of my other cookbooks, you are likely already familiar with these indispensable keto grits. I find that they have a million uses and go with just about any flavor or type of cuisine.

4 large eggs

¼ cup beef broth

½ teaspoon fine sea salt

¼ cup (½ stick) unsalted butter

¼ cup shredded sharp cheddar cheese (about 1 ounce)

1   In a small bowl, whisk together the eggs, broth, and salt.

2   Melt the butter in a medium saucepan over medium heat. Add the egg mixture and cook until the mixture thickens and small curds form, scraping the bottom of the pan and stirring to keep large curds from forming. (A whisk works well for this task.)

3   Add the cheese and stir until well combined. Remove from the heat and transfer to a serving bowl.

4   Store leftovers in an airtight container in the refrigerator for up to 4 days. To reheat, place in a greased skillet over medium heat, stirring often, for 5 minutes or until heated through.

NUTRITIONAL INFORMATION

per serving	36 calories	2 g fat
4 g protein	0.5 g carbs	0 g fiber

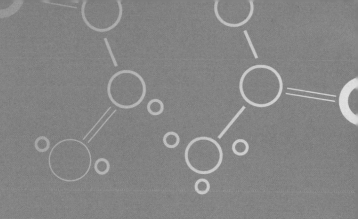

MAIN DISHES

WALLEYE
IN LEMON CREAM

OPTION

YIELD: 4 servings   **PREP TIME:** 5 minutes   **COOK TIME:** 10 minutes

2 tablespoons ghee or unsalted butter (or coconut oil if dairy-free)

½ cup diced onions

1 clove garlic, smashed to a paste

1 pound walleye fillets, cut into 2-ounce pieces

1 teaspoon fine sea salt

¼ teaspoon ground black pepper

¼ cup fish or chicken broth

¼ cup heavy cream (or full-fat coconut milk if dairy-free)

2 tablespoons chopped fresh parsley leaves, plus more for garnish

2 lemons

1   Melt the ghee in a large cast-iron skillet over medium heat. Add the onions and garlic and sauté until fragrant, 2 to 3 minutes.

2   Season the fish fillets on both sides with the salt and pepper. Add the fish, broth, cream, and parsley to the skillet. Simmer, uncovered, for 7 minutes, or until the fillets are opaque in the center and start to flake.

3   Juice one of the lemons and thinly slice the remaining lemon. Line a serving platter with the lemon slices, then pour the juice into the pan with the fish.

4   Top the sliced lemons on the serving platter with the fish and cover with the sauce. Garnish with the additional parsley. (*Note:* If you prefer a thicker sauce, remove the fish from the pan and place it on the platter; boil the sauce for 10 minutes or until thickened to your liking, then pour it over the fish and garnish with parsley.)

5   Store leftovers in an airtight container in the refrigerator for up to 3 days. To reheat, place in a greased skillet over medium heat for a few minutes, until warmed to your liking.

NUTRITIONAL INFORMATION		
per serving	245 calories	15 g fat
23 g protein	4 g carbs	1 g fiber

CHICKEN, BACON, AND RANCH ZUCCHINI BOATS

OPTION

YIELD: 4 servings   **PREP TIME:** 5 minutes   **COOK TIME:** 20 minutes

2 (12-inch) zucchini

2 cups chopped cooked chicken

6 tablespoons mayonnaise

Fine sea salt and ground black pepper

¼ cup diced tomatoes

1 cup shredded sharp cheddar or Monterey Jack cheese (omit for dairy-free)

4 slices bacon, diced

½ cup Ranch Dressing (page 208) (or dairy-free ranch if dairy-free), for drizzling

Chopped fresh chives, for garnish

1   Preheat the oven to 375°F.

2   Cut the zucchini in half lengthwise and scoop out the middle where the seeds are. Place the zucchini, cut side up, on a rimmed baking sheet.

3   Place the chopped chicken and mayonnaise in a medium bowl. Stir well to combine. Season to taste with salt and pepper.

4   Fill the zucchini with the chicken salad. Cover each boat with diced tomato and cheese. Bake for 20 minutes, or until the zucchini is fork-tender.

5   Meanwhile, cook the bacon in a cast-iron skillet over medium heat until it's crisp and cooked through, about 4 minutes. Use a slotted spoon to remove the bacon from the pan and set aside.

6   Remove the zucchini from the oven and garnish with the ranch dressing, reserved bacon, and chives.

7   Store leftovers in an airtight container in the refrigerator for up to 3 days. To reheat, place on a baking sheet in a 375°F oven for 5 minutes or until heated through.

> **NOTE:** A good store-bought option for dairy-free ranch is the Primal Kitchen brand.

NUTRITIONAL INFORMATION		
per serving	667 calories	51 g fat
47 g protein	5 g carbs	1 g fiber

GREEK PORK CHOPS

YIELD: 4 servings   **PREP TIME:** 15 minutes   **COOK TIME:** 7 minutes

PORK CHOPS:

4 (4-ounce) boneless pork chops, about 1 inch thick

2 tablespoons coconut oil or ghee

Fine sea salt and ground black pepper

FETA CHEESE SAUCE:

Makes 1 cup (3 tablespoons per serving)

3 ounces feta cheese

¼ to ½ cup beef or chicken broth

¼ cup MCT oil or extra-virgin olive oil

2 tablespoons coconut vinegar

¼ teaspoon minced garlic, or ½ head roasted garlic, cloves squeezed from the head

1 teaspoon dried oregano leaves

½ teaspoon fine sea salt

FOR SERVING:

1 cup chopped cucumbers

1 cup pitted black olives, chopped

¼ cup capers

¼ cup finely diced red onions

¼ cup crumbled feta cheese

1. Preheat a cast-iron skillet over medium-high heat. Generously season both sides of the pork chops with salt and pepper. Heat the oil in the hot pan, then sear the chops for about 3½ minutes. Flip the chops over and continue to cook for another 3½ minutes or until there is barely any pink visible in the center (or the internal temperature of the chops reaches 145°F on an instant-read thermometer).

2. While the chops cook, make the sauce: Place all the sauce ingredients in a jar and shake vigorously until very smooth.

3. Plate the chops with one-quarter each of the chopped cucumber and black olives. Drizzle each chop with 3 tablespoons of the sauce and sprinkle the plates with the capers, red onions, and feta cheese.

4. Store leftover chops in an airtight container in the refrigerator for up to 3 days, and store extra sauce in a separate airtight container in the refrigerator for up to 1 week. To reheat, place the chops in a greased skillet over medium heat for a few minutes, until warmed to your liking.

> **NOTE:** This recipe makes more feta cheese sauce than you'll need for four pork chops. Store the extra sauce in an airtight container in the refrigerator for up to 1 week. It tastes great over a bed of greens! Shake well before using.

NUTRITIONAL INFORMATION

per serving	424 calories	30 g fat
33 g protein	4 g carbs	1 g fiber

TURKEY LEGS WITH LEMON GRAVY AND CAULIFLOWER PILAF

OPTION

YIELD: 4 servings **PREP TIME:** 15 minutes **COOK TIME:** 1 hour 55 minutes

TURKEY LEGS:

4 turkey legs

1½ teaspoons fine sea salt

1 teaspoon ground black pepper

2 tablespoons ghee (or coconut oil if dairy-free)

½ cup diced onions

¼ cup diced celery

2 sprigs fresh thyme

1 sprig fresh rosemary

2 bay leaves

1½ cups turkey or chicken broth

2 lemons

⅛ teaspoon guar gum (optional, for thickening)

CAULIFLOWER PILAF:

1 small head cauliflower, cut into florets (about 3 cups)

2 tablespoons butter or ghee (or coconut oil if dairy-free)

2 tablespoons diced onions

1 clove garlic, minced

Fine sea salt and ground black pepper

Freshly ground black pepper, for garnish (optional)

1 Preheat the oven to 300°F.

2 Preheat a large cast-iron skillet over medium-high heat. Season the turkey legs on all sides with the salt and pepper. Place the ghee in the hot pan. Add the legs and sear on all sides until golden brown, about 3 minutes per side. Remove the turkey legs from the skillet and set aside.

3 Place the onions, celery, and herbs in the skillet and cook over medium-high heat for 4 minutes, or until the onions are translucent. Place the veggies in a roasting pan and top with the turkey legs.

4 Add the broth to the roasting pan. Cut the lemons in half and squeeze the juice into the pan; then add the cut lemons to the pan. Roast, uncovered, for about 1 hour 40 minutes.

5 When there is about 30 minutes of roasting time left for the turkey legs, make the cauliflower pilaf: Place the cauliflower florets in a food processor and pulse a few times until the cauliflower is the size of small grains of rice. Alternatively, you can use the largest holes on a box grater to grate the cauliflower into small pieces.

6 Place the butter in the same skillet and heat over medium heat. Add the onions and sauté for 4 minutes, or until the onions are translucent. Add the garlic and cook for 1 more minute. Add the riced cauliflower and cook for 4 minutes, until softened. Remove from the heat. Stir well and season to taste with salt and pepper.

7 To serve, divide the pilaf among 4 plates. Place a turkey leg on each plate, along with half a roasted lemon, if desired. If you prefer a thicker gravy, whisk in the guar gum and heat the gravy on the stovetop over medium-high heat for 1 minute. Divide the gravy among the plates and garnish with freshly ground black pepper, if desired.

8 Store leftover turkey legs in an airtight container in the refrigerator for up to 3 days. To reheat, place on a rimmed baking sheet in a preheated 300°F oven for a few minutes, until warmed to your liking.

NUTRITIONAL INFORMATION		
per serving	563 calories	21 g fat
78 g protein	14 g carbs	5 g fiber

GREEK MEATLOAF

YIELD: 6 servings   **PREP TIME:** 15 minutes   **COOK TIME:** 55 minutes

When I was little, I dreaded meatloaf night. I probably would have liked it if I would have given it a chance, but I seriously think the name turned me off! I love meatloaf now. It's like a gigantic hamburger. Who wouldn't want that? I officially am renaming meatloaf "Gigantic Hamburger Loaf"! Instead of using breadcrumbs or cracker crumbs, I use an egg for the binder, along with finely chopped mushrooms (don't worry, you can't even taste them, but they make the meatloaf very moist) and grated Parmesan cheese. Mushrooms and aged cheeses have something called umami, which is a pleasant, savory taste produced by glutamate and ribonucleotides—chemicals that occur naturally in many foods. Umami is subtle and not generally identified by people when they encounter it, but it blends well with other tastes to intensify and enhance flavors and plays an important role in making food taste delicious.

MEATLOAF:

1½ pounds ground lamb or beef

1½ cups ¼-inch-diced feta cheese

¾ cup finely chopped button mushrooms

½ cup diced red onions

½ cup powdered Parmesan cheese (see page 180)

¼ cup tomato sauce

1 large egg

¼ cup diced black olives

1 teaspoon Greek seasoning

1 teaspoon dried oregano leaves

1 clove garlic, minced

GLAZE:

¼ cup tomato sauce

2 tablespoons whole-grain mustard

1 teaspoon freshly squeezed lemon juice

2 tablespoons Swerve confectioners'-style sweetener or equivalent amount of liquid or powdered sweetener

1 teaspoon smoked paprika

¼ teaspoon cayenne pepper

¼ teaspoon ground cinnamon

1   Preheat the oven to 350°F.

2   Put all the ingredients for the meatloaf in a large bowl. Using your hands, mix everything together until well combined. Press the meatloaf mixture into an 8 by 4-inch loaf pan.

3   Make the glaze: Place all the ingredients for the glaze in a small bowl and whisk until well combined.

4   Spread the glaze on the meatloaf and bake for 55 minutes, or until the internal temperature reaches 160°F.

5   Store leftovers in an airtight container in the refrigerator for up to 3 days. To reheat, place ½-inch-thick slices of the meatloaf on a rimmed baking sheet in a preheated 375°F oven for a few minutes, until warmed to your liking.

NUTRITIONAL INFORMATION		
per serving	390 calories	28 g fat
27 g protein	6 g carbs	1 g fiber

BRAISED DUCK LEGS
WITH LEMON AND THYME

OPTION

YIELD: 4 servings **PREP TIME:** 7 minutes **COOK TIME:** 25 minutes

4 bone-in, skin-on duck legs
(about 2 pounds)

Fine sea salt and ground black
pepper

¼ cup ghee or coconut oil

2 tablespoons minced shallots

2 sprigs fresh thyme, plus more
for garnish

1 bay leaf

1 lemon, sliced thin

Freshly ground black pepper, for
garnish

1 Preheat a large heavy skillet over medium-high heat. Season the duck legs liberally on all sides with salt and pepper. Place the ghee in the hot pan. When the ghee is hot, place the legs in the skillet, skin side down. Cook until the skin is golden brown and crisp, about 8 minutes. Flip the legs and cook for another 5 minutes, or until golden.

2 Add the shallots, thyme, and bay leaf and cook for 2 more minutes. Cut the lemon into wedges. Squirt in the juice from 1 lemon and add the wedges to the skillet; cook for another 10 minutes, or until the duck is no longer pink in the center (or the internal temperature reaches 180°F on an instant-read thermometer).

3 Remove the legs from the skillet and place on a serving platter to rest for 10 minutes. Spoon the drippings from the skillet over the legs. Garnish with freshly ground black pepper and sprigs of thyme.

4 Store leftovers in an airtight container in the refrigerator for up to 3 days. To reheat, place in a baking dish in a preheated 350°F oven for 5 minutes, or until warmed to your liking.

> **VARIATION: Braised Chicken Thighs with Lemon and Thyme.** You can make this recipe with chicken thighs instead of duck legs, if you prefer. Simply replace the duck legs with 2 pounds of bone-in, skin-on chicken thighs and follow the recipe as written.

NUTRITIONAL INFORMATION

per serving	435 calories	30 g fat
37 g protein	2 g carbs	1 g fiber

EASY BEEF BRISKET WITH KETO GREMOLATA

OPTION

YIELD: 12 servings   **PREP TIME:** 4 minutes   **COOK TIME:** 3½ to 4 hours

4 pounds beef brisket

2½ tablespoons fine sea salt

1 tablespoon ground black pepper

1 tablespoon garlic powder

1 tablespoon onion powder

3 cups beef broth

GREMOLATA:

½ cup avocado oil or melted unsalted butter

¼ cup finely chopped fresh parsley leaves and stems

3 teaspoons minced garlic

Grated zest of 1 lemon (about 3 tablespoons)

1 Preheat the oven to 350°F.

2 Pat the brisket dry and season with the salt, pepper, garlic powder, and onion powder. Place in a large roasting pan that snugly fits the brisket and set aside for 10 to 15 minutes to allow the meat to come to room temperature.

3 Bake the brisket, uncovered, for 1 hour. Remove from the oven and add the broth. Lower the oven temperature to 300°F, cover the pan with foil or a lid, and bake for another 2½ hours, or until the brisket is fork-tender. If the brisket isn't tender enough at this point, continue to cook (still covered) for an additional 30 minutes.

4 Meanwhile, make the gremolata: Place the oil, parsley, minced garlic, and lemon zest in a food processor or blender and purée until smooth.

5 When the brisket is tender, remove it to a cutting board and allow to rest for 10 minutes. Slice the meat across the grain into ⅛-inch slices and serve with the sauce.

6 Store leftovers in an airtight container in the refrigerator for up to 3 days. To reheat, place on a rimmed baking sheet, cover with foil, and bake in a preheated 350°F oven for 5 minutes, or until warmed through.

NUTRITIONAL INFORMATION		
per serving	611 calories	49 g fat
39 g protein	2 g carbs	0.4 g fiber

TOM KA GAI
PANNA COTTA

YIELD: 4 servings **PREP TIME:** 5 minutes, plus 2 hours to chill **COOK TIME:** 3 minutes

2 teaspoons grass-fed powdered gelatin

¼ cup freshly squeezed lime juice, chilled

1 (14-ounce) can full-fat coconut milk

1 teaspoon grated fresh ginger

1 stalk lemongrass, cut into 1-inch pieces

1 teaspoon fine sea salt

¼ teaspoon cayenne pepper

½ teaspoon turmeric powder

Fresh cilantro leaves or sprigs, for garnish

Thinly sliced green onions, for garnish

1 Sift the gelatin over the cold lime juice and set aside for 10 minutes to soften.

2 Meanwhile, place the coconut milk, ginger, lemongrass, salt, cayenne pepper, and turmeric in a saucepan over medium heat. Stir gently until hot.

3 Add the softened gelatin to the hot coconut milk mixture and stir well to completely dissolve the gelatin. Remove the lemongrass pieces.

4 Pour the panna cotta mixture into four 8-ounce ramekins. Cover and chill in the refrigerator for at least 2 hours to set. Before serving, garnish with the cilantro and green onions.

5 Store leftovers, covered tightly with plastic wrap, in the refrigerator for up to 3 days.

> **TIP:** Using gelatin is an easy way to make tasty treats, but foods made with gelatin can easily get too rubbery if they sit in the refrigerator overnight. If you plan on making this recipe ahead of time and aren't serving it the same day it is made, I suggest using ¼ teaspoon less gelatin than called for. This quantity will ensure a perfect creamy texture even after the panna cotta has rested in the refrigerator for a day or two.

NUTRITIONAL INFORMATION		
per serving	192 calories	18 g fat
3 g protein	3 g carbs	0.2 g fiber

SAVORY CHICKEN DANISH

YIELD: 4 servings   **PREP TIME:** 15 minutes   **COOK TIME:** 19 minutes

The Ranch Dressing on page 208 tastes great drizzled over this Danish. Because the dressing needs to chill for a couple of hours, make it first, before starting work on this tasty Danish.

DOUGH:

1¾ cups shredded mozzarella cheese

1 ounce cream cheese (2 tablespoons)

¾ cup blanched almond flour

1 large egg

⅛ teaspoon fine sea salt

FILLING:

2 strips bacon, diced

1½ cups diced cooked chicken

½ cup diced green bell peppers (optional)

¼ cup mayonnaise

½ cup shredded cheddar cheese

3 tablespoons Ranch Dressing (page 208), for serving

Fresh herbs, for garnish

1   Preheat the oven to 400°F. Line a pizza stone or cookie sheet with parchment paper and grease the paper. (A pizza stone creates a crispier bottom.)

2   To make the dough, place the mozzarella and cream cheese in a microwave-safe bowl and microwave on high for 1 to 2 minutes, until the cheese is entirely melted. Stir well.

3   Add the almond flour, egg, and salt to the cheese mixture and use a hand mixer to combine. (*Note:* If the dough is too sticky, chill it in the refrigerator for an hour or overnight.)

4   Put the dough on the greased parchment paper and pat it out with your hands to form a large oval, about 12 by 8 inches. Position the oval so one of the short sides is facing you.

5   Make the filling: Fry the diced bacon in a cast-iron skillet over medium heat for 4 minutes, or until crispy and cooked through; remove the bacon from the pan and set aside. While the bacon is cooking, place the diced chicken, green peppers (if using), and mayonnaise in a bowl and stir to combine, making sure to coat the chicken evenly with the mayonnaise.

6   Starting 3 inches from the top of the dough oval and working toward you, pour the chicken mixture down the middle of the oval, ending 3 inches from the edge nearest you. Spread the filling into an oval shape, leaving 1½ inches along the sides exposed. Top the chicken mixture with the shredded cheese, then place the bacon on top of the cheese.

7   To braid the Danish, cut 1½-inch long, ¾-inch-wide flaps along the long sides of the dough oval, cutting only into the part that doesn't have any filling on it. Fold the top and bottom short ends over the top of the chicken filling. Then, starting at the top of the oval, fold the right flap over the chicken filling, then the left flap; continue folding the flaps over the filling until the whole Danish is wrapped. Some of the filling will be exposed.

NUTRITIONAL INFORMATION		
per serving	676 calories	52 g fat
49 g protein	6 g carbs	2 g fiber

8　Place the pizza stone or cookie sheet with the braid in the oven and bake for 15 minutes, or until the braid is golden brown and the dough is fully cooked. Remove from the oven and allow to cool for 10 minutes.

9　Once the braid is cool, drizzle with the ranch dressing and garnish with herbs.

10　Store leftover Danish in an airtight container in the refrigerator for up to 4 days, or freeze for up to a month. To reheat, place on a baking sheet in a preheated 375°F oven for 10 minutes or until heated through. Drizzle with ranch.

SMOKED CHICKEN DRUMSTICKS

YIELD: 12 servings   **PREP TIME:** 5 minutes, plus 30 minutes to soak the wood chips
COOK TIME: 1 hour 15 minutes to 1 hour 30 minutes

Smoking foods sounds intimidating, but it is really quite simple! If you are a visual learner like me, check out MariaMindBodyHealth.com/videos for a simple video tutorial.

4 pounds chicken drumsticks

1 teaspoon fine sea salt

½ teaspoon ground black pepper

BBQ SAUCE:

2 cups tomato sauce

2 tablespoons coconut vinegar or apple cider vinegar

½ teaspoon garlic powder

½ teaspoon onion powder

Pinch of fine sea salt

½ teaspoon ground black pepper

¼ cup Swerve confectioners'-style sweetener or equivalent amount of liquid or powdered sweetener

1½ teaspoons liquid smoke

1   Thirty minutes before you're ready to smoke the chicken, soak the wood chips in water and remove the chicken from the refrigerator. Season the chicken with the salt and pepper.

2   To smoke the chicken: Read the manufacturer's directions for your smoker before you begin. There are wood, electric, propane, and charcoal smokers, and each type works differently. Start the smoker and, if your smoker came with a water bowl, add water to it. When slow-cooking meat, it is essential that you have a thermometer to monitor the temperature of the smoker. When the temperature reaches 180°F, you can start smoking the chicken.

3   Drain the wood chips and place them in the smoker. Place the chicken in the smoker. Secure the lid so that it is airtight and no smoke escapes. Smoke the chicken for 30 minutes, then increase the heat to 230°F. Cook for an additional 45 minutes to 1 hour, until the internal temperature reaches 165°F. Remove the chicken from the smoker. Cover tightly and let it cool and until you're ready to serve it. You can store it in the refrigerator for up to 10 days. If you vacuum-seal it, the smoked chicken will keep for up to 3 weeks.

4   To make the BBQ sauce, place all the ingredients for the sauce in a large bowl and stir well to combine. Store leftover sauce in an airtight container in the refrigerator for up to 8 days.

5   Serve the smoked chicken with the BBQ sauce.

NUTRITIONAL INFORMATION		
per serving	263 calories	10 g fat
38 g protein	2 g carbs	0.4 g fiber

SPECIAL EQUIPMENT:
Smoker

4 cups wood chips of choice

NOTE: When it comes to tomato products, opt for jarred (the best choice) or BPA-free canned products. The linings of cans often contain BPA, a chemical that's associated with several health problems and may affect children's development, and tomatoes' high acidity can cause more BPA to leach into the food.

MEXICAN HAND PIES

YIELD: 2 servings   **PREP TIME:** 8 minutes   **COOK TIME:** 10 minutes

DOUGH:

1¾ cups shredded mozzarella cheese

2 tablespoons unsalted butter

1 large egg

⅛ teaspoon fine sea salt

¾ cup blanched almond flour

FILLING:

¼ pound ground beef

½ teaspoon fine sea salt

½ teaspoon chili powder

½ teaspoon ground cumin

½ teaspoon garlic powder

½ teaspoon onion powder

4 tablespoons shredded sharp cheddar cheese, divided

Salsa, for serving

1 Preheat the oven to 425°F. Line a pizza stone or cookie sheet with parchment paper and grease the paper. (A pizza stone creates a crispier bottom.)

2 To make the dough, place the mozzarella and butter in a microwavable bowl and microwave on high for 1 to 2 minutes, or until the cheese is entirely melted. Stir well.

3 Add the egg and salt then use a hand mixer to combine well. Add the almond flour and combine well. Use your hands and work it like traditional dough, kneading for about 3 minutes. Set aside.

4 Make the filling: Place the ground beef, salt, chili powder, ground cumin, onion powder, and garlic powder in a skillet over medium heat. Sauté until the beef is no longer pink; set aside.

5 Place one-quarter of the dough on the greased piece of parchment paper and pat it out with your hands to make a small circle, about 4 inches in diameter. Repeat with the remaining dough. Fill each circle with a tablespoon of the shredded cheese and divide the cooked beef mixture among the circles. Fold the dough over the filling and seal the edges with your fingers to make pockets.

6 Place the stone with the hand pies in the oven. Bake for 10 minutes or until the pies are golden brown and the dough is fully cooked. Serve with salsa.

7 Store leftovers in an airtight container in the refrigerator for up to 3 days. To reheat, place on a cookie sheet in a preheated 375°F oven for a few minutes, until warmed to your liking.

NUTRITIONAL INFORMATION		
per serving	798 calories	67 g fat
47 g protein	11 g carbs	5 g fiber

SHREDDED BEEF
MEXICAN LASAGNA

 YIELD: 8 servings **PREP TIME:** 8 minutes **COOK TIME:** 20 minutes, plus 8 hours in a slow cooker

Instead of noodles, tortillas are used for the layers when making a traditional Mexican lasagna. Here, the keto stand-ins are cabbage leaves!

1¾ pounds boneless beef roast

1½ teaspoons fine sea salt

2 teaspoons ground black pepper

2 teaspoons ground cumin

2 teaspoons paprika

½ cup chopped onions

1 (7-ounce) can chopped green chiles

2½ cups salsa or tomato sauce, divided

10 large cabbage leaves

2 cups shredded Monterey Jack cheese (see Note)

Fresh cilantro, for garnish (optional)

1   Season the beef roast on all sides with the salt, pepper, cumin, and paprika. Place in a 4-quart slow cooker. Add the onions, green chiles, and ½ cup of the salsa. Cook on low for 7 to 8 hours, until the meat is fork-tender. Shred the meat and set aside.

2   Meanwhile, blanch the cabbage leaves: Bring a large pot of water to a boil, then add the cabbage leaves and boil them for 5 minutes, or until tender. Drain and rinse the cabbage leaves with cold water to stop the cooking. Drain well and set the leaves aside.

3   When you're ready to assemble the lasagna, preheat the oven to 350°F.

4   Layer the bottom of a 13 by 9-inch baking dish with ½ cup of the salsa, then top it with one-third of the meat mixture. If the cabbage leaves aren't completely dry, pat them dry with a paper towel. Place a layer of blanched cabbage leaves on top of the meat. Sprinkle the cabbage leaves with ½ cup each of the salsa and shredded cheese. Repeat these layers two more times.

5   Bake for 20 minutes, or until the cheese is melted and bubbly. Serve garnished with cilantro, if desired.

6   Store leftovers in an airtight container in the refrigerator for up to 5 days, or freeze individual portions for up to a month. To reheat, place on a rimmed baking sheet in a preheated 300°F oven for a few minutes, until warmed to your liking.

NOTE: If you use part-skim mozzarella in place of Monterey Jack cheese, the lasagna will have excess moisture after it bakes. The recipe will still work, but you might have to drain some of the moisture.

BUSY FAMILY TIP: Steps 1 and 2 can be completed up to 3 days ahead. Store the cooked meat and blanched cabbage leaves in separate airtight containers in the refrigerator until ready to assemble the lasagna.

NUTRITIONAL INFORMATION

per serving	435 calories	30 g fat
26 g protein	11 g carbs	4 g fiber

KIELBASA CASEROLE

OPTION

YIELD: 8 servings   **PREP TIME:** 8 minutes   **COOK TIME:** 40 minutes

This simple dish makes fantastic leftovers!

1 pound ground pork

1 large bell pepper (any color), diced

½ cup diced onions

2 cloves garlic, minced

1 cup diced tomatoes (preferably fresh)

1 cup tomato sauce

1 cup beef broth

1 teaspoon fine sea salt

2 teaspoons chili powder

½ teaspoon ground cumin

¼ teaspoon ground black pepper

1 (1-pound) smoked kielbasa sausage link, sliced into ¼-inch pieces

1 cup shredded Monterey Jack or cheddar cheese (omit for dairy-free)

Freshly ground black pepper, for garnish

1   Preheat the oven to 375°F.

2   Cook the ground pork, bell peppers, onions, and garlic in a large cast-iron skillet or other oven-safe skillet over medium heat, breaking up the pork as it cooks. When the pork is cooked through, about 5 minutes, add the tomatoes, tomato sauce, broth, salt, and spices and stir. Simmer, uncovered, for 20 minutes.

3   Slide the slices of kielbasa into the skillet and stir to combine. Cover the casserole with the shredded cheese. Transfer the skillet to the oven and bake for 15 minutes, or until the cheese is bubbly and melted. Sprinkle with freshly ground black pepper and serve.

4   Store leftovers in an airtight container in the refrigerator for up to 3 days. To reheat, place in a baking dish in a preheated 350°F oven for few minutes, until warmed to your liking.

> **NOTE:** If you don't own a large oven-safe skillet, you can bake the casserole in an 8-inch square baking dish. After completing Step 2, transfer the ground sausage mixture to the baking dish. Then top with the kielbasa and cheese and bake as directed in Step 3.

NUTRITIONAL INFORMATION		
per serving	233 calories	17 g fat
15 g protein	5 g carbs	1 g fiber

THAI NUTTY SHORT RIBS

YIELD: 12 servings   **PREP TIME:** 5 minutes   **COOK TIME:** 7 to 8 hours in a slow cooker

1 cup beef broth

¼ cup chopped onions

¼ cup unsweetened almond butter

2 tablespoons Swerve confectioners'-style sweetener or equivalent amount of liquid or powdered sweetener

1 tablespoon freshly squeezed lime juice

2 cloves garlic, minced

4 beef short ribs (4 pounds)

Sliced green onions, for garnish

Chopped raw pili nuts or macadamia nuts, for garnish

3 batches Keto Grits made without cheese (page 226) (optional)

1   Place the broth, onions, almond butter, sweetener, lime juice, and garlic in a 6-quart slow cooker and stir well to combine. Add the ribs and cook on low for 7 to 8 hours, until the meat is tender and easily pulls away from the bone. Place the ribs on a serving platter. Cut into ⅓-pound sections for serving (12 equal-sized rib sections).

2   Pour the sauce in the slow cooker into a small saucepan and bring to a boil over high heat. Whisk and boil for 2 minutes, or until thickened to your liking. Serve the ribs with the sauce, garnished with sliced green onions and chopped nuts, and with a spoonful of keto grits, if desired.

3   Store leftovers in an airtight container in the refrigerator for up to 3 days. To reheat, place on a rimmed baking sheet in a preheated 400°F oven for a few minutes, until warmed to your liking.

NUTRITIONAL INFORMATION		
per serving	741 calories	66 g fat
34 g protein	2 g carbs	1 g fiber

TOMATO BASIL CHICKEN SALAD

OPTION

YIELD: 6 servings **PREP TIME:** 8 minutes, plus time to chill cooked chicken **COOK TIME:** 10 minutes

2 tablespoons ghee or unsalted butter (or coconut oil if dairy-free)

½ cup diced onions

1 cup diced celery

3 cloves garlic, minced

4 boneless, skinless chicken thighs, cut into ½-inch cubes

1 teaspoon fine sea salt

¼ teaspoon ground black pepper

½ cup mayonnaise

1 cup grape tomatoes, halved

1 bunch fresh basil, chopped, plus more leaves for garnish

½ cup cubed fresh mozzarella cheese (omit for dairy-free)

Extra-virgin olive oil or avocado oil, for drizzling

Freshly ground black pepper, for garnish

1 Heat 2 tablespoons ghee in a large cast-iron skillet over medium-high heat. Add the onions and celery and sauté for 2 minutes, stirring often. Add the garlic and sauté for 1 more minute.

2 Season the chicken well with salt and pepper. Add the chicken to the skillet and sauté for 7 minutes, or until the chicken pieces are cooked through. Remove the chicken and vegetables to a serving bowl, allow to cool, then cover and place in the refrigerator for 1 hour, or until chilled.

3 Remove the chicken from the refrigerator and add the mayonnaise, cherry tomatoes, basil, and mozzarella cheese. Garnish with additional basil and drizzle olive oil over the bowl.

4 Store leftovers in an airtight container in the refrigerator for up to 4 days.

NUTRITIONAL INFORMATION		
per serving	421 calories	38 g fat
17 g protein	3 g carbs	1 g fiber

MEATBALL CARBONARA

 YIELD: 4 servings   **PREP TIME:** 10 minutes   **COOK TIME:** 15 minutes

MEATBALLS:

1 pound ground beef

1 large egg, beaten

½ cup finely chopped button mushrooms

2 tablespoons finely chopped onions

1 teaspoon fine sea salt

1 clove garlic, smashed to a paste

"NOODLES":

4 strips bacon, cut into ¼-inch dice

2 cups thinly sliced green or red cabbage

¼ cup chopped onions

½ teaspoon minced garlic

½ cup grated Parmesan cheese (about 2 ounces), plus more for garnish (optional)

2 large eggs, beaten

Fine sea salt and ground black pepper

1   Preheat the oven to 400°F.

2   Put the ingredients for the meatballs in a large bowl. Using your hands, mix everything together until well combined. Shape into 1-inch meatballs and place on a rimmed baking sheet.

3   Bake for 15 minutes, or until the meatballs are cooked through and no longer pink inside.

4   While the meatballs are baking, make the noodles: Fry the bacon in a large cast-iron skillet over medium heat until crisp, about 5 minutes.

5   Use a slotted spoon to remove the bacon pieces from the skillet and set them aside, reserving the bacon drippings in the pan.

6   Add the cabbage "noodles," onions, and garlic to the bacon grease and cook over medium heat until the onion is translucent and the "noodles" are soft, about 4 minutes.

7   Return the bacon to the skillet. Stir well to combine and heat through. Add the Parmesan cheese and toss until the cheese is melted. Add the beaten eggs and cook, tossing constantly with tongs or a large fork until the eggs are just set. Taste for seasoning and add additional salt or pepper if needed. Serve immediately with the meatballs. Garnish with additional grated Parmesan, if desired.

8   Store leftovers in an airtight container in the refrigerator for up to 4 days, or freeze for up to a month. To reheat, place in a lightly greased skillet over medium heat, stirring occasionally, for 5 minutes, or until heated through.

NUTRITIONAL INFORMATION

per serving	466 calories	35 g fat
32 g protein	5 g carbs	1 g fiber

EASY SHREDDED BEEF DINNER

YIELD: 8 servings   **PREP TIME:** 5 minutes   **COOK TIME:** 4 or 8 hours in a slow cooker

3 teaspoons fine sea salt

2 teaspoons paprika

1 teaspoon ground black pepper

1 pound boneless beef roast, cut into 4 equal pieces

2 cups beef broth

1 cup diced onions

1 tomato, diced

½ head green or purple cabbage, cut into 8 wedges

1 lime, halved, for juicing

FOR SERVING (OPTIONAL):

Lime wedges

Fresh cilantro

1   Place the salt, paprika, and pepper in a small bowl and mix well to combine; then sprinkle the mixture all over the roast. Place the roast in a 4-quart slow cooker. Add the broth, onions, tomato, and cabbage wedges.

2   Cover the slow cooker and cook on low for 8 hours or high for 4 hours, or until the meat is fork-tender. When the beef is tender, use two forks to shred it. Stir well to coat the meat in the sauce in the slow cooker. Squeeze the lime halves into the slow cooker and stir well again. Taste and add salt, if desired. Serve garnished with lime wedges and fresh cilantro, if desired.

3   Store leftovers in an airtight container in the refrigerator for up to 4 days. To reheat, place in a baking dish in a preheated 350°F oven for 5 minutes or until heated through.

NUTRITIONAL INFORMATION		
per serving	375 calories	25 g fat
23 g protein	13 g carbs	4 g fiber

BROILED SHRIMP

 YIELD: 4 servings   **PREP TIME:** 8 minutes   **COOK TIME:** 5 minutes

This shrimp tastes great over greens with my Ranch Dressing (see page 208).

½ cup (1 stick) plus 2 tablespoons melted unsalted butter, divided

1 tablespoon freshly squeezed lemon or lime juice

1 teaspoon fine sea salt

1 clove garlic, smashed to a paste

½ pound large shrimp, peeled and deveined

Lemon or lime wedges, for serving (optional)

Freshly ground black pepper, for garnish (optional)

Fresh parsley, for garnish (optional)

1 Preheat the broiler.

2 Place 2 tablespoons of the melted butter, the lime juice, salt, and smashed garlic in a large bowl. Stir well to combine. Add the shrimp and stir well to coat the shrimp.

3 Place the shrimp on a rimmed baking sheet and broil for 5 minutes, or until the shrimp has turned pink.

4 Serve the remaining ½ cup of melted butter alongside the shrimp for dipping. If desired, serve with lemon wedges and garnish with freshly ground black pepper and fresh parsley.

5 Store leftovers in an airtight container in the refrigerator for up to 4 days. To reheat, place in a lightly greased skillet over medium heat, stirring occasionally, for 5 minutes, or until heated through.

NUTRITIONAL INFORMATION		
per serving	294 calories	29 g fat
8 g protein	1 g carbs	0.3 g fiber

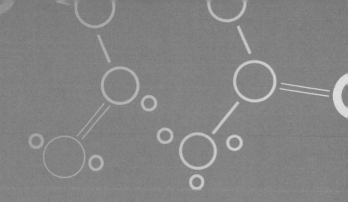

SWEET ENDINGS

MINI CHOCOLATE RASPBERRY CUPCAKES

 YIELD: 24 cupcakes (1 per serving)   **PREP TIME:** 20 minutes   **COOK TIME:** 10 minutes

CUPCAKES:

2 large eggs

¼ cup sour cream

2 tablespoons unsalted butter or coconut oil, softened, plus more for the pan

½ cup Swerve confectioners'-style sweetener or equivalent amount of liquid or powdered sweetener

½ cup unsweetened cocoa powder

1 tablespoon coconut flour

1 teaspoon baking powder

¼ teaspoon fine sea salt

2 teaspoons raspberry extract

FROSTING:

½ cup (1 stick) unsalted butter or coconut oil, softened

4 ounces cream cheese (½ cup), softened

½ cup Swerve confectioners'-style sweetener or equivalent amount of liquid or powdered sweetener

2 teaspoons raspberry extract

⅛ teaspoon fine sea salt

1. Preheat the oven to 325°F. Grease a 24-well mini-muffin pan or line it with mini cupcake liners.

2. In a large bowl, combine the eggs, sour cream, softened butter, and sweetener. Mix until well combined.

3. In a medium bowl, whisk together the cocoa powder, coconut flour, baking powder, and salt.

4. Add the dry mixture to the egg mixture and stir to combine well. Add the raspberry extract and stir to combine.

5. Spoon the batter into the greased muffin pan, filling the wells about two-thirds full. Bake for 10 to 12 minutes, until a toothpick inserted in the middle of a cupcake comes out clean. Remove the cupcakes to a cooling rack and allow to cool completely.

6. While the cupcakes are cooling, make the frosting: Place all the frosting ingredients in a medium bowl and use a hand mixer to combine until smooth. Taste and add more sweetener, if desired.

7. When the cupcakes are cool, frost them using a piping bag or small frosting knife. Store extra cupcakes in an airtight container in the refrigerator for up to 5 days.

NUTRITIONAL INFORMATION

per serving	188 calories	17 g fat
4 g protein	5 g carbs	2 g fiber

PEACHES AND CREAM
ICE POPS

OPTION   OPTION

YIELD: 8 pops (1 per serving)   **PREP TIME:** 3 minutes, plus time to freeze

1 cup heavy cream (or coconut oil if dairy-free)

1 cup strong-brewed peach tea, chilled (see Note)

¼ teaspoon liquid peach stevia

1 teaspoon peach extract (optional)

3 tablespoons Swerve confectioners'-style sweetener or equivalent amount of liquid or powdered sweetener (or to desired sweetness)

½ teaspoon fine sea salt

2 ounces cream cheese (¼ cup), (optional, for an extra-creamy texture) (omit for dairy-free)

1   Place all the ingredients in a blender and blend until smooth. Pour the mixture into the ice pop molds and freeze until set.

2   Store the ice pops in an airtight container in the freezer for up to 1 month.

> **NOTE:** A convenient substitute for brewed peach tea is Bai's Panama Peach drink. I often use this instead of taking the time to brew tea.

NUTRITIONAL INFORMATION		
per serving	125 calories	4 g fat
0.5 g protein	0.5 g carbs	0 g fiber

SPECIAL EQUIPMENT:
8 (2-ounce) ice pop molds

NO-BAKE PUMPKIN SPICE CHEESECAKE IN JARS

 YIELD: 4 servings **PREP TIME:** 5 minutes

½ cup heavy cream

4 ounces cream cheese or mascarpone cheese (½ cup), softened

¼ cup Swerve confectioners'-style sweetener or equivalent amount of liquid or powdered sweetener (or to desired sweetness)

1 teaspoon pumpkin pie spice

1 teaspoon vanilla extract

Natural orange food coloring (optional)

¼ cup chopped raw walnuts (omit for nut-free)

1 Place a large stainless-steel bowl and beaters for a hand mixer in the freezer until they're cold.

2 Place the cream in the chilled bowl and whip it with the hand mixer until firm peaks form. Add the softened cream cheese, sweetener, pumpkin pie spice, vanilla, and natural food coloring, if using. Using the hand mixer, beat until very smooth.

3 Divide the chopped walnuts among four 4-ounce serving jars or cups and top with the pumpkin cheesecake mixture.

4 The jars can be made up to 5 days ahead. Store covered in the refrigerator until ready to serve.

NUTRITIONAL INFORMATION		
per serving 267 calories		26 g fat
3 g protein	2 g carbs	1 g fiber

EASY VANILLA ICE CREAM CUPS

YIELD: 12 ice cream cups (3 per serving)   **PREP TIME:** 5 minutes, plus time to freeze

1 cup heavy cream, chilled

1 (8-ounce) package cream cheese, softened

¼ cup Swerve confectioners'-style sweetener or equivalent amount of liquid or powdered sweetener (or to desired sweetness)

Seeds scraped from 1 vanilla bean (about 8 inches long), or 1 teaspoon vanilla extract

CHOCOLATE DRIZZLE:

¼ cup heavy cream

½ ounce unsweetened baking chocolate, finely chopped

2 tablespoons Swerve confectioners'-style sweetener or equivalent amount of liquid or powdered sweetener (or to desired sweetness)

½ teaspoon vanilla extract

FOR GARNISH (OPTIONAL):

Coarse rock or sea salt

1   Line a 12-well muffin pan with muffin liners. Place a large stainless-steel bowl and beaters for a hand mixer in the freezer until they're cold.

2   Place the heavy cream in the chilled bowl and whip until stiff peaks form. Add the softened cream cheese, sweetener, and vanilla and beat with the hand mixer until smooth.

3   Spoon the mixture into the muffin liners, filling each about one-quarter full. Place the pan in the freezer for 3 hours, or until the cups are set.

4   Make the chocolate drizzle: Place the cream, chopped chocolate, and sweetener in a double boiler or a heat-safe bowl over a pan of simmering water. (Make sure the bowl fits snugly in the saucepan, allowing no steam to escape, and that the bottom of the bowl isn't touching the water.) Heat on low heat, stirring constantly, just until the chocolate melts. Remove the bowl from the pan. Add the vanilla and stir to combine. Taste and adjust the sweetness to your liking.

5   Before serving the cups, allow them to defrost on the counter for 3 minutes before removing the liners; otherwise, the liners will stick to the ice cream. Garnish with a sprinkle of coarse salt and a drizzle of chocolate, if desired.

6   Store the cups in an airtight container in the freezer for up to 1 month.

NUTRITIONAL INFORMATION		
per serving	400 calories	42 g fat
4 g protein	2 g carbs	0 g fiber

NO-BAKE
RHUBARB CRISPS

OPTION

YIELD: 4 servings   **PREP TIME:** 8 minutes, plus 20 minutes to chill

⅔ cup diced rhubarb

1 (8-ounce) package cream cheese or mascarpone cheese (or Kite Hill brand cream cheese–style spread if dairy-free), softened

¼ cup unsweetened cashew or almond milk

⅓ cup Swerve confectioners'-style sweetener or equivalent amount of liquid or powdered sweetener (or to desired sweetness)

1 teaspoon strawberry extract or vanilla extract

⅛ teaspoon fine sea salt

½ cup crushed raw almonds, for topping

1   Place the rhubarb in a large microwavable bowl and microwave on high for 2 minutes or until soft. Add the cream cheese, cashew milk, sweetener, extract, and salt and use a hand mixer to combine until the cream cheese is smooth.

2   Divide the mixture among four 4-ounce ramekins and smooth the tops. Cover and place in the refrigerator to chill for at least 20 minutes. Just before serving, sprinkle the crushed nuts over the ramekins.

3   Cover the leftover crisps and store them in the refrigerator for up to 4 days.

NUTRITIONAL INFORMATION		
per serving 286 calories		25 g fat
7 g protein	6 g carbs	2 g fiber

MINT CHOCOLATE CAKE

YIELD: One 9-inch single-layer cake (25 servings)   **PREP TIME:** 10 minutes, plus time to refrigerate
COOK TIME: 40 minutes

CAKE:

4 cups blanched almond flour

½ cup unsweetened cocoa powder

1 teaspoon baking powder

½ teaspoon fine sea salt

1 cup unsweetened cashew or almond milk

5 large eggs

1 cup Swerve confectioners'-style sweetener or equivalent amount of liquid or powdered sweetener

BROWNED BUTTER CHOCOLATE FROSTING:

1 cup (2 sticks) unsalted butter

1 (8-ounce) package mascarpone or cream cheese

½ cup unsweetened cashew or almond milk

¼ cup unsweetened cocoa powder

¼ cup Swerve confectioners'-style sweetener or equivalent amount of liquid or powdered sweetener (or to desired sweetness)

FOR GARNISH (OPTIONAL):

Pink rock salt

Fresh mint leaves

1 Preheat the oven to 350°F. Grease the bottom and sides of a 9-inch square cake pan, line the bottom with parchment paper, and then grease the paper (this will make it easy to remove the cake from the pan).

2 Make the cake: In a large bowl, whisk together the almond flour, cocoa powder, baking powder, and salt until well combined. In a medium bowl, whisk together the milk, eggs, sweetener, and mint extract until well combined.

3 Pour the wet ingredients into the almond flour mixture and use a hand mixer to mix until thoroughly combined. Transfer the batter to the prepared cake pan.

4 Bake for 30 to 32 minutes, until a toothpick inserted in the center of the cake comes out clean. Let cool in the pan for 1 hour.

5 While the cake is cooling, make the frosting: Heat the butter in a saucepan over high heat until the butter sizzles and you see lots of brown (not black) flecks. Remove the pan from the heat and add the mascarpone cheese, milk, cocoa powder, and sweetener. Using a hand mixer, beat until very smooth. Set aside to cool for a bit before you frost the cake.

6 Remove the cake from the pan and spread the frosting over the top and sides. Put the cake in the refrigerator for a few hours or overnight before serving.

7 To serve, cut the cake into 25 squares by making 4 equal-spaced cuts in each direction. Garnish with pink salt and/or fresh mint leaves, if desired.

8 Store leftovers in an airtight container in the refrigerator for up to 4 days.

NUTRITIONAL INFORMATION		
per serving	241 calories	23 g fat
7 g protein	5 g carbs	3 g fiber

VANILLA BEAN ICE CREAM

YIELD: 2½ cups (½ cup per serving)   **PREP TIME:** 5 minutes, plus time to churn and freeze

This is a delicious vanilla ice cream, but you can mix it up by stirring in a swirl of your favorite flavor or other add-ins.

5 large egg yolks

½ cup Swerve confectioners'-style sweetener or equivalent amount of liquid or powdered sweetener (or to desired sweetness)

1 cup heavy cream

1 cup unsweetened cashew or almond milk

Seeds scraped from 1 vanilla bean (about 8 inches long), or 1 teaspoon vanilla extract

¼ teaspoon fine sea salt

1   If you plan to cook the egg yolks to make a custard-style ice cream, place the egg yolks and sweetener in a medium saucepan; if you'd like to omit the cooking step (and are comfortable consuming raw egg yolks), place the yolks and sweetener in the mixing bowl.

2   Using a hand mixer on high speed, whip the yolks until they're light in color and doubled in size. Stir in the cream. If you're not cooking the eggs, jump ahead to Step 4.

3   To cook the egg mixture, place the saucepan over medium heat and cook, stirring constantly. Stir until the mixture has thickened into a custard (it will coat the back of a spoon). Remove the saucepan from the heat and strain the custard through a fine-mesh sieve into a mixing bowl.

4   Stir in the cashew milk, vanilla bean seeds, and salt. Place the ice cream base in the refrigerator to chill it completely before churning it.

5   Pour the chilled mixture into an ice cream maker and churn according to the manufacturer's instructions, generally 15 to 30 minutes, depending on the machine. Serve immediately or transfer to a storage container and freeze for up to 1 month.

NUTRITIONAL INFORMATION		
per serving	220 calories	24 g fat
3 g protein	1 g carbs	0 g fiber

CHOCOLATE WHOOPIE PIES

YIELD: 8 pies (1 per serving) **PREP TIME:** 20 minutes **COOK TIME:** 12 minutes

CAKE:

1¼ cups blanched almond flour, or ½ cup coconut flour

¼ cup unsweetened cocoa powder

½ teaspoon baking soda

¼ teaspoon fine sea salt

2 tablespoons unsalted butter or coconut oil, softened

⅓ cup Swerve confectioners'-style sweetener or equivalent amount of liquid or powdered sweetener

3 large eggs (if using coconut flour, use 6 large eggs and ¼ cup unsweetened almond milk)

1 teaspoon vanilla extract

FILLING:

¾ cup (1½ sticks) unsalted butter, softened

6 ounces cream cheese or mascarpone cheese (¾ cup), softened

¾ cup Swerve confectioners'-style sweetener or equivalent amount of liquid or powdered sweetener (or to desired sweetness)

1 tablespoon heavy cream or full-fat coconut milk

1 teaspoon vanilla extract

CHOCOLATE DRIZZLE (page 274)

Fresh raspberries, for garnish (optional)

1 Preheat the oven to 350°F. Grease 16 wells of 2 whoopie pie pans.

2 In a mixing bowl, whisk together the almond flour, baking soda, and salt. In a separate bowl, use a hand mixer to beat the butter, sweetener, eggs, and extract until smooth. Stir the wet ingredients into the dry ingredients until well combined.

3 Spoon the batter into the greased wells of the pans, filling the wells two-thirds full. Place in the oven and bake for 12 minutes or until a toothpick inserted in the center of a cake comes out clean. Remove the cakes from the pan and allow to cool completely.

4 Meanwhile, make the filling: Using a hand mixer, cream the butter, cream cheese, and sweetener in a medium bowl until fluffy, about 2 minutes. Add the heavy cream and extract and mix to combine. Set the frosting aside.

5 Make the chocolate drizzle (page 274).

6 Assemble the whoopie pies: Place one cake upside down on a plate (so the flat side is facing up). Spread 2 tablespoons of the filling onto the cake and then top the filling with another cake (with the flat side facing the filling). Repeat with the remaining cakes and filling. Drizzle the top of each pie with the melted chocolate. Garnish with fresh raspberries, if desired.

7 Store the whoopie pies in an airtight container in the refrigerator for up to 4 days.

> **VARIATION: Mint Chocolate Whoopie Pies.**
> Replace the vanilla extract used in the cake and the filling with the same quantity of mint extract or a few drops of mint oil. Garnish with fresh mint leaves, if desired.

 **SPECIAL EQUIPMENT:** 2 (12-well) whoopie pie pans

NUTRITIONAL INFORMATION		
per serving	439 calories	43 g fat
9 g protein	6 g carbs	3 g fiber

BUCKEYES

YIELD: 45 buckeyes (1 per serving) **PREP TIME:** 30 minutes

ALMOND BUTTER BALLS:

1 (18-ounce) jar unsweetened, natural almond butter, room temperature

1 cup Swerve confectioners'-style sweetener or equivalent amount of liquid or powdered sweetener

½ cup (1 stick) unsalted butter, softened

½ teaspoon vanilla extract

CHOCOLATE COATING:

1 cup heavy cream

½ cup Swerve confectioners'-style sweetener or equivalent amount of liquid or powdered sweetener (or to desired sweetness)

1 teaspoon vanilla extract (or another extract, such as cherry)

3 ounces unsweetened baking chocolate, finely chopped

1 Drain off any oil from the top of the almond butter, then place the almond butter in a medium bowl. Add the sweetener, butter, and vanilla extract. Use a hand mixer to combine until smooth. Place the bowl in the freezer or refrigerator to completely chill the mixture, about 20 minutes.

2 Line a rimmed baking sheet with wax paper, parchment paper, or foil. Use a cookie scoop to form the almond butter mixture into 1-inch balls and set them on the lined baking sheet. Set the baking sheet in the freezer for 5 to 7 minutes to chill (which makes the balls easier to dip).

3 While the balls are chilling, make the chocolate coating: In a small saucepan over medium heat, stir together the heavy cream, sweetener, and extract. Bring to a light simmer, then remove the pan from the heat and add the finely chopped chocolate. Stir until the mixture is smooth and the chocolate is completely melted. Allow the coating to cool a little before dipping the almond butter balls in it.

4 Line a second rimmed baking sheet with wax paper, parchment paper, or foil.

5 Remove the balls from the freezer. Insert a toothpick or wooden skewer into a ball and then dip it in the chocolate, turning the ball quickly to cover it. (*Note:* For traditional buckeyes, as pictured, leave a circle of almond butter visible on top.) Place the dipped balls onto the second baking sheet. Allow the buckeyes to sit at room temperature until the chocolate coating dries and hardens; you can refrigerate them to speed the drying process.

6 Store the buckeyes in an airtight container in the refrigerator for up to 4 days, or freeze for up to a month.

NUTRITIONAL INFORMATION		
per serving	115 calories	11 g fat
3 g protein	3 g carbs	2 g fiber

NOTE: The buckeyes in the photo are plated with one of my favorite holiday cookies, called "Cookie Cut Outs." You can find the recipe for them on my site, MariaMindBodyHealth.com.

MAPLE BACON SHORTBREAD COOKIES

OPTION

YIELD: 24 cookies (1 per serving)   **PREP TIME:** 7 minutes   **COOK TIME:** 18 minutes

2 strips bacon, cut into ¼-inch dice

6 tablespoons (¾ stick) unsalted butter (or butter-flavored coconut oil if dairy-free), softened

⅓ cup Swerve confectioners'-style sweetener or equivalent amount of liquid or powdered sweetener

2 cups blanched almond flour or pecan meal

1 teaspoon maple extract

Pinch of fine sea salt

CHOCOLATE DIP:

¾ cup heavy cream (or full-fat coconut milk if dairy-free)

2 ounces unsweetened baking chocolate, finely chopped

⅓ cup Swerve confectioners'-style sweetener or equivalent amount of liquid or powdered sweetener

1 teaspoon vanilla extract or maple extract

1   Preheat the oven to 350°F. Line a cookie sheet with parchment paper.

2   Cook the diced bacon in a cast-iron skillet over medium heat until cooked through, about 4 minutes. Remove the bacon from the skillet with a slotted spoon and set aside.

3   In a medium bowl, use a hand mixer to cream the butter and sweetener until fluffy, about 2 minutes. Add the almond flour, extract, and salt and mix until well combined.

4   Roll the dough between 2 sheets of parchment paper into a ¼-inch-thick square. Cut into 1½-inch squares and place them ½ inch apart on the lined cookie sheet. Press the cooked diced bacon into the top of the cookies. Bake for 15 minutes, or until the cookies are starting to turn golden brown. Cool the cookies completely before removing from cookie sheet.

5   While the cookies cool, make the chocolate dip: Place the cream in a saucepan and heat on medium heat until simmering. Remove the saucepan from the heat and add the chopped chocolate and sweetener; stir until the chocolate is completely melted. Add the extract and stir to combine. Allow the dip to cool a few minutes before dipping the cookies.

6   Dip one end of a cookie in the melted chocolate and place the cookie on a piece of parchment paper to dry.

7   Store the cookies in an airtight container in the refrigerator for up to 5 days, or freeze for up to 1 month.

NUTRITIONAL INFORMATION		
per serving	125 calories	12 g fat
3 g protein	3 g carbs	2 g fiber

ACKNOWLEDGMENTS

From Dr. Nally

First, I must express my gratitude to thousands of patients who have been a part of almost two decades of private practice. Each has taught me what it means to be a healer. I appreciate every patient who has trusted my advice to put down the cereal bowl and "have a piece of bacon" (or an egg). It takes great courage to place trust in someone who's asking you to disregard popular medical belief and swim upstream. To each of you who has been weighed, measured, and examined and with whom I've laughed, cried, and shared successes and failures, thank you. Without you, the possible successes of a ketogenic lifestyle and the knowledge we've shared in this text would never be known.

Second, I must thank Jimmy Moore. He has been a wonderful friend for many years. I never would have imagined that a friendship created across a conference hall at an obesity medicine lecture would lead to a project of this magnitude. I found a unique connection to Jimmy through his love of people and as a seeker of truth. This is apparent in his many podcasts and interviews with thousands of thought leaders around the world. I had the pleasure of getting to know him as his cohost on KetoTalk.com, and though our time podcasting together was short, I will be ever grateful for his insight, advice, and trust.

Third, thanks go to Maria for the hard work and love that she put into this book. I've said it before, and I will say it again: Maria Emmerich replaced Betty Crocker in my home. In the Nally kitchen, the pages of Maria's books are worn, tattered, and often covered in almond flour. Her talent for creating amazing ketogenic meals is second to none. She epitomizes the keto lifestyle, and when I was asked who could create recipes for our readers, I could think of no one I'd be more honored to work with than Maria. I have learned much from her and her amazing family.

Fourth, I am grateful to the new friends I have made at Victory Belt Publishing. It is rare to find such professionalism and precision in an organization. I am so impressed and so thankful for my association with each of them. Writing a book is no simple task, and they were incredibly patient with me as I found time to squeeze in writing time between personal and business challenges. Thank you for putting your trust in me, for taking a risk on someone unknown, and for holding my hand through the process.

Above all, I want to thank my beautiful, brilliant, and patient wife, Tiffini, and my two amazing children. They have cheered me on and been my support when no one else was around. Tiffini has been there through my education and supported me through the grueling process of medical school, residency, and opening a private medical practice. She and my children have endured hours upon hours of Dad's absence as I took care of patients, worked on charts, and wrote blogs and book chapters, and they've patiently endured it all with smiles and hugs. Fifteen years ago, I announced that if I didn't do something drastic for my health, I probably wouldn't be around for long. Tiffini set out to revamp the Nally household to conform to the science I was learning about and sharing with my patients. It was Tiffini who educated us about how to make food preparation and nutrition a reality in our home. She is my best friend, my confidant, my partner, and my eternal companion. She is the epitome of a virtuous woman, and she is the one and only ketogenic domestic goddess. Thank you, Tiffini!

From Jimmy Moore

What a thrill to be one of the coauthors on this book that is a natural sequel to my hit 2014 book *Keto Clarity* with two of my favorite people and all-stars in the ketogenic community—Dr. Adam Nally and Maria Emmerich.

Adam has been a longtime friend ever since I met him many moons ago at the various obesity medicine conferences we attended. I always felt a connection to him for his ability to make complex biochemistry and physiological mechanisms understandable to the layperson. When we started a podcast together in 2016 called *Keto Talk with Jimmy Moore & The Doc* (www.ketotalk.com), it quickly became apparent that this book needed to be written sooner rather than later so people can understand the how and why of nutritional ketosis. Although he's no longer doing the podcast, that trademark charisma and extensive practical keto knowledge people came to love and expect continues on now in *The Keto Cure.* Thank you, Adam, for sharing your special gift with the entire world. I'm so proud to call you a friend and now a coauthor!

Maria and I collaborated on a book in 2015 called *The Ketogenic Cookbook,* and it quickly became an international bestseller. She is without question the most talented ketogenic recipe maker on the planet. Adam and his family have long been huge fans of Maria's cookbooks, so when we needed someone to help us create some recipes for the readers of this book, choosing Maria was a no-brainer. Maria, you are one of hardest-working, kindest, most compassionate, and most loving people I've ever met, and I'm honored and privileged to be your friend and to once again collaborate with you on a life-changing book!

To my Victory Belt Publishing family, what can I say? You've got me addicted to writing books now, and I have no plans to slow down or stop anytime soon. Even with three straight international bestsellers in *Keto Clarity, The Ketogenic Cookbook,* and *The Complete Guide to Fasting,* the best is yet to come. Thank you for believing in me and my ability when others wouldn't give me a chance. I'll never forget the day you asked me to start writing books for you in 2012 and I said I wanted to write about ketogenic diets. Although you were initially skeptical of the keto concept, we're now seeing that the hunger and thirst for this way of eating is stronger than ever before. Victory Belt is blazing a trail by staying on the cutting edge of nutritional health.

And last but certainly not least, none of this would be possible without my rock and always supportive wife, Christine, who has stood by my side throughout this wild and crazy ketogenic journey. After earning her Nutritional Therapy Practitioner certification in 2017, she's ready to take on the world helping her clients embrace a whole foods-based ketogenic lifestyle to health and healing . . . and writing a book all about it with me called *Real Food Keto,* coming soon. I couldn't imagine going through life without you. Love you, Christine!

END NOTES

Chapter 1

1. Davis, Richard C. "Frederick Schwatka (1849–1892)." *Arctic* 37, no. 3 (1984): 302–303. http://arctic. journalhosting.ucalgary.ca/arctic/index.php/arctic/article/view/2209.

Chapter 2

1. "The Healthcare Costs of Obesity." *The State of Obesity* website, accessed February 24, 2017. https://stateofobesity.org/healthcare-costs-obesity/.
2. Laprete, Jay. "U.S. Farm Bill." *The New York Times* website, Times Topics. December 31, 2012.
3. "U.S. Farm Bill: Frequently Asked Questions." *SNAP to Health* website, Farm Bill & USDA, accessed November 29, 2017. www.snaptohealth.org/farm-bill-usda/u-s-farm-bill-faq/.
4. Monke, Jim. "Farm Commodity Programs: Base Acreage and Planting Flexibility." *CRS Report for Congress*, September 14, 2005. http://nationalaglawcenter.org/wp-content/uploads/assets/crs/ RS21615.pdf.
5. Ogden, C. L., M. D. Carroll, B. K. Kit, and K. M. Flegal. "Prevalence of Obesity in the United States, 2009–2010." *NCHS Data Brief* 82 (2012): 1–8. www.ncbi.nlm.nih.gov/pubmed/22617494.
6. United States Department of Agriculture. "National School Lunch Program." Last updated November 2017. https://fns-prod.azureedge.net/sites/default/files/cn/NSLPFactSheet.pdf.
7. United States Department of Agriculture. *Dietary Guidelines for Americans 2010*. Washington, DC: USDA. December 2010. www.cnpp.usda.gov/sites/default/files/dietary_guidelines_for_ americans/PolicyDoc.pdf.
8. Lovett, Edward. "School Lunch Showdown: 850-Calorie Meals Compared." *ABC News* website, September 30, 2012. http://abcnews.go.com/Health/school-lunch-showdown-850-calorie-meals-compared/blogEntry?id=17358834.
9. Drewnowski, A., and S. E. Specter. "Poverty and Obesity: The Role of Energy Density and Energy Costs." *American Journal of Clinical Nutrition* 79, no. 1 (2004): 6–16. www.ncbi.nlm.nih.gov/ pubmed/14684391.
10. "Surprising Facts About Arizona Agriculture." *Arizona Farm Bureau* website. November 2, 2012. www.azfb.org/Article/Surprising-Facts-About-Arizona-Agriculture.
11. "Farm Subsidy Information." *EWG* website, accessed November 29, 2017. http://farm.ewg.org/ region.php?fips=00000.
12. Smith, Aaron. "Children of the Corn: The Renewable Fuels Disaster." *The American*, January 4, 2012. www.aei.org/publication/children-of-the-corn-the-renewable-fuels-disaster/.
13. "Agricultural Policies Versus Health Policies." *Physicians Committee for Responsible Medicine* website, accessed November 29, 2017. www.pcrm.org/health/reports/agriculture-and-health-policies-ag-versus-health.
14. Ohio State University. "Food Stamp Use Linked to Weight Gain, Study Finds." *ScienceDaily*, August 12, 2009. www.sciencedaily.com/releases/2009/08/090810122139.htm.
15. Drewnowski, A., and S. E. Specter. "Poverty and Obesity: The Role of Energy Density and Energy Costs." *American Journal of Clinical Nutrition* 79, no. 1 (2004): 6–16. http://ajcn.nutrition.org/ content/79/1/6.full.
16. Powell, L. M., and F. J. Chaloupka. "Food Prices and Obesity: Evidence and Policy Implications for Taxes and Subsidies." *The Milbank Quarterly* 87, no. 1 (2009): 229–257. www.ncbi.nlm.nih.gov/ pubmed/19298422.
17. Todd, Jessica, and Biing-Hwan Lin. "What Role Do Food and Beverage Prices Have on Diet and Health Outcomes?" *Amber Waves,* September 20, 2012. www.ers.usda.gov/amber-waves/2012/ september/what-role-do-food-and-beverage-prices/.

18. Ogden, Cynthia, and Margaret Carroll. "Prevalence of Overweight, Obesity, and Extreme Obesity Among Adults: United States, Trends 1960–1962 Through 2007–2008." *Centers for Disease Control and Prevention National Center for Health Statistics* website, June 2010. www.cdc.gov/nchs/data/hestat/obesity_adult_07_08/obesity_adult_07_08.pdf.

19. Kelly, T., W. Yang, C. S. Chen, K. Reynolds, and J. He. "Global Burden of Obesity in 2005 and Projections to 2030." *International Journal of Obesity* 32, no. 9 (2008): 1431–1437. www.ncbi.nlm.nih.gov/pubmed/18607383.

20. Hite, A. H., R. D. Feinman, G. E. Guzman, M. Satin, P. A. Schoenfeld, and R. J. Wood. "In the Face of Contradictory Evidence: Report of the Dietary Guidelines for Americans Committee." *Nutrition* 25, no. 10 (2010): 915–924. www.ncbi.nlm.nih.gov/pubmed/20888548.

21. Howard, D. V., J. E. Manson, M. L. Stefanick, S. A. Beresford, G. Frank, B. Jones, R. J. Rodabough, et al. "Low-Fat Dietary Pattern and Weight Change over 7 Years: The Women's Health Initiative Dietary Modification Trial." *Journal of the American Medical Association* 295, no. 1 (2006): 39–49. www.ncbi.nlm.nih.gov/pubmed/16391215.

22. McGeary, Judith. "Policy Update: Farm Bill and GMOs." *The Weston A. Price Foundation* website, Get Involved. December 12, 2012. www.westonaprice.org/policy-update-farm-bill-and-gmos/.

23. Reuters. "US Senate, House Ag Committees in Deal to Avert Milk Price Spike." *Reuters* website, December 30, 2012. www.reuters.com/article/farm-bill-compromise/refile-update-3-us-senate-house-ag-committees-in-deal-to-avert-milk-price-spike-idUSL1E8NU15O20121231.

24. Cornell University. "Obesity Accounts for 21 Percent of U.S. Health Care Costs, Study Finds." *ScienceDaily* website, April 9, 2012. www.sciencedaily.com/releases/2012/04/120409103247.htm.

25. Kahn, Katherine. "Obese Employees Cost Employers Thousands in Extra Medical Costs." *CFAH Center for Advancing Health* website. May 13, 2014. www.cfah.org/hbns/2014/obese-employees-cost-employers-thousands-in-extra-medical-costs.

26. Begley, Sharon. "As America's Waistline Expands, Costs Soar." *Reuters* website, April 30, 2012. www.reuters.com/article/us-obesity/as-americas-waistline-expands-costs-soar-idUSBRE83T0C820120430.

27. Gaudette, É., B. Tysinger, A. Cassil, and D. P. Goldman. "Health and Health Care of Medicare Beneficiaries in 2030." *Forum for Health & Economics Policy* 18, no. 2 (2015): 75–96. www.ncbi.nlm.nih.gov/pubmed/27127455.

28. Ungar, Rick. "Obesity Now Costs Americans More in HealthCare Spending Than Smoking." *Forbes* website, April 30, 2012. www.forbes.com/sites/rickungar/2012/04/30/obesity-now-costs-americans-more-in-healthcare-costs-than-smoking/#40ad90d053d7.

29. Centers for Disease Control and Prevention. Overweight & Obesity, Adult Obesity Facts, accessed January 31, 2018. www.cdc.gov/obesity/data/adult.html.

30. "The Lipid Research Clinics Coronary Primary Prevention Trial Results. I. Reduction in Incidence of Coronary Heart Disease." *Journal of the American Medical Association* 251, no. 3 (1984): 351–364. www.ncbi.nlm.nih.gov/pubmed/6361299.

31. Schatz, I. J., K. Masaki, K. Yano, R. Chen, B. L. Rodriguez, and J. D. Curb. "Cholesterol and All-Cause Mortality in Elderly People from the Honolulu Heart Program: A Cohort Study." *The Lancet* 358, no. 9279 (2001): 351–355. www.ncbi.nlm.nih.gov/pubmed/11502313.

32. Taubes, Gary. *Good Calories, Bad Calories: Fats, Carbs, and the Controversial Science of Diet and Health.* New York: Anchor Books, 2007.

33. U.S. Department of Agriculture. "Dietary Guidelines for Americans 2010." December 2010. https://health.gov/dietaryguidelines/dga2010/DietaryGuidelines2010.pdf.

34. Walsh, Bryan. "Ending the War on Fat." *TIME*, June 12, 2014.

35. Reaven, G., R. Lerner, M. Stern, and J. Farquhar. "Role of Insulin in Endogenous Hypertriglyceridemia." *Journal of Clinical Investigation* 46, no. 11 (1967): 1756–1767. www.ncbi.nlm.nih.gov/pmc/articles/PMC292926/.

36. Kolkata, G. "High-Carb Diets Questioned." *Science* 235, no. 4785 (1987): 164. http://science.sciencemag.org/content/235/4785/164.

37. Ahrens, Jr., E. H., J. Hirsch, K. Oette, J. W. Farquhar, and Y. Stein. "Carbohydrate-Induced and Fat-Induced Lipemia." *Transactions of the Association of American Physicians* 74 (1961): 134–146. www.researchgate.net/publication/9706857_Carbohydrate-induced_and_fat-induced_lipemia.

38. Harlan Jr., W. R., J. Graham, and E. H. Estes. "Familial Hypercholesterolemia: A Genetic and Metabolic Study." *Annals of Internal Medicine* 63, no. 5 (1965): 915–916. http://annals.org/aim/article-abstract/680362/familial-hypercholesterolemia-genetic-metabolic-study.

Chapter 4

1. Allam, A., R. Thompson, S. Wann, M. Miyamoto, and G. Thomas. "Computed Tomographic Assessment of Atherosclerosis in Ancient Egyptian Mummies." *Journal of the American Medical Association* 302, no. 19 (2009): 2091–2094. https://jamanetwork.com/journals/jama/fullarticle/184891.
2. Kraft, Joseph. *Diabetes Epidemic & You: Should Everyone Be Tested?* Bloomington, IN: Trafford Publishing, 2008.
3. Ibid.
4. Boyle, J., T. Thompson, E. Gregg, L. Barker, and D. Williamson. "Projection of the Year 2050 Burden of Diabetes in the US Adult Population: Dynamic Modeling of Incidence, Mortality, and Prediabetes Prevalence." *Population Health Metrics* 8, no. 29 (2010): https://pophealthmetrics.biomedcentral.com/articles/10.1186/1478-7954-8-29.

Part 2

1. Bryans, J. A., P. A. Judd, and P. R. Ellis. "The Effect of Consuming Instant Black Tea on Postprandial Plasma Glucose and Insulin Concentrations in Healthy Humans." *Journal of the American College of Nutrition* 26, no. 5 (2007): 471–477. www.ncbi.nlm.nih.gov/pubmed/17914136.
2. Stote, K. S., and D. J. Baer. "Tea Consumption May Improve Biomarkers of Insulin Sensitivity and Risk Factors for Diabetes." *Journal of Nutrition* 138, no. 8 (2008): 1584S–1588S. www.ncbi.nlm.nih.gov/pubmed/18641211.
3. Floyd, Jr., J. C., S. S. Fajans, J. W. Conn, R. F. Knopf, and J. Rull. "Stimulation of Insulin Secretion by Amino Acids." *Journal of Clinical Investigation* 45, no. 9 (1966): 1487–1502. www.ncbi.nlm.nih.gov/pmc/articles/PMC292828/.

Chapter 5

1. Cryer, P. E. "Glucose Counterregulation: Prevention and Correction of Hypoglycemia in Humans." *American Journal of Physiology* 264, no. 2 pt. 1 (1993): E149–E155. www.ncbi.nlm.nih.gov/pubmed/8447379.
2. Ibid.
3. Horton, W. B., and J. S. Subauste. "Care of the Athlete with Type 1 Diabetes Mellitus: A Clinical Review." *International Journal of Endocrinology & Metabolism* 14, no. 2 (2016): e36091. www.ncbi.nlm.nih.gov/pmc/articles/PMC5035675/.
4. Sprague, J. E., and A. M. Arbeláez. "Glucose Counterregulatory Responses to Hypoglycemia." *Pediatric Endocrinology Reviews* 9, no. 1 (2011): 463–475. www.ncbi.nlm.nih.gov/pmc/articles/PMC3755377/.
5. Mitrakou, A., C. Ryan, T. Veneman, M. Mokan, T. Jenssen, I. Kiss, J. Durrant, et al. "Hierarchy of Glycemic Thresholds for Counterregulator Hormone Secretion, Symptoms, and Cerebral Dysfunction." *American Journal of Physiology* 260, no. 1 pt. 1 (1991): E67–E74. www.ncbi.nlm.nih.gov/pubmed/1987794.
6. Cryer, P. E. "Hierarchy of Physiological Responses to Hypoglycemia: Relevance to Clinical Hypoglycemia in Type I (Insulin Dependent) Diabetes Mellitus." *Hormone and Metabolic Research* 29, no. 3 (1997): 92–96. www.ncbi.nlm.nih.gov/pubmed/9137976.
7. Cryer, P. E., S. N. Davis, and H. Shamoon. "Hypoglycemia in Diabetes." *Diabetes Care* 26, no. 6 (2003): 1902–1912. www.ncbi.nlm.nih.gov/pubmed/12766131.

8. Riddell, M., and B. A. Perkins. "Exercise and Glucose Metabolism in Persons with Diabetes Mellitus: Perspectives on the Role for Continuous Glucose Monitoring." *Journal of Diabetes Science and Technology* 3, no. 4 (2009): 914–923. www.ncbi.nlm.nih.gov/pmc/articles/PMC2769951/.

Chapter 6

1. U.S. Department of Health and Human Services, National Institutes of Health. "The Seventh Report of the Joint National Committee on Prevention, Detection, Evaluation, and Treatment of High Blood Pressure." NIH Publication No. 04-5230, August 2004. www.nhlbi.nih.gov/files/docs/guidelines/jnc7full.pdf.
2. James, P., S. Oparil, B. Carter, W. Cushman, C. Dennison-Himmelfarb, J. Handler, D. Lackland, et al. "2014 Evidence-Based Guideline for the Management of High Blood Pressure in Adults: Report from the Panel Members Appointed to the Eighth Joint National Committee (JNC 8)." *Journal of the American Medical Association* 311, no. 5 (2014): 507–520. https://jamanetwork.com/journals/jama/fullarticle/1791497.
3. Tiwari, S., S. Riazi, and C. Ecelbarger. "Insulin's Impact on Renal Sodium Transport and Blood Pressure in Health, Obesity, and Diabetes." *American Journal of Physiology–Renal Physiology* 293, no. 4 (2007): F974–F984. http://ajprenal.physiology.org/content/293/4/F974.
4. Anderson, R. A., and M. M. Polansky. "Tea Enhances Insulin Activity." *Journal of Agricultural and Food Chemistry* 50, no. 24 (2002): 7182–7186. www.ncbi.nlm.nih.gov/pubmed/12428980.
5. Forman, J. P., M. J. Stampfer, and G. C. Curhan. "Diet and Lifestyle Risk Factors Associated with Incident Hypertension in Women." *Journal of the American Medical Association* 302, no. 4 (2009): 401–411. www.ncbi.nlm.nih.gov/pubmed/19622819.
6. Ascherio, A., E. B. Rimm, E. L. Giovannucci, G. A. Colditz, B. Rosner, W. C. Willett, F. Sacks, and M. J. Stampfer. "A Prospective Study of Nutritional Factors and Hypertension Among US Men." *Circulation* 88, no. 5 (1992): 1475–1485. www.ncbi.nlm.nih.gov/pubmed/1330360.
7. Dhawan, V., and S. Jain. "Garlic Supplementation Prevents Oxidative DNA Damage in Essential Hypertension." *Molecular and Cellular Biochemistry* 275, no. 1–2 (2005): 85–97. www.ncbi.nlm.nih.gov/pubmed/16335787.
8. Hasrat, J. A., L. Pieters, and A. J. Vlietinck. "Medicinal Plants in Suriname: Hypotensive Effect of *Gossypium Barbadense*." *Journal of Pharmacy and Pharmacology* 56, no. 3 (2004): 381–387. www.ncbi.nlm.nih.gov/pubmed/15025864.
9. Burke, V., J. M. Hodgson, L. J. Beilin, N. Giangiulioi, P. Rogers, and I. B. Puddey. "Dietary Protein and Soluble Fiber Reduce Ambulatory Blood Pressure in Treated Hypertensives." *Hypertension* 38, no. 4 (2001): 821–826. www.ncbi.nlm.nih.gov/pubmed/11641293.
10. Mashour, N. H., G. I. Lin, and W. H. Frishman. "Herbal Medicine for the Treatment of Cardiovascular Disease: Clinical Considerations." *Archives of Internal Medicine* 158, no. 20 (1998): 2225–2234. www.ncbi.nlm.nih.gov/pubmed/9818802.
11. Engelhard, Y. N., B. Gazer, and E. Paran. "Natural Antioxidants from Tomato Extract Reduce Blood Pressure in Patients with Grade-1 Hypertension: A Double-Blind, Placebo-Controlled Pilot Study." *American Heart Journal* 151, no. 1 (2006): 100. www.ncbi.nlm.nih.gov/pubmed/16368299.
12. Liu, X., J. Wei, S. Zhou, G. Würthwein, and P. Rohdewald. "Pycnogenol, French Maritime Pine Bark Extract, Improves Endothelial Function of Hypertensive Patients." *Life Sciences* 74, no. 7 (2004): 855–862. www.ncbi.nlm.nih.gov/pubmed/14659974.
13. Jerie, P. "Milestones of Cardiovascular Therapy. IV. Reserpine." *Journal of Czech Physicians (Casopis Lékaru Ceských)* 146, no. 7 (2007): 573–577. www.ncbi.nlm.nih.gov/pubmed/17722843.
14. Taubert, D., R. Berkels, R. Roesen, and W. Klaus. "Chocolate and Blood Pressure in Elderly Individuals with Isolated Systolic Hypertension." *Journal of the American Medical Association* 290, no. 8 (2003): 1029–1030. www.ncbi.nlm.nih.gov/pubmed/12941673.
15. Amaechina, F. C., and E. K. Omogbai. "Hypotensive Effect of Aqueous Extract of the Leaves of Phyllanthus Amarus Schum and Thonn (Euphorbiaceae)." *Acta Poloniae Pharmaceutica* 64, no. 6 (2007): 547–552. www.ncbi.nlm.nih.gov/pubmed/18323250.

16. Fugh-Berman, A. "Herbs and Dietary Supplements in the Prevention and Treatment of Cardiovascular Disease." *Preventive Cardiology* 3, no. 1 (2000): 24–32. www.ncbi.nlm.nih.gov/pubmed/11834913.
17. Ghayur, M. N., and A. H. Gilani. "Ginger Lowers Blood Pressure Through Blockade of Voltage-Dependent Calcium Channels." *Journal of Cardiovascular Pharmacology* 45, no. 1 (2005): 74–80. www.ncbi.nlm.nih.gov/pubmed/15613983.

Chapter 7

1. Ahrens Jr., E. H. "The Diet-Heart Questions in 1985: Has It Really Been Settled?" *The Lancet* 328, no. 8437 (1985): 1085–1087. www.sciencedirect.com/science/article/pii/S0140673685923815.
2. Ahrens Jr., E. H., H. Hirsch, K. Oette, J. W. Farquhar, and Y. Stein. "Carbohydrate-Induced and Fat-Induced Lipemia." *Transactions of the Association of American Physicians* 74 (1961): 134–146. www.researchgate.net/publication/9706857_Carbohydrate-induced_and_fat-induced_lipemia.
3. Ahrens Jr., E. H. "The Diet-Heart Questions in 1985: Has It Really Been Settled?" *The Lancet* 328, no. 8437 (1985): 1085–1087. www.sciencedirect.com/science/article/pii/S0140673685923815.
4. Ferrières, Jean. "The French Paradox: Lessons for Other Countries." *Heart* 90, no. 1 (2004): 107–111. www.ncbi.nlm.nih.gov/pmc/articles/PMC1768013/.
5. Schatz, I. J., K. Masaki, K. Yano, R. Chen, B. L. Rodriguez, and J. D. Curb. "Cholesterol and All-Cause Mortality in Elderly People from the Honolulu Heart Program: A Cohort Study." *The Lancet* 358, no. 9279 (2001): 351–355. www.ncbi.nlm.nih.gov/pubmed/11502313.
6. Ravnskov, U., D. Diamond, R. Hama, T. Hamazaki, B. Hammarskjöld, N. Hynes, M. Kendrick, et al. "Lack of an Association or an Inverse Association Between Low-Density-Lipoprotein Cholesterol and Mortality in the Elderly: A Systematic Review." *BMJ Open* 6 (2016): http://bmjopen.bmj.com/content/6/6/e010401.
7. The Lipid Research Clinics Coronary Primary Prevention Trial (LRC-CPPT). "The Lipid Research Clinics Coronary Primary Prevention Trial Results. I. Reduction in Incidence of Coronary Heart Disease." *Journal of the American Medical Association* 251, no. 3 (1984): 351–364. www.ncbi.nlm.nih.gov/pubmed/6361299.
8. Parker, T. S., B. R. Gordon, S. D. Saal, A. L. Rubin, and E. H. Ahrens, Jr. "Plasma High Density Lipoprotein Is Increased in Man When Low Density Lipoprotein (LDL) Is Lowered by LDL-Pheresis." *Proceedings of the National Academy of Sciences of the United States of America* 83, no. 3 (1986): 777–781. www.ncbi.nlm.nih.gov/pmc/articles/PMC322948/.
9. Hoogeveen, R. C., J. W. Gaubatz, W. Sun, R. C. Dodge, J. R. Crosby, J. Jiang, D. Couper, et al. "Small Dense Low-Density Lipoprotein-Cholesterol Concentrations Predict Risk for Coronary Heart Disease: The Atherosclerosis Risk In Communities (ARIC) Study." *Arteriosclerosis, Thrombosis, and Vascular Biology* 34, no. 5 (2014): 1069–1077. www.ncbi.nlm.nih.gov/pubmed/24558110.
10. Ivanova, E., V. Myasoedova, A. Melnichenko, A. Grechko, and A. Orekhov. "Small Dense Low-Density Lipoprotein as Biomarker for Atherosclerotic Diseases." *Oxidative Medicine and Cellular Longevity 2017* (2017). www.hindawi.com/journals/omcl/2017/1273042/.
11. Williams, P., X. Zhao, S. Marcovina, J. Otvos, B. G. Brown, and R. Krauss. "Comparison of Four Methods of Analysis of Lipoprotein Particle Subfractions for Their Association with Angiographic Progression of Coronary Artery Disease." *Atherosclerosis* 233, no. 2 (2014): 713–720. www.ncbi.nlm.nih.gov/pmc/articles/PMC3990359/.
12. Griffin, B. A., A. M. Minihane, N. Furlonger, C. Chapman, M. Murphy, D. Williams, J. J. Wright, et al. "Inter-Relationships Between Small, Dense Low-Density Lipoprotein (LDL), Plasma Triacylglycerol and LDL Apoprotein B in an Atherogenic Lipoprotein Phenotype in Free-Living Subjects." *Clinical Science* 97, no. 3 (1999): 269–276. www.ncbi.nlm.nih.gov/pubmed/10464051.
13. Ibid.
14. Ravnskov, U. D., M. Diamond, R. Hama, T. Hamazaki, B. Jammarskjöld, N. Hynes, M. Kendrick, et al. "Lack of an Association or an Inverse Association Between Low-Density-Lipoprotein Cholesterol and Mortality in the Elderly: A Systematic Review." *BMJ Open* 6 (2016): e010401. http://bmjopen.bmj.com/content/6/6/e010401.

15. Mensink, R. "Effects of Saturated Fatty Acids on Serum Lipids and Lipoproteins: A Systematic Review and Regression Analysis." Geneva: World Health Organization. 2016.

16. The Multiple Risk Factor Intervention Trial. "Multiple Risk Factor Intervention Trial. Risk Factor Changes and Mortality Results. Multiple Risk Factor Intervention Trial Research Group." *Journal of the American Medical Association* 248, no. 12 (1982): 1465–1477. www.ncbi.nlm.nih.gov/pubmed/7050440.

17. Mayor, S. "Statin Side Effects Are Strongest Predictor of Inadequate Cholesterol Control, Study Shows." *BMJ* 356 (2017). www.bmj.com/content/356/bmj.j869.

18. Bradberry, J. C., and D. E. Hillman. "Overview of Omega-3 Fatty Acid Therapies." *P&T Journal* 39, no. 11 (2013): 681–691. www.ncbi.nlm.nih.gov/pubmed/24391388.

19. Weitz, D., H. Weintraub, E. Fisher, and A. Z. Schwartzbard. "Fish Oil for the Treatment of Cardiovascular Disease." *Cardiology in Review* 18, no. 5 (2010): 258–263. www.ncbi.nlm.nih.gov/pubmed/20699674.

20. Ranasinghe, P., W. S. Wathurapathy, M. H. Ishara, R. Jayawardana, P. Galappatthy, P. Katulanda, and G. R. Constantine. "Effects of Zinc Supplementation on Serum Lipids: A Systematic Review and Meta-Analysis." *Nutrition & Metabolism* 12, no. 26 (2015). https://nutritionandmetabolism.biomedcentral.com/articles/10.1186/s12986-015-0023-4.

22. Kesl, S. L., A. M. Poff, N. P. Ward, T. N. Fiorelli, C. Ari, A. J. Van Putten, J. W. Sherwood, et al. "Effects of Exogenous Ketone Supplementation on Blood Ketone, Glucose, Triglyceride, and Lipoprotein Levels in Sprague-Dawley Rats." *Nutrition & Metabolism* 13, no. 9 (2016). https://nutritionandmetabolism.biomedcentral.com/articles/10.1186/s12986-016-0069-y.

Chapter 8

1. Zhao, Xue-Qiao. "Pathogenesis of Atherosclerosis." *UpToDate* website. October 9, 2017. www.uptodate.com/contents/pathogenesis-of-atherosclerosis.

2. Dogan, S., Y. Plantinga, J. R. Crouse III, G. W. Evans, J. S. Raichlen, D. H. O'Leary, M. K. Palmer, et al. "Algorithms to Measure Carotid Intima-Media Thickness in Trials: A Comparison of Reproducibility, Rate of Progression and Treatment Effect." *Journal of Hypertension* 29, no. 11 (2011): 2181–2193. www.ncbi.nlm.nih.gov/pubmed/21918474.

3. Shai, I., J. D. Spence, D. Schwarzfuchs, Y. Henkin, G. Parraga, A. Rudich, A. Fenster, et al. "Dietary Intervention to Reverse Carotid Atherosclerosis." *Circulation* 121, no. 10 (2010): 1200–1208. www.ncbi.nlm.nih.gov/pubmed/20194883.

4. Takayama, T., T. Hiro, M. Yamagishi, H. Daida, A. Hirayama, S. Saito, T. Yamaguchi, et al. "Effect of Rosuvastatin on Coronary Atheroma in Stable Coronary Artery Disease: Multicenter Coronary Atherosclerosis Study Measuring Effects of Rosuvastatin Using Intravascular Ultrasound in Japanese Subjects (COSMOS)." *Circulation Journal* 73, no. 11 (2009): 2110–2117. www.ncbi.nlm.nih.gov/pubmed/19801853/.

5. Bradberry, J. C., and D. E. Hilleman. "Overview of Omega-3 Fatty Acid Therapies." *P&T Journal* 38, no. 11 (2013): 681–691. www.ncbi.nlm.nih.gov/pubmed/24391388.

6. Weitz, D., H. Weintraub, E. Fisher, and A. Z. Schwartzbard. "Fish Oil for the Treatment of Cardiovascular Disease." *Cardiology in Review* 18, no. 5 (2010): 258–263. www.ncbi.nlm.nih.gov/pubmed/20699674.

7. Moss, J., and D. Ramji. "Nutraceutical Therapies for Atherosclerosis." *Nature Reviews Cardiology* 13, no. 9 (2016): 513–532. www.ncbi.nlm.nih.gov/pmc/articles/PMC5228762/.

8. Heiss, C., R. Sansone, H. Karimi, M. Krabbe, D. Schuler, A. Rodriguez-Mateos, and T. Kraemer. "Impact of Cocoa Flavanol Intake on Age-Dependent Vascular Stiffness in Healthy Men: A Randomized, Controlled, Double-Masked Trial." *Age* 37, no. 3 (2015): 9794. www.ncbi.nlm.nih.gov/pubmed/26013912.

9. Kong, W. J., J. Wei, Z. Y. Zuo, Y. M. Wang, D. Q. Song, X. F. You, L. X. Zhao, et al. "Combination of Simvastatin with Berberine Improves the Lipid-Lowering Efficacy." *Metabolism: Clinical and Experimental* 57, no. 8 (2008): 1029–1037. www.ncbi.nlm.nih.gov/pubmed/18640378.

10. de Courten, B., M. Jakubova, M. P. de Courten, I. J. Kukurova, S. Vallova, P. Krumpolec, L. Valkovic, et al. "Effects of Carnosine Supplementation on Glucose Metabolism: Pilot Clinical Trial." *Obesity* 24, no. 5 (2016): 1027–1034. www.ncbi.nlm.nih.gov/pubmed/27040154.

11. Kesl, S. L., A. M. Poff, N. P. Ward, T. N. Fiorelli, C. Ari, A. J. Van Putten, J. W. Sherwood, et al. "Effects of Exogenous Ketone Supplementation on Blood Ketone, Glucose, Triglyceride, and Lipoprotein Levels in Sprague-Dawley Rats." *Nutrition & Metabolism* 13, no. 9 (2016). https://nutritionandmetabolism.biomedcentral.com/articles/10.1186/s12986-016-0069-y.

12. Akazawa, N., Y. Choi, A. Miyaki, Y. Tanabe, J. Sugawara, R. Ajisaka, and S. Maeda. "Curcumin Ingestion and Exercise Training Improve Vascular Endothelial Function in Postmenopausal Women." *Nutrition Research* 32, no. 10 (2012): 795–799. www.ncbi.nlm.nih.gov/pubmed/23146777.

13. Pereira, M. A., E. O'Reilly, K. Augustsson, G. E. Fraser, U. Goldbourt, B. L. Heitmann, G. Hallmans, et al. "Dietary Fiber and Risk of Coronary Heart Disease: A Pooled Analysis of Cohort Studies." *Archives of Internal Medicine* 164, no. 4 (2004): 370–376. www.ncbi.nlm.nih.gov/pubmed/14980987.

Chapter 9

1. Hall, A., P. Barry, T. Dawber, and P. McNamara. "Epidemiology of Gout and Hyperuricemia: A Long-Term Population Study." *American Journal of Medicine* 42, no. 1 (1967): 27–37. www.amjmed.com/article/0002-9343(67)90004-6/pdf.

2. Campion, E. W., R. J. Glynn, and L. O. DeLabry. "Asymptomatic Hyperuricemia. Risks and Consequences in the Normative Aging Study." *American Journal of Medicine* 82, no. 3 (1987): 421–426. www.ncbi.nlm.nih.gov/pubmed/3826098.

3. Hollander, J., E. Stoner, E. Brown, Jr., and P. de Moor. "Joint Temperature Measurement in the Evaluation of Anti-Arthritic Agents." *Journal of Clinical Investigation* 30, no. 7 (1951): 701–706. www.ncbi.nlm.nih.gov/pmc/articles/PMC436300/.

4. Loeb, J. "The Influence of Temperature on the Solubility of Monosodium Urate." *Arthritis & Rheumatism* 15, no. 2 (2005): 189–192. http://onlinelibrary.wiley.com/doi/10.1002/art.1780150209/pdf.

5. Youm, Y. H., K. Y. Nguyen, R. W. Grant, E. L. Goldberg, M. Bodogai, D. Kim, D. D'Agostino, et al. "The Ketone Metabolite β-Hydroxybutyrate Blocks NLRP3 Inflammasome-Mediated Inflammatory Disease." *Nature Medicine* 21, no. 3 (2015): 263–269. www.ncbi.nlm.nih.gov/pmc/articles/PMC4352123/.

6. Howatson, G., M. P. McHugh, J. A. Hill, J. Brouner, A. P. Jewell, K. A. van Someren, R. E. Shave, et al. "Influence of Tart Cherry Juice on Indices of Recovery Following Marathon Running." *Scandinavian Journal of Medicine & Science in Sports* 20, no. 6 (2010): 843–852. www.ncbi.nlm.nih.gov/pubmed/19883392.

7. Kelley, D. S., R. Rasooly, R. A. Jacob, A. A. Kader, and B. E. Mackey. "Consumption of Bing Sweet Cherries Lowers Circulating Concentrations of Inflammation Markers in Healthy Men and Women." *Journal of Nutrition* 136, no. 4 (2006): 981–986. www.ncbi.nlm.nih.gov/pubmed/16549461.

8. Stein, H. B., A. Hasan, and I. H. Fox. "Ascorbic Acid-Induced Uricosuria. A Consequency of Megavitamin Therapy." *Annals of Internal Medicine* 84, no. 4 (1976): 385–388. www.ncbi.nlm.nih.gov/pubmed/1259282.

9. Choi, H. K., X. Gao, and G. Curhan. "Vitamin C Intake and the Risk of Gout in Men: A Prospective Study." *Archives of Internal Medicine* 169, no. 5 (2009): 502–507. www.ncbi.nlm.nih.gov/pubmed/19273781.

10. Caspi, D., E. Lubart, E. Graff, B. Habot, M. Yaron, and R. Segal. "The Effect of Mini-Dose Aspirin on Renal Function and Uric Acid Handling in Elderly Patients." *Arthritis & Rheumatism* 43, no. 1 (2000): 103–108. www.ncbi.nlm.nih.gov/pubmed/10643705.

11. Yarnell, E. "Herbs for Gout." *Alternative and Complementary Therapies* 22, no. 5 (2016): 218–225. http://online.liebertpub.com/doi/abs/10.1089/act.2016.29075.eya.

12. Poff, A., S. Kesl, N. Ward, and D. D'Agostino. "Metabolic Effects of Exogenous Ketone Supplementation—An Alternative or Adjuvant to the Ketogenic Diet as a Cancer Therapy?" *FASEB Journal* 30, no. 1 (2016). www.fasebj.org/content/30/1_Supplement/1167.2.

Chapter 10

1. Scales Jr., C. D., A. C. Smith, J. M. Hanley, and C. S. Saigal. "Prevalence of Kidney Stones in the United States." *European Urology* 62, no. 1 (2012): 160–165. www.ncbi.nlm.nih.gov/pubmed/22498635.
2. Coe, F., J. Parks, and J. Asplin. "The Pathogenesis and Treatment of Kidney Stones." *New England Journal of Medicine* 327, no. 16 (1992): 1141–1152. www.nejm.org/doi/full/10.1056/NEJM199210153271607.
3. Lemann Jr., J., W. F. Piering, and E. J. Lennon. "Possible Role of Carbohydrate-Induced Calciuria in Calcium Oxalate Kidney-Stone Formation." *New England Journal of Medicine* 280, no. 5 (1969): 232–237.
4. Taylor, E. N., and G. C. Curhan. "Fructose Consumption and the Risk of Kidney Stones." *Kidney International* 73, no. 2 (2008): 207–212. www.ncbi.nlm.nih.gov/pubmed/17928824.
5. Maalouf, N., O. Moe, B. Adams-Huet, and K. Sakhaee. "Hypercalciuria Associated with High Dietary Protein Intake Is Not Due to Acid Load." *Journal of Clinical Endocrinology & Metabolism* 96, no. 12 (2011): 3733–3740. www.ncbi.nlm.nih.gov/pmc/articles/PMC3232614/.
6. Howatson, G., M. P. McHugh, J. A. Hill, J. Brouner, A. P. Jewell, K. A. van Someren, R. E. Shave, et al. "Influence of Tart Cherry Juice on Indices of Recovery Following Marathon Running." *Scandinavian Journal of Medicine & Science in Sports* 20, no. 6 (2010): 843–852. www.ncbi.nlm.nih.gov/pubmed/19883392.
7. Kelley, D. S., R. Rasooly, R. A. Jacob, A. A. Kader, and B. E. Mackey. "Consumption of Bing Sweet Cherries Lowers Circulating Concentrations of Inflammation Markers in Healthy Men and Women." *Journal of Nutrition* 136, no. 4 (2006): 981–986. www.ncbi.nlm.nih.gov/pubmed/16549461.
8. Yarnell, E. "Herbs for Gout." *Alternative and Complementary Therapies* 22, no. 5 (2016): 218–225. http://online.liebertpub.com/doi/abs/10.1089/act.2016.29075.eya.

Chapter 11

1. Bhala, N., T. Usherwood, and J. George. "Non-Alcoholic Fatty Liver Disease." *BMJ* 339 (2009). www.bmj.com/content/339/bmj.b2474.
2. Xu, A., Y. Wang, L. Y. Xu, K. S. Lam, and G. J. Cooper. "The Fat-Derived Hormone Adiponectin Alleviates Alcoholic and Nonalcoholic Fatty Liver Diseases in Mice." *Journal of Clinical Investigation* 112, no. 1 (2003): 91–100. www.ncbi.nlm.nih.gov/pubmed/12840063.
3. Musso, G., R. Gambino, M. Durazzo, G. Biroli, M. Carello, E. Faga, G. Pacini, et al. "Adipokines in NASH: Postprandial Lipid Metabolism as a Link Between Adiponectin and Liver Disease." *Hepatology* 42, no. 5 (2005): 1175–1183. www.ncbi.nlm.nih.gov/pubmed/16231364.
4. Boursier, J., O. Mueller, M. Barret, M. Machado, L. Fizanne, F. Araujo-Perez, C. D. Guy, et al. "The Severity of Nonalcoholic Fatty Liver Disease Is Associated with Gut Dysbiosis and Shift in the Metabolic Function of the Gut Microbiota." *Hepatology* 63, no. 3 (2016): 764–775. www.ncbi.nlm.nih.gov/pubmed/26600078.
5. Cope, K., T. Risby, and A. M. Diehl. "Increased Gastrointestinal Ethanol Production in Obese Mice: Implications for Fatty Liver Disease Pathogenesis." *Gastroenterology* 119, no. 5 (2000): 1340–1347. www.ncbi.nlm.nih.gov/pubmed/11054393.
6. Zamora-Valdés, D., and N. Méndez-Sánchez. "Experimental Evidence of Obstructive Sleep Apnea Syndrome as a Second Hit Accomplice in Nonalcoholic Steatohepatitis Pathogenesis." *Annals of Hepatology* 6, no. 4 (2007): 281–283. www.medigraphic.com/pdfs/hepato/ah-2007/ah074q.pdf.

7. Aron Wisnewsky, J., C. Minville, J. Tordjman, J. L. Bouillot, A. Basdevant, P. Bedossa, K. Clément, et al. "Chronic Intermittent Hypoxia Is a Major Trigger for Non-Alcoholic Fatty Livery Disease in Morbid Obese." *Journal of Hepatology* 26, no. 1 (2012): 225–233. www.ncbi.nlm.nih.gov/pubmed/21703181.

8. Basaranoglu, M., G. Basaranoglu, and E. Bugianesi. "Carbohydrate Intake and Nonalcoholic Fatty Liver Disease: Fructose as a Weapon of Mass Destruction." *Hepatobiliary Surgery and Nutrition* 4, no. 2 (2015): 109–116. www.ncbi.nlm.nih.gov/pmc/articles/PMC4405421/.

9. Ibid.

10. Ruhl, C. E., and J. E. Everhart. "Joint Effects of Body Weight and Alcohol on Elevated Serum Alanine Aminotransferase in the United States Population." *Clinical Gastroenterology and Hepatology* 3, no. 12 (2005): 1260–1208. www.ncbi.nlm.nih.gov/pubmed/16361053.

11. Rakoski, M. O., A. G. Singal, M. A. Rogers, and H. Conjeevaram. "Meta-Analysis: Insulin Sensitizers for the Treatment of Non-Alcoholic Steatohepatitis." *Alimentary Pharmacology & Therapeutics* 32, no. 10 (2010): 1211–1221. www.ncbi.nlm.nih.gov/pubmed/20955440.

12. Boettcher, E., G. Csako, F. Pucino, R. Wesley, and R. Loomba. "Meta-Analysis: Pioglitazone Improves Liver Histology and Fibrosis in Patients with Non-Alcoholic Steatohepatitis." *Alimentary Pharmacology & Therapeutics* 35, no. 1 (2012): 66–75. www.ncbi.nlm.nih.gov/pubmed/22050199.

13. Armstrong, M. J., P. Gaunt, G. P. Aithal, D. Barton, D. Hull, R. Parker, J. M. Hazlehurst, et al. "Liraglutide Safety and Efficacy in Patients with Non-Alcoholic Steatohepatitis (LEAN): A Multicentre, Double-Blind, Randomised, Placebo-Controlled Phase 2 Study." *The Lancet* 387, no. 10019 (2016): 679–690. www.ncbi.nlm.nih.gov/pubmed/26608256.

14. Zhang, B., D. Xu, Y. Guo, J. Ping, L. Chen, and H. Wang. "Protection by and Anti-Oxidant Mechanism of Berberine Against Rat Liver Fibrosis Induced by Multiple Heptotoxic Factors." *Clinical and Experimental Pharmacology and Physiology* 35, no. 3 (2008): 243–360. http://onlinelibrary.wiley.com/doi/10.1111/j.1440-1681.2007.04819.x/full.

15. Di Pierro, F., N. Villanova, F. Agostini, R. Marzocchi, V. Soverini, and G. Marchesini. "Pilot Study on the Additive Effects of Berberine and Oral Type 2 Diabetes Agents for Patients with Suboptimal Glycemic Control." *Diabetes, Metabolic Syndrome and Obesity: Targets and Therapy* 5 (2012): 213–217. www.researchgate.net/publication/230742844_Pilot_study_on_the_additive_effects_of_berberine_and_oral_type_2_diabetes_agents_for_patients_with_suboptimal_glycemic_control.

16. Xia, X., J. Yan, J. Shen, K. Tang, J. Yin, Y. Zhang, D. Yang, et al. "Berberine Improves Glucose Metabolism in Diabetic Rats by Inhibition of Hepatic Gluconeogenesis." *PLoS One* 6, no. 2 (2011): e16556. www.ncbi.nlm.nih.gov/pmc/articles/PMC3033390/.

17. Yan, H. M., M. F. Xia, Y. Wang, X. X. Chang, X. Z. Yao, S. X. Rao, M. S. Zeng, et al. "Efficacy of Berberine in Patients with Non-Alcoholic Fatty Liver Disease." *PLoS One* 10, no. 8 (2015): e0134172. www.ncbi.nlm.nih.gov/pubmed/26252777.

18. Parker, H. M., N. A. Johnson, C. A. Burdon, J. S. Cohn, H. T. O'Connor, and J. George. "Omega-3 Supplementation and Non-Alcoholic Fatty Liver Disease: A Systematic Review and Meta-Analysis." *Journal of Hepatology* 56, no. 4 (2012): 944–951. www.ncbi.nlm.nih.gov/pubmed/22023985.

19. Radiya, R., T. Khatua, P. Bagul, M. Kuncha, and S. Banerjee. "Garlic Improves Insulin Sensitivity and Associated Metabolic Syndromes in Fructose Fed Rats." *Nutrition & Metabolism* 8 (2011): 53. www.ncbi.nlm.nih.gov/pmc/articles/PMC3168415/.

20. Xiao, J., Y. P. Ching, E. Liong, A. Nanji, M. L. Fung, and G. Tipoe. "Garlic-Derived S-Allylmercaptocysteine Is a Hepato-Protective Agent in Non-Alcoholic Fatty Liver Disease in Vivo Animal Model." *European Journal of Nutrition* 52 (2013): 179–191. https://link.springer.com/content/pdf/10.1007/s00394-012-0301-0.pdf.

21. Kesl, S. L., A. M. Poff, N. P. Ward, T. N. Fiorelli, C. Ari, A. J. Van Putten, J. W. Sherwood, et al. "Effects of Exogenous Ketone Supplementation on Blood Ketone, Glucose, Triglyceride, and Lipoprotein Levels in Sprague-Dawley Rats." *Nutrition & Metabolism* 13 (2016). www.ncbi.nlm.nih.gov/pubmed/26855664.

Chapter 12

1. Ortiz, L., M. Zannini, R. DiLauro, and P. Santisteban. "Transcriptional Control of the Forkhead Thyroid Transcription Factor TTF-2 by Thyrotropin, Insulin, and Insulin-Like Growth Factor I." *Journal of Biological Chemistry* 272, no. 37 (1997): 23334–23339. www.ncbi.nlm.nih.gov/pubmed/9287345.

2. Lartey, L., J. P. Werneck-de-Castro, I. O-Sullivan, T. Unterman, and A. Bianco. "Coupling Between Nutrient Availability and Thyroid Hormone Activation." *Journal of Biological Chemistry* 290, no. 51 (2015): 30551–30561. www.jbc.org/content/290/51/30551.short.

3. Coelho, M., T. Oliveira, and R. Fernandes. "Biochemistry of Adipose Tissue: An Endocrine Organ." *Archives of Medical Science* 9, no. 2 (2013): 191–200. www.ncbi.nlm.nih.gov/pubmed/23671428.

4. Wilcox, G. "Insulin and Insulin Resistance." *Clinical Biochemist Reviews* 26, no. 2 (2005): 19–39. www.ncbi.nlm.nih.gov/pubmed/10278749.

5. Arahaf, B. "Increased Need for Thyroxine in Women with Hypothyroidism During Estrogen Therapy." *New England Journal of Medicine* 344, no. 23 (2001): 1743–1749. www.nejm.org/doi/full/10.1056/NEJM200106073442302#t=article.

6. Duntas, L. H. "Selenium and the Thyroid: A Close-Knit Connection." *Journal of Clinical Endocrinology and Metabolism* 95, no. 12 (2010): 180–188. www.ncbi.nlm.nih.gov/pubmed/20810577.

Chapter 13

1. Annegers, J. F., W. A. Hauser, J. R. Lee, and W. A. Rocca. "Incidence of Acute Symptomatic Seizures in Rochester, Minnesota, 1935–1984." *Epilepsia* 36, no. 4 (1995): 327–333. www.ncbi.nlm.nih.gov/pubmed/7607110.

2. Hauser, W. A., J. F. Annegers, and L. T. Kurland. "Incidence of Epilepsy and Unprovoked Seizures in Rochester, Minnesota: 1935–1984." *Epilepsia* 34, no. 3 (1993): 453–468. www.ncbi.nlm.nih.gov/pubmed/8504780.

3. Huff, J. S., D. L. Morris, R. U. Kothari, M. A. Gibbs, and Emergency Medicine Seizure Study Group. "Emergency Department Management of Patients with Seizures: A Multicenter Study." *Academic Emergency Medicine* 8, no. 6 (2001): 622–628. www.ncbi.nlm.nih.gov/pubmed/11388937.

4. Bough, K. J., J. Wetherington, B. Hassel, J. F. Pare, J. W. Gawryluk, J. G. Greene, R. Shaw, et al. "Mitochondrial Biogenesis in the Anticonvulsant Mechanism of the Ketogenic Diet." *Annals of Neurology* 60, no. 2 (2006): 223–235. www.ncbi.nlm.nih.gov/pubmed/16807920.

5. Soukupova, M., A. Binaschi, C. Falcicchia, E. Palma, P. Roncon, S. Zucchini, and M. Simonato. "Increased Extracellular Levels of Glutamate in the Hippocampus of Chronically Epileptic Rats." *Neuroscience* 301 (2015): 246–253. www.ncbi.nlm.nih.gov/m/pubmed/26073699/.

6. Krumholz, A., S. Wiebe, G. S. Gronseth, D. S. Gloss, A. M. Sanchez, A. A. Kabir, A. T. Liferidge, et al. "Evidence-Based Guideline: Management of an Unprovoked First Seizure in Adults: Report of the Guideline Development Subcommittee of the American Academy of Neurology and the American Epilepsy Society." *Neurology* 84, no. 16 (2015): 1705–1713. www.ncbi.nlm.nih.gov/pubmed/25901057.

7. Barborka, C. "Ketogenic Diet Treatment of Epilepsy in Adults." *Journal of the American Medical Association* 91, no. 2 (1928): 73–78. https://jamanetwork.com/journals/jama/article-abstract/258113?redirect=true.

8. Martin, K., C. F. Jackson, R. G. Levy, and P. N. Cooper. "Ketogenic Diet and Other Dietary Treatments for Epilepsy." *Cochrane Database of Systemic Reviews* 2 (2016). www.ncbi.nlm.nih.gov/pubmed/26859528.

9. Lefevre, F., and N. Aronson. "Ketogenic Diet for the Treatment of Refractory Epilepsy in Children: A Systematic Review of Efficacy." *Pediatrics* 105, no. 4 (2000): E46. www.ncbi.nlm.nih.gov/pubmed/10742367.

10. Kossoff, E. H., L. C. Laux, R. Blackford, P. F. Morrison, P. L Pyzik, R. M. Hamdy, Z. Turner, et al. "When Do Seizures Usually Improve with the Ketogenic Diet?" *Epilepsia* 49, no. 2 (2008): 329–333. www.ncbi.nlm.nih.gov/pubmed/18028405.

11. Villeneuve, N., F. Pinton, N. Bahi-Buisson, O. Dulac, C. Chiron, and R. Nabbout. "The Ketogenic Diet Improves Recently Worsened Focal Epilepsy." *Developmental Medicine and Child Neurology* 51, no. 4 (2009): 276–281. www.ncbi.nlm.nih.gov/pubmed/19191829.

12. D'Agostino, D. P., R. Pilla, H. E. Held, C. S. Landon, M. Puchowicz, H. Brunengraber, C. Ari, et al. "Therapeutic Ketosis with Ketone Ester Delays Central Nervous System Oxygen Toxicity Seizures in Rats." *American Journal of Physiology* 304, no. 10 (2013): R829–R836. www.ncbi.nlm.nih.gov/pubmed/23552496.

13. Pearce, J. M. S. "Historical Descriptions of Multiple Sclerosis." *European Neurology* 54, no. 1 (2005): 49–53. www.karger.com/Article/Fulltext/87387.

14. Castellano, C. A., S. Nugent, N. Paquet, S. Tremblay, C. Bocti, G. Lacombe, H. Imbeault, et al. "Lower Brain 18F-Fluorodeoxyglucose Uptake but Normal 11C-Acetoacetate Metabolism in Mild Alzheimer's Disease Dementia." *Journal of Alzheimer's Disease* 43, no. 4 (2015): 1343–1353. www.ncbi.nlm.nih.gov/pubmed/25147107.

15. Nugent, S., S. Tremblay, K. W. Chen, N. Ayutyanont, C. A. Castellano, M. Fortier, M. Roy, et al. "Brain Glucose and Acetoacetate Metabolism: A Comparison of Young and Older Adults." *Neurobiology of Aging* 35, no. 6 (2014): 1386–1395. www.ncbi.nlm.nih.gov/pubmed/24388785.

16. Lassman, H., W. Brück, and C. F. Lucchinetti. "The Immunopathology of Multiple Sclerosis: An Overview." *Brain Pathology* 17, no. 2 (2007): 210–218. www.ncbi.nlm.nih.gov/pubmed/17388952.

17. Confavreux, C., and S. Vukusic. "Natural History of Multiple Sclerosis: A Unifying Concept." *Brain* 129, no. 3 (2006): 606–616. www.ncbi.nlm.nih.gov/pubmed/16415308.

18. Stys, P. K., G. W. Zamponi, J. van Minnen, and J. J. G. Geurts. "Will the Real Multiple Sclerosis Please Stand Up?" *Nature Reviews Neuroscience* 13, no. 7 (2012): 507–514. www.ncbi.nlm.nih.gov/pubmed/22714021.

19. Storoni, M., and G. T. Plant. "The Therapeutic Potential of the Ketogenic Diet in Treating Progressive Multiple Sclerosis." *Multiple Sclerosis International* 2015 (2015): Article ID 681289. www.hindawi.com/journals/msi/2015/681289/.

20. Sullivan, P. G., J. E. Springer, E. D. Hall, and S. W. Scheff. "Mitochondrial Uncoupling as a Therapeutic Target Following Neuronal Injury." *Journal of Bioenergetics and Biomembranes* 36, no. 4 (2004): 353–356. www.ncbi.nlm.nih.gov/pubmed/15377871.

21. Sullivan, P. G., N. A. Rippy, K. Dorenbos, R. C. Concepcion, A. K. Agarwal, and J. M. Rho. "The Ketogenic Diet Increases Mitochondrial Uncoupling Protein Levels and Activity." *Annals of Neurology* 55, no. 4 (2004): 576–580. www.ncbi.nlm.nih.gov/pubmed/15048898.

22. Shimazu, T., M. D. Hirschey, J. Newman, W. He, K. Shirakawa, N. Le Moan, C. A. Grueter, et al. "Suppression of Oxidative Stress by β-Hydroxybutyrate, an Endogenous Histone Deacetylase Inhibitor." *Science* 339, no. 6116 (2013): 211–214. www.ncbi.nlm.nih.gov/pubmed/23223453.

23. Dupuis, N., N. Curatolo, J. F. Benoist, and S. Auvin. "Ketogenic Diet Exhibits Anti-Inflammatory Properties." *Epilepsia* 56, no. 7 (2015): e95–e98. www.ncbi.nlm.nih.gov/pubmed/26011473.

24. Kim, D. Y., J. Hao, R. Liu, G. Turner, F.-D. Shi, and J. M. Rho. "Inflammation-Mediated Memory Dysfunction and Effects of a Ketogenic Diet in a Murine Model of Multiple Sclerosis." *PLoS One* 7, no. 5 (2012). www.ncbi.nlm.nih.gov/pubmed/22567104.

25. Youm, Y. H., K. Y. Nguyen, R. W. Grant, E. L. Goldberg, M. Bodogai, D. Kim, D. D'Agostino, et al. "The Ketone Metabolite β-Hydroxybutyrate Blocks NLRP3 Inflammasome—Mediated Inflammatory Disease." *Nature Medicine* 21, no. 3 (2015): 263–269. www.ncbi.nlm.nih.gov/pubmed/25686106.

26. Paoli, A., A. Bianco, E. Damiani, and G. Bosco. "Ketogenic Diet in Neuromuscular and Neurodegenerative Diseases." *BioMed Research International* 2014 (2014). www.hindawi.com/journals/bmri/2014/474296/.

27. Ridge, P. G., M. T. W. Ebbert, and J. S. K. Kauwe. "Genetics of Alzheimer's disease." *BioMed Research International* 2013 (2013). www.hindawi.com/journals/bmri/2013/254954/.

28. Akter, K., E. A. Lanza, S. A. Martin, N. Myronyuk, and R. B. Raffa. "Diabetes Mellitus and Alzheimer's Disease: Shared Pathology and Treatment?" *British Journal of Clinical Pharmacology* 71, no. 3 (2011): 365–376. www.ncbi.nlm.nih.gov/pubmed/21284695.

29. Srikanth, V., A. Maczurek, T. Phan, M. Steele, B. Westcott, D. Juskiw, and G. Münch. "Advanced Glycation Endproducts and Their Receptor RAGE in Alzheimer's Disease." *Neurobiology of Aging* 32, no. 5 (2011): 763–777. www.ncbi.nlm.nih.gov/pubmed/19464758.

30. Kashiwaya, Y., C. Bergman, J. H. Lee, R. Wan, M. T. King, M. R. Mughal, E. Okun, et al. "A Ketone Ester Diet Exhibits Anxiolytic and Cognition-Sparing Properties, and Lessens Amyloid and Tau Pathologies in a Mouse Model of Alzheimer's Disease." *Neurobiology of Aging* 34, no. 6 (2013): 1530–1539. www.ncbi.nlm.nih.gov/pubmed/23276384.

31. Beckett, T. L., C. M Studzinski, J. N. Keller, M. Paul Murphy, and D. M. Niedowicz. "A Ketogenic Diet Improves Motor Performance but Does Not Affect β-Amyloid Levels in a Mouse Model of Alzheimer's Disease." *Brain Research* 1505 (2013): 61–67. www.ncbi.nlm.nih.gov/pubmed/23415649.

32. Paoli, A., A. Bianco, E. Damiani, and G. Bosco. "Ketogenic Diet in Neuromuscular and Neurodegenerative Diseases." *BioMed Research International* 2014 (2014). www.ncbi.nlm.nih.gov/pubmed/25101284.

33. Zhao, Z., D. J. Lange, A. Voustianiouk, D. MacGrogan, L. Ho, J. Suh, N. Humala, et al. "A Ketogenic Diet as a Potential Novel Therapeutic Intervention in Amyotrophic Lateral Sclerosis." *BMC Neuroscience* 2006 (2006). www.ncbi.nlm.nih.gov/pubmed/16584562.

34. Tieu, K., C. Perier, C. Caspersen, P. Teismann, D. C. Wu, S. D. Yan, A. Naini, et al. "D-Beta-Hydroxybutyrate Rescues Mitochondrial Respiration and Mitigates Features of Parkinson Disease." *The Journal of Clinical Investigation* 112, no. 6 (2003): 892–901. www.ncbi.nlm.nih.gov/pubmed/12975474.

35. Vanitallie, T. B., C. Nonas, A. Di Rocco, K. Boyar, K. Hyams, and S. B. Heymsfield. "Treatment of Parkinson Disease with Diet-Induced Hyperketonemia: A Feasibility Study." *Neurology* 64, no. 4 (2005): 728–730. www.ncbi.nlm.nih.gov/pubmed/15728303.

36. Vorgerd, M., and J. Zange. "Treatment of Glycogenosys Type V (McArdle Disease) with Creatine and Ketogenic Diet with Clinical Scores and with 31P-MRS on Working Leg Muscle." *Acta Myologica* 26, no. 1 (2007): 61–63. www.ncbi.nlm.nih.gov/pubmed/17915573.

37. Valayannopoulos, V., F. Bajolle, J. B. Arnoux, S. Dubois, N. Sannier, C. Baussan, F. Petit, et al. "Successful Treatment of Severe Cardiomyopathy in Glycogen Storage Disease Type III with D, L-3-Hydroxybutyrate, Ketogenic and High-Protein Diet." *Pediatric Research* 70, no. 6 (2011): 638–641. www.ncbi.nlm.nih.gov/pubmed/21857385.

38. Huttenlocher, P. R., A. J. Wilbourn, and J. M. Signore. "Medium-Chain Triglycerides as a Therapy for Intractable Childhood Epilepsy." *Neurology* 21, no. 11 (1971): 1097–1103. www.ncbi.nlm.nih.gov/pubmed/5166216.

39. Huttenlocher, P. R. "Ketonemia and Seizures: Metabolic and Anticonvulsant Effects of Two Ketogenic Diets in Childhood Epilepsy." *Pediatric Research* 10, no. 5 (1976): 536–540. www.ncbi.nlm.nih.gov/pubmed/934725.

40. Checkoway, H., K. Powers, T. Smith Wollor, G. M. Franklin, W. T. Longstreth, Jr., and P. D. Swanson. "Parkinson's Disease Risks Associated with Cigarette Smoking, Alcohol Consumption, and Caffeine Intake." *American Journal of Epidemiology* 155, no. 8 (2002): 732–738. www.ncbi.nlm.nih.gov/pubmed/11943691.

41. Bryans, J. A., P. A. Judd, and P. R. Ellis. "The Effect of Consuming Instant Black Tea on Postprandial Plasma Glucose and Insulin Concentrations in Healthy Humans." *Journal of the American College of Nutrition* 26, no. 5 (2007): 471–477. www.ncbi.nlm.nih.gov/pubmed/17914136.

42. Stote, K. S., and D. J. Baer. "Tea Consumption May Improve Biomarkers of Insulin Sensitivity and Risk Factors for Diabetes." *Journal of Nutrition* 138, no. 8 (2008): 1584S–1588S. www.ncbi.nlm.nih.gov/pubmed/18641211.

43. Ashok, P. K., and K. Upadhyaya. "Tannins Are Astringent." *Journal of Pharmacognosy and Phytochemistry* 1, no. 3 (2012): 45–50. https://pdfs.semanticscholar.org/e03e/263f777c2feada435136bec684db86c3a3b.pdf.

44. Ricardo-da-Silva, J. M., V. Cheynier, J. M. Souquet, M. Moutounet, J. C. Cabanis, and M. Bourzeix. "Interaction of Grape Seed Procyanidins with Various Proteins in Relation to Wine Fining." *Journal of the Science of Food and Agriculture* 57 (1991): 111–125.

45. Clarke, R., D. Bennett, S. Parish, S. Lewington, M. Skeaff, S. J. Eussen, C. Lewerin, et al. "Effects of Homocysteine Lowering with B Vitamins on Cognitive Aging: Meta-Analysis of 11 Trials with Cognitive Data on 22,000 Individuals." *American Journal of Clinical Nutrition* 100, no. 2 (2014): 657–666. www.ncbi.nlm.nih.gov/pubmed/24965307.

46. Selhub, J., P. F. Jacques, A. G. Bostom, R. B. D'Agostino, P. W. Wilson, A. J. Belanger, D. H. O'Leary, et al. "Relationship Between Plasma Homocysteine, Vitamin Status and Extracranial Carotid-Artery Stenosis in the Framingham Study Population." *Journal of Nutrition* 126, no. 4 Suppl. (1996): 1258S–1265S. www.ncbi.nlm.nih.gov/pubmed/8642467.

47. Sano, M., C. Ernesto, R. G. Thomas, M. R. Klauber, K. Schaefer, M. Grundman, P. Woodbury, et al. "A Controlled Trial of Selegiline, Alpha-Tocopherol, or Both as Treatment for Alzheimer's Disease. The Alzheimer's Disease Cooperative Study." *New England Journal of Medicine* 336, no. 17 (1997): 1216–1222. www.ncbi.nlm.nih.gov/pubmed/9110909.

48. Dysken, M. W., M. Sano, S. Asthana, J. E. Vertrees, M. Pallaki, M. Llorente, S. Love, et al. "Effect of Vitamin E and Memantine on Functional Decline in Alzheimer Disease: The TEAM-AD VA Cooperative Randomized Trial." *Journal of the American Medical Association* 311, no. 1 (2014): 33–44. www.ncbi.nlm.nih.gov/pubmed/24381967.

49. Birks, J., and L. Flicker. "Selegiline for Alzheimer's Disease." *Cochrane Database of Systemic Reviews* 2003, no. 1 (2003). www.ncbi.nlm.nih.gov/pubmed/12535396.

50. Quinn, J. F., R. Raman, R. G. Thomas, K. Yurko-Mauro, E. B. Nelson, C. Van Dyck, J. E. Galvin, et al. "Docosahexaenoic Acid Supplementation and Cognitive Decline in Alzheimer Disease: A Randomized Trial." *Journal of the American Medical Association* 304, no. 17 (2010): 1903–1911. www.ncbi.nlm.nih.gov/pubmed/21045096.

51. Tieu, K., C. Perier, C. Caspersen, P. Teismann, D. C. Wu, S. D. Yan, A. Naini, et al. "D-Beta-Hydroxybutyrate Rescues Mitochondrial Respiration and Mitigates Features of Parkinson Disease." *Journal of Clinical Investigation* 112, no. 6 (2003): 892–901. www.ncbi.nlm.nih.gov/pubmed/12975474.

52. Srivastava, R. A., S. L. Pinkosky, S. Filippov, J. C. Hanselman, C. T. Cramer, and R. S. Newton. "AMP-Activated Protein Kinase: An Emerging Drug Target to Regulate Imbalances in Lipid and Carbohydrate Metabolism to Treat Cardio-Metabolic Diseases." *Journal of Lipid Research* 53, no. 12 (2012): 2490–2514. www.ncbi.nlm.nih.gov/pubmed/22798688.

53. Izumi, Y., K. Ishii, H. Katsuki, A. M. Benz, and C. F. Zorumski. "Beta-Hydroxybutyrate Fuels Synaptic Function During Development. Histological and Physiological Evidence in Rat Hippocampal Slices." *Journal of Clinical Investigation* 101, no. 5 (1998): 1121–1132. www.ncbi.nlm.nih.gov/pubmed/9486983.

54. D'Agostino, D. P., R. Pilla, H. E. Held, C. S. Landon, M. Puchowicz, H. Brunengraber, C. Ari, et al. "Therapeutic Ketosis with Ketone Ester Delays Central Nervous System Oxygen Toxicity Seizures in Rats." *American Journal of Physiology* 304, no. 10 (2013): R829–R836. www.ncbi.nlm.nih.gov/pubmed/23552496.

Chapter 14

1. Ballester, J., M. C. Muñoz, J. Domínguez, T. Rigau, J. J. Guinovart, and J. E. Rodríguez-Gil. "Insulin-Dependent Diabetes Affects Testicular Function by FSH- and LH-Linked Mechanisms." *Journal of Andrology* 25, no. 5 (2004). 706–719. www.ncbi.nlm.nih.gov/pubmed/15292100.

2. Morin-Papunen, L.C., I. Vauhkonen, R. M. Koivunen, A. Ruokonen, and J. S. Tapanainen. "Insulin Sensitivity, Insulin Secretion, and Metabolic and Hormonal Parameters in Healthy Women and Women with Polycystic Ovarian Syndrome." *Human Reproduction* 15, no. 6 (2000): 1266–1274. www.ncbi.nlm.nih.gov/pubmed/10831553.

3. Wilcox, G. "Insulin and Insulin Resistance." *Clinical Biochemist Reviews* 26, no. 2 (2005): 19–39. www.ncbi.nlm.nih.gov/pmc/articles/PMC1204764/.

4. Wu, F. C., A. Tajar, S. R. Pye, A. J. Silman, J. D. Finn, T. W. O'Neill, G. Bartfai, et al. "Hypothalamic-Pituitary-Testicular Axis Disruptions in Older Men Are Differentially Linked to Age and Modifiable Risk Factors: The European Male Aging Study." *Journal of Clinical Endocrinology and Metabolism* 93, no. 7 (2008): 2737–2745. www.ncbi.nlm.nih.gov/pubmed/18270261.

5. Kiddey, D. S., D. Hamilton-Fairley, M. Seppälä, R. Koistinen, V. H. James, M. J. Reed, and S. Franks. "Diet-Induced Changes in Sex Hormone Binding Globulin and Dree Testosterone in Women with Normal or Polycystic Ovaries: Correlation with Serum Insulin-Like Growth Factor-1." *Clinical Endocrinology* 31, no. 6 (1989): 757–763. www.ncbi.nlm.nih.gov/pubmed/2697481.

6. Strauss, R. H., R. R. Lanese, and W. B. Malarkey. "Weight Loss in Amateur Wrestlers and Its Effect on Serum Testosterone Levels." *Journal of the American Medical Association* 254, no. 23 (1985): 3337–3338. www.ncbi.nlm.nih.gov/pubmed/4068168.

7. Roemmich, J. N., and W. E. Sinning. "Weight Loss and Wrestling Training: Effects on Nutrition, Growth, Maturation, Body Composition, and Strength." *Journal of Applied Physiology* 82, no. 6 (1997): 1751–1759. www.ncbi.nlm.nih.gov/pubmed/9173937.

8. Volek, J. S. "Secrets to Supercharged Muscle Growth." *Nutrition Express* website, accessed January 30, 2018. www.nutritionexpress.com/article+index/sports+nutrition/testosterone+boosters/showarticle.aspx?id=222.

9. Metha, P. H., and R. A. Josephs. "Testosterone and Cortisol Jointly Regulate Dominance: Evidence for a Dual-Hormone Hypothesis." *Hormones and Behavior* 58, no. 5 (2010): 898–906. www.ncbi.nlm.nih.gov/pubmed/20816841.

10. Skorupskaite, K., J. T. George, and R. A. Anderson. "The Kisspeptin-GnRH Pathway in Human Reproductive Health and Disease." *Human Reproduction Update* 20, no. 4 (2014): 485–500. www.ncbi.nlm.nih.gov/pmc/articles/PMC4063702/.

11. Li, X. F., J. E. Bowe, J. C. Mitchell, S. D. Brain, S. I. Lightman, and K. T. O'Byrne. "Stress-Induced Suppression of the Gonadotropin-Releasing Hormone Pulse Generator in the Female Rat: A Novel Neural Action for Calcitonin-Gene-Related Peptide." *Endocrinology* 145, no. 4 (2004): 1556–1563. www.ncbi.nlm.nih.gov/pubmed/14736738.

12. Muff, R., W. Born, and J. A. Fischer. "Calcitonin, Calcitonin Gene-Related Peptide, Adrenomedullin and Amylin: Homologous Peptides, Separate Receptors and Overlapping Biological Actions." *European Journal of Endocrinology* 133, no. 1 (1995): 17–20. www.ncbi.nlm.nih.gov/pubmed/7627335.

13. Simo, R., C. Saez-Lopez, A. Lecube, C. Hernandez, J. M. Fort, and D. M. Selva. "Adiponectin Upregulates SHBG Production: Molecular Mechanisms and Potential Implications." *Endocrinology* 155, no. 8 (2014): 2820–2830. https://doi.org/10.1210/en.2014-1072.

14. Arazi, H., A. Damirchi, H. Faraji, and R. Rahimi. "Hormonal Responses to Acute and Chronic Resistance Exercise in Middle-Age Versus Young Men." *Sport Sciences for Health* 8, no. 2–3 (2012): 59–65. https://link.springer.com/article/10.1007/s11332-012-0131-8.

15. Kraemer, W. J., A. C. Fry, B. J. Warren, M. H. Stone, S. J. Fleck, J. T. Kearney, B. P. Conroy, et al. "Acute Hormonal Responses in Elite Junior Weightlifters." *International Journal of Sports Medicine* 13, no. 2 (1992): 103–109. www.ncbi.nlm.nih.gov/pubmed/1555898.

16. Nimptsch, K., E. A. Platz, W. C. Willett, and E. Giovannucci. "Association Between Plasma 25-OH Vitamin D and Testosterone Levels in Men." *Clinical Endocrinology* 77, no. 1 (2012): 106–112. www.ncbi.nlm.nih.gov/pubmed/22220644.

17. Wehr, E., S. Pilz, B. O. Boehm, W. März, and B. Obermayer-Pietsch. "Association of Vitamin D Status with Serum and Androgen Levels in Men." *Clinical Endocrinology* 73, no. 2 (2010): 243–248. www.ncbi.nlm.nih.gov/pubmed/20050857.

18. Prasad, A. S., C. S. Mantzoros, F. W. Beck, J. W. Hess, and G. J. Brewer. "Zinc Status and Serum Testosterone Levels of Healthy Adults." *Nutrition* 12, no. 5 (1996): 344–348. www.ncbi.nlm.nih.gov/pubmed/8875519.

19. Gunnelo, T. A., and R. J. Bloomer. "Increasing Circulating Testosterone: Impact of Herbal Dietary Supplements." *Journal of Plant Biochemistry & Physiology* 2, no. 130 (2014). www.omicsonline.org/open-access/increasing-circulating-testosterone-impact-of-herbal-dietary-supplements.2329-9029.1000130.php?aid=28009.

20. Mohammed, H. A., L. A. Ba, T. Burkholz, E. Schumann, B. Diesel, J. Zapp, A. K. Kiemer, et al. "Facile Synthesis of Chrysin-Derivatives with Promising Activities as Aromatase Inhibitors." *Natural Product Communications* 6, no. 1 (2011): 31–34. www.ncbi.nlm.nih.gov/pubmed/21366040.

21. Lambert, J. D., J. Hong, D. H. Kim, V. M. Mishin, and C. S. Yang. "Piperine Enhances the Bioavailability of the Tea Polyphenol (-)- Epigallocatechin-3-Gallate in Mice." *Journal of Nutrition* 134, no. 8 (2004): 1948–1952. www.researchgate.net/publication/8426332_Piperine_Enhances_the_Bioavailability_of_the_Tea_Polyphenol_--Epigallocatechin-3-gallate_in_Mice.

22. Shoba, G., D. Joy, T. Joseph, M. Majeed, R. Rajendran, and P. S. Srinivas. "Influence of Piperine on the Pharmacokinetics of Curcumin in Animals and Human Volunteers." *Planta Medica* 64, no. 4 (1998): 353–356. www.ncbi.nlm.nih.gov/pubmed/9619120.

23. Tambi, M. I., M. K. Imran, and R. R. Henkel. "Standardised Water-Soluble Extract of Eurycoma Longifolia, Tongkat Ali, As Testosterone Booster for Managing Men with Late-Onset Hypogonadism?" *Andrologia* 44, no. 1 (2012): 226–230. www.ncbi.nlm.nih.gov/pubmed/21671978.

24. Hamzah, S., and A. Yusof. "The Ergogenic Effects of Eurycoma Longifolia Jack: A Pilot Study." *British Journal of Sports Medicine* 37 (2003): 464–470. http://supermanherbs.com/wp-content/uploads/2014/08/ELJ_BJSM.pdf.

25. Henkel, R. R., R. Wang, S. H. Bassett, T. Chen, N. Liu, Y. Zhu, and M. I. Tambi. "Tongkat Ali as a Potential Herbal Supplement for Physically Active Male and Female Seniors—A Pilot Study." *Phytotherapy Research* 28, no. 4 (2014): 544–550. www.ncbi.nlm.nih.gov/pubmed/23754792.

Chapter 15

1. Franks, S. "Polycystic Ovary Syndrome: A Changing Perspective." *Clinical Endocrinology* 31, no. 1 (1989): 87–120. www.ncbi.nlm.nih.gov/pubmed/2513151.

2. Reinehr, T., G. de Sousa, C. L. Roth, and W. Andler. "Androgens Before and After Weight Loss in Obese Children." *Journal of Clinical Endocrinology and Metabolism* 90, no. 10 (2005): 5588–5595. www.ncbi.nlm.nih.gov/pubmed/16014405.

3. McCartney, C. R., K. A. Prendergast, S. Chhabra, C. A. Eagleson, R. Yoo, R. J. Chang, C. M. Foster, et al. "The Association of Obesity and Hyperandrogenemia During the Pubertal Transition in Girls: Obesity as a Potential Factor in the Genesis of Postpubertal Hyperandrogenism." *Journal of Clinical Endocrinology and Metabolism* 91, no. 5 (2006): 1714–1722. www.ncbi.nlm.nih.gov/pubmed/16492701.

4. Rosenfield, R. L., and D. A. Ehrmann. "The Pathogenesis of Polycystic Ovary Syndrome (PCOS): The Hypothesis of PCOS as Functional Ovarian Hyperandrogenism Revisited." *Endocrine Reviews* 37, no. 5 (2016): 467–520. www.ncbi.nlm.nih.gov/pubmed/27459230.

5. Mavropoulous, J. C., W. S. Yancy, J. Hepburn, and E. C. Westman. "The Effects of a Low-Carbohydrate, Ketogenic Diet on the Polycystic Ovary Syndrome: A Pilot Study." *Nutrition & Metabolism* 2 (2005): 35. www.ncbi.nlm.nih.gov/pmc/articles/PMC1334192/.

6. Dunaif, A., K. R. Segal, W. Futterweit, and A. Dobrjansky. "Profound Peripheral Insulin Resistance, Independent of Obesity, in Polycystic Ovary Syndrome." *Diabetes* 38, no. 9 (1989): 1165–1174. www.ncbi.nlm.nih.gov/pubmed/2670645.

7. DeUgarte, C. M., A. A. Bartolucci, and R. Azziz. "Prevalence of Insulin Resistance in the Polycystic Ovary Syndrome Using the Homeostasis Model Assessment." *Fertility and Sterility* 83, no. 5 (2005): 1454–1460. www.ncbi.nlm.nih.gov/pubmed/15866584.

8. Mason, H. D., B. S. Willis, R. W. Beard, R. M. Winston, R. Margara, and S. Franks. "Estradiol Production by Granulosa Cells of Normal and Polycystic Ovaries: Relationship to Menstrual Cycle History and Concentrations of Gonadotropins and Sex Steroids in Follicular Fluid." *Journal of Clinical Endocrinology and Metabolism* 79, no. 5 (1994): 1355–1360. www.ncbi.nlm.nih.gov/pubmed/7962330.

9. Simó, R., C. Saez-Lopez, A. Lecube, C. Hernandez, J. M. Fort, and D. M. Selva. "Adiponectin Upregulates SHBG Production: Molecular Mechanisms and Potential Implications." *Endocrinology* 155, no. 8 (2014): 2820–2830. https://doi.org/10.1210/en.2014-1072.

10. Legro, R. S., S. A. Arslanian, D. A. Ehrmann, K. M. Hoeger, M. H. Murad, R. Pasquali, and C. K. Welt. "Diagnosis and Treatment of Polycystic Ovary Syndrome: An Endocrine Society Clinical Practice Guideline." *Journal of Clinical Endocrinology and Metabolism* 98, no. 12 (2013): 4565–4592. https://academic.oup.com/jcem/article/98/12/4565/2833703.

11. Tasali, E., F. Chapotot, R. Leproult, H. Whitmore, and D. A. Ehrmann. "Treatment of Obstructive Sleep Apnea Improves Cardiometabolic Function in Young Obese Women with Polycystic Ovary Syndrome." *Journal of Clinical Endocrinology and Metabolism* 96, no. 2 (2011): 365–374. www.ncbi.nlm.nih.gov/pubmed/21123449.

12. Misra, A., N. K. Alappan, N. K. Vikram, K. Goel, N. Gupta, K. Mittal, S. Bhatt, et al. "Effect of Supervised Progressive Resistance-Exercise Training Protocol on Insulin Sensitivity, Glycemia, Lipids, and Body Composition in Asian Indians with Type 2 Diabetes." *Diabetes Care* 31, no. 7 (2008): 1282–1287. http://care.diabetesjournals.org/content/31/7/1282.

13. Armanini, D., M. J. Mattarello, C. Fiore, G. Bonanni, C. Scaroni, P. Sartorato, and M. Palermo. "Licorice Reduces Serum Testosterone in Healthy Women." *Steroids* 69, no. 11–12 (2004): 763–766. www.ncbi.nlm.nih.gov/pubmed/15579328.

14. Maharjan, R., P. S. Nagar, and L. Nampoothiri. "Effect of Aloe Barbadensis Mill. Formulation on Letrozole Induced Polycystic Ovarian Syndrome Rat Model." *Journal of Ayurveda and Integrative Medicine* 1, no. 4 (2010): 273–279. www.ncbi.nlm.nih.gov/pubmed/21731374.

15. Luo, J., T. I. Yin, Y. Wanb, et al. "Influence of Astragalus Polysaccharides Plus Diane-35 on Insulin Resistance and Androgen Levels and Lipid Metabolism of Patients with Polycystic Ovary Syndrome." *Chinese Journal of Misdiagnostics.* Accessed January 30, 2018. http://en.cnki.com.cn/Article_en/CJFDTOTAL-ZWZX200928006.htm.

16. Rizk, A. K., M. A. Bedaiwy, and H. G. Al-Inany. "N-Acetyl-Cysteine Is a Novel Adjuvant to Clomiphene Citrate in Clomiphene Citrate-Resistant Patients with Polycystic Ovary Syndrome." *Fertility and Sterility* 83, no. 2 (2005): 367–370. www.ncbi.nlm.nih.gov/pubmed/15705376.

17. Nestler, J. E., D. J. Jakubowicz, P. Reamer, R. D. Gunn, and G. Allan. "Ovulatory and Metabolic Effects of D-Chiro-Inositol in the Polycystic Ovary Syndrome." *New England Journal of Medicine* 340, no. 17 (1999): 1314–1320. www.ncbi.nlm.nih.gov/pubmed/10219066.

18. Westphal, L. M., M. L. Polan, and A. S. Trant. "Double-Blind, Placebo-Controlled Study of FertilityBlend: A Nutritional Supplement for Improving Fertility in Women." *Clinical and Experimental Obstetrics & Gynecology* 33, no. 4 (2006): 205–208. www.ncbi.nlm.nih.gov/pubmed/17211965.

Chapter 16

1. Lustig, R. H. "Fructose: Metabolic, Hedonic, and Societal Parallels with Ethanol." *Journal of the American Dietetic Association* 110, no. 9 (2010): 1307–1321. www.ncbi.nlm.nih.gov/pubmed/20800122.

2. Johnston, C. A., and J. P. Foreyt. "Robust Scientific Evidence Demonstrates Benefits of Artificial Sweeteners." *Trends in Endocrinology and Metabolism* 25, no. 1 (2014). www.ncbi.nlm.nih.gov/pubmed/24182455.

3. Swithers, S. E. "Artificial Sweeteners Produce the Counterintuitive Effect of Inducing Metabolic Derangements." *Trends in Endocrinology and Metabolism* 24, no. 9 (2013). www.ncbi.nlm.nih.gov/pubmed/23850261

4. de Koning, L., V. S. Malik, E. B. Rimm, W. C. Willett, and F. B Hu. "Sugar-Sweetened and Artificially Sweetened Beverage Consumption and Risk of Type 2 Diabetes in Men." *American Journal of Clinical Nutrition* 93, no. 6 (2011): 1321–1327. www.ncbi.nlm.nih.gov/pubmed/21430119.

5. Dhingra, R., L. Sullivan, P. F. Jacques, T. J. Wang, C. S. Fox, J. B Meigs, R. B. D'Agostino, et al. "Soft Drink Consumption and Risk of Developing Cardiometabolic Risk Factors and the Metabolic Syndrome in Middle-Aged Adults in the Community." *Circulation* 116, no. 5 (2007): 480–487. www.ncbi.nlm.nih.gov/pubmed/17646581.

6. Lutsey, P. L., L. M. Steffen, and J. Stevens. "Dietary Intake and the Development of the Metabolic Syndrome: The Atherosclerosis Risk in Communities Study." *Circulation* 117, no. 6 (2008): 754–761. www.ncbi.nlm.nih.gov/pubmed/18212291.

7. Nettleton, J. A., P. L. Lutsey, Y. Wang, J. A. Lima, E. D. Michos, and D. R. Jacobs, Jr. "Diet Soda Intake and Risk of Incident Metabolic Syndrome and Type 2 Diabetes in the Multi-Ethnic Study of Atherosclerosis (MESA)." *Diabetes Care* 32, no. 4 (2009): 688–694. www.ncbi.nlm.nih.gov/pubmed/19151203.

8. EFSA Panel on Food Additives and Nutrient Sources Added to Food. "Scientific Opinion on the Re-Evaluation of Aspartame (E 951) as a Food Additive." *EFSA Journal* 11, no. 12 (2013): 3496. http://onlinelibrary.wiley.com/doi/10.2903/j.efsa.2013.3496/full.

9. Van Den Eeden, S. K., T. D. Koepsell, W. T. Longstreth, G. van Belle, J. R. Daling, and B. McKnight. "Aspartame Ingestion and Headaches: A Randomized Crossover Trial." *Neurology* 44, no. 10 (1994): 1787–1793. www.ncbi.nlm.nih.gov/pubmed/7936222.

10. Palmnäs, M., T. Cowan, M. Bomhof, J. Su, R. Reimer, H. Vogel, D. Hittel, et al. "Low-Dose Aspartame Consumption Differentially Affects Gut Microbiota-Host Metabolic Interactions in the Diet-Induced Obese Rat." *PLoS One* (2014). http://journals.plos.org/plosone/article?id=10.1371/journal.pone.0109841.

11. Ashok, I., and R. Sheeladevi. "Biochemical Responses and Mitochondrial Mediated Activation of Apoptosis on Long-Terms Effect of Aspartame in Rat Brain." *Redox Biology* 2 (2014): 820–831. www.ncbi.nlm.nih.gov/pmc/articles/PMC4085354/.

12. Liang, Y., G. Steinbach, V. Maier, and E. F. Pfeiffer. "The Effect of Artificial Sweetener on Insulin Secretion. I. The Effect of Acesulfame K on Insulin Secretion in the Rat (Studies in Vivo)." *Hormone and Metabolic Research* 19, no. 6 (1987): 233–238. www.ncbi.nlm.nih.gov/pubmed/2887500.

13. Liang, Y., G. Steinback, L. Lalić, and E. F. Pfeiffer. "The Effect of Artificial Sweetener on Insulin Secretion. II. Stimulation of Insulin Release from Isolated Rat Islets by Acesulfame K (in Vitro Experiments)." *Hormone and Metabolic Research* 19, no. 7 (1987): 285–289. www.ncbi.nlm.nih.gov/pubmed/2887503.

14. Raida, M., H. Mestrom, and H. Delbrück. "Maltodextrin Supplemented Diet Prevents Postoperative Weight Loss During the First Months After Gastrectomy for Gastric Cancer." *Journal of Clinical Oncology* 25, no. 18_suppl. 15127 (2007): 15127. http://ascopubs.org/doi/abs/10.1200/jco.2007.25.18_suppl.15127.

15. Berthoud, H. R., E. R. Trimble, E. G. Siegel, D. A. Bereiter, and B. Jeanrenaud. "Cephalic-phase Insulin Secretion in Normal and Pancreatic Islet-Transplanted Rats." *American Journal of Physiology—Endocrinology and Metabolism* 238, no. 4 (1980): E336–E340. www.physiology.org/doi/abs/10.1152/ajpendo.1980.238.4.E336.

16. Weihrauch, M. R., and V. Diehl. "Artificial Sweeteners—Do They Bear a Carcinogenic Risk?" *Annals of Oncology* 15, no. 10 (2004): 1460–1465. https://academic.oup.com/annonc/article/15/10/1460/170200.

17. Moisés, R. S., C. R. Carvalho, D. Shiota, and M. J. Saad. "Evidence for a Direct Effect of Captopril on Early Steps of Insulin Action in BC3H-1 Myocytes." *Metabolism* 52, no. 3 (2003): 273–278. www.ncbi.nlm.nih.gov/pubmed/12647262.

18. Zhou, Y., Y. Zheng, J. Ebersole, and C. F. Huang. "Insulin Secretion Stimulating Effects of Mogroside V and Fruit Extract of Luo Han Kuo (Siraitia Grosvenori Swingle) Fruit Extract." *Yao Xue Xue Bao* 44, no. 11 (2009): 1252–1257. www.ncbi.nlm.nih.gov/pubmed/21351724.

19. Daubioul, C. A., Y. Horsmans, P. Lambert, E. Danse, and N. M. Delzenne. "Effects of Oligofructose on Glucose and Lipid Metabolism in Patients with Nonalcoholic Steatohepatitis: Results of a Pilot Study." *European Journal of Clinical Nutrition* 59, no. 5 (2005): 723–726. www.ncbi.nlm.nih.gov/pubmed/15770222.

20. Natah, S. S., K. R. Hussien, J. A. Tuominen, and V. A. Koivisto. "Metabolic Response to Lactitol and Xylitol in Healthy Men." *American Journal of Clinical Nutrition* 64, no. 4 (1997): 947–950. http://ajcn.nutrition.org/content/65/4/947.abstract.

21. Zhang, X. Z., G. W. Meijer, and A. C. Beynen. "Dietary Maltitol Causes Serum and Liver Cholesterol Concentrations in Rats." *International Journal for Vitamin and Nutrition Research* 60, no. 3 (1990): 296–297. www.cabdirect.org/cabdirect/abstract/19911431031.

22. Munroa, I. C., W. O. Berntb, J. F. Borzellecac, G. Flammd, B. S. Lyncha, E. Kennepohla, E. A. Bäre, et al. "Erythritol: An Interpretive Summary of Biochemical, Metabolic, Toxicological and Clinical Data." *Food and Chemical Toxicology* 36, no. 12 (1998): 1139–1174. www.sciencedirect.com/science/article/pii/S027869159800091X.

23. Kim, Y. "Studies on the Glycemic Index of Raisins and on the Intestinal Absorption of Fructose." Electronic Thesis or Dissertation. Ohio State University, 2007. https://etd.ohiolink.edu/pg_10?0::NO:10:P10_ACCESSION_NUM:osu1180462637.

24. Hossain, A., F. Yamagochi, K. Hirose, T. Matsunaga, L. Sui, Y. Hirata, C. Noguchi, et al. "Rare Sugar D-Psicose Prevents Progression and Development of Diabetes in T2DM Model Ostuka Long-Evans Tokushima Fatty Rats." *Dovepress* 2015, no. 9 (2015): 525–535. www.dovepress.com/rare-sugar-d-psicose-prevents-progression-and-development-of-diabetes--peer-reviewed-article-DDDT.

25. Iida, T., Y. Kishimoto, Y. Yoshikawa, N. Hayashi, K. Okuma, M. Tohi, T. Matsuo T, et al. "Acute D-Psicose Administration Decreases the Glycemic Response to Oral Maltodextrin Tolerance Test in Normal Adults." *Journal of Nutritional Science and Vitaminology* 54, no. 6 (2008): 511–514. www.ncbi.nlm.nih.gov/pubmed/19155592.

26. Hayashi, N., T. Iida, T. Yamada, K. Okuma, I. Takehara, T. Yamamoto, K. Yamada, et al. "Study on the Postprandial Blood Glucose Suppression Effect of D-Psicose in Borderline Diabetes and the Safety of Long-Term Ingestion by Normal Human Subjects." *Bioscience, Biotechnology, and Biochemistry* 74, no. 3 (2010): 510–519. www.ncbi.nlm.nih.gov/pubmed/20208358.

27. Shintani, T., T. Yamada, N. Hayashi, T. Iida, Y. Nagata, N. Ozaki, and Y. Toyoda. "Rare Sugar Syrup Containing D-Allulose but Not High Fructose Corn Syrup Maintains Glucose Tolerance and Insulin Sensitivity Partial via Hepatic Glucokinase Translocation in Wistar Rats." *Journal of Agricultural and Food Chemistry* 65, no. 13 (2017): 2888–2894. www.ncbi.nlm.nih.gov/pubmed/28209058.

28. Iwasaki, Y., M. Sendo, K. Dezaki, T. Hira, T. Sato, M. Nakata, C. Goswami, et al. "GLP-1 Release and Vagal Afferent Activation Mediate the Beneficial Metabolic and Chronotherapeutic Effects of D-Allulose." *Nature Communications* 9 (2018): 113. www.ncbi.nlm.nih.gov/pmc/articles/PMC5760716/.

HANDY KETOGENIC REFERENCES

Low-Carb and Keto Science Books

The Alzheimer's Antidote
Amy Berger

The Art And Science of Low Carbohydrate Living
Jeff Volek, PhD, and Stephen Phinney, MD

The Art And Science of Low Carbohydrate Performance
Jeff Volek, PhD, and Stephen Phinney, MD

The Big Fat Surprise
Nina Teicholz

Cholesterol Clarity
Jimmy Moore and Eric Westman, MD

The Diabetes Code
Jason Fung, MD

Eat Rich, Live Long
Ivor Cummins and Jeffry Gerber, MD

Good Calories, Bad Calories
Gary Taubes

Keto Clarity
Jimmy Moore and Eric C. Westman, MD

Keto for Cancer
Miriam Kalamian

Keto: The Complete Guide to Success on the Ketogenic Diet
Maria Emmerich and Craig Emmerich

The Ketogenic Bible
Jacob Wilson, PhD, and Ryan Lowery

Lies My Doctor Told Me
Ken Berry, MD

A Low Carbohydrate, Ketogenic Diet Manual: No Sugar, No Starch Diet
Eric Westman, MD

The Obesity Code
Jason Fung, MD

Primal Fat Burner
Nora Gedgaudas, CNS, NTP, BCHN

Why We Get Fat
Gary Taubes

Low-Carb and Keto Podcasts

2 Keto Dudes
www.2ketodudes.com

40+ Fitness Podcast
40plusfitnesspodcast.com

Be Well, Be Keto with Tracee Gluhaich
highenergygirl.com/podcast

Fast Keto with Ketogenic Girl
www.ketogenicgirl.com/pages/podcast-fast-keto-with-ketogenic-girl

Fat Chat with Ryan Lowery
fat.chat

Fit for the Kingdom
www.trentholbertfitness.com/podcast

Fit2Fat2Fit Experience with Drew Manning
www.fit2fat2fit.com/podcast

High Intensity Health Radio with Mike Mutzel
www.highintensityhealth.com

The Keto Answers Podcast with Dr. Anthony Gustin
www.perfectketo.com/category/podcast

Keto Diet Podcast with Leanne Vogel
www.healthfulpursuit.com/podcast

Keto for Normies
ketoconnect.net/libsyn.com

The Keto for Women Show with Shawn Mynar, NTP, CPT
www.shawnmynar.com/ketoforwomen

Keto Lifestyle with Jessica Tye
www.jessicatye.com

Keto Naturopath
www.facebook.com/groups/ketonaturopath

Keto Savage Podcast
ketosavage.com/podcasts

Keto Talk with Jimmy Moore & Dr. Will Cole
www.ketotalk.com

Keto Woman Podcast
www.ketowomanpodcast.com

Ketogeek Podcast
www.ketogeek.com/pages/podcast

The Ketohacking MD Podcast with Dr. John Limansky & Jimmy Moore
www.ketohackingmd.com

Ketovangelist Podcast
www.ketovangelist.com/category/podcast

The Livin' La Vida Low-Carb Show with Jimmy Moore
www.thelivinlowcarbshow.com

Low Carb Conversations with Leah Williamson, NTP & Guests
www.lowcarbconversations.com

The Low Carb Leader with Daniel Perryman
thelowcarbleader.com/category/best-low-carb-leader-podcasts/

Naturally Nourished Podcast
www.alimillerrd.com/podcast

The Obesity Code Podcast with Dr. Jason Fung and Megan Ramos
obesitycodepodcast.com

Low-Carb and Keto Science Blogs and Websites

The Charlie Foundation
www.charliefoundation.org

Diet Doctor
www.dietdoctor.com

DocMuscles
www.docmuscles.com

Keto Connect
www.ketoconnect.net

Ketogenic.com
ketogenic.com

Ketogenic Diet Resource
www.ketogenic-diet-resource.com

KetoSchool
ketoschool.com

Ketovangelist
www.ketovangelist.com

Livin' La Vida Low Carb
livinlavidalowcarb.com/blog

Perfect Keto
www.perfectketo.com/blog

Ruled.me
www.ruled.me

Low-Carb and Keto Recipe Blogs and Websites

All Day I Dream About Food
alldayidreamaboutfood.com

Beauty and the Foodie
beautyandthefoodie.com

Castaway Kitchen
thecastawaykitchen.com

Daily Ketosis
www.dailyketosis.net/home

Ditch the Carbs
www.ditchthecarbs.com

DJ Foodie
www.djfoodie.com

Eat Fat Lose Fat
eatfatlosefatblog.com

Go Keto with Casey
caseydurango.com

Grass Fed Girl
www.grassfedgirl.com

Healthful Pursuit
www.healthfulpursuit.com

Holistically Engineered
holisticallyengineered.com

I Breathe I'm Hungry
www.ibreatheimhungry.com

Keto Diet Blog
ketodietapp.com/blog

Keto in the City
ketointhecity.com

Keto Karma
ketokarma.com

Ketogasm
ketogasm.com

Ketogenic Girl
www.ketogenicgirl.com

Low Carb Dietician
www.lowcarbdietitian.com/blog

Low Carb Maven
www.lowcarbmaven.com

Low Carb Yum
lowcarbyum.com

Maria Mind Body Health LLC & KetoAdapted
mariamindbodyhealth.com

My Keto Kitchen
www.myketokitchen.com

No Bun Please
nobunplease.com

Nourished Caveman
thenourishedcaveman.com

Peace Love and Low Carb
peaceloveandlowcarb.com

Splendid Low Carbing
low-carb-news.blogspot.com

Vida Low Carb
www.vidalowcarb.com.br

Wholesome Yum
www.wholesomeyum.com

Wicked Stuffed Keto
www.wickedstuffed.com

Low-Carb and Keto Films and Documentaries

The Big Fat Fix
www.thebigfatfix.com

Carb-Loaded: A Culture Dying to Eat
carbloaded.com

Cereal Killers
www.cerealkillersmovie.com

Cereal Killers 2: Run on Fat
www.runonfatmovie.com

Fat Head
www.fathead-movie.com

Fed Up
fedupmovie.com

My Big Fat Diet
www.drjaywortman.com

The Perfect Human Diet
cjhuntreports.com/documentary

Sugar Coated
sugarcoateddoc.com

That Sugar Film
thatsugarfilm.com

Find a Keto Physician

Jimmy Moore's Ketogenic Practitioners
www.ketogenicdocs.com

Ketogenic Clinicians
ketogenic.com/tools/keto-clinicians-finder/

INDEX